CW00541300

NO TIME TO DIE

"Surviving Cancer & America's Failing Justice System"

Richard Sabb

TrueStoryNetwork.com   Colorado

Online publishing by:
TrueStoryNetwork.com
P. O. Box 3699
Breckenridge, CO 80424

ISBN 0-9704429-0-4 (Soft Cover)
ISBN 0-9704429-1-2 (Hard Cover)

Printed & Bound in Korea through Bolton Associates, Inc., San Rafael, CA

The paper in this book meets the guidelines for permanence and durability of the Committee on Production Guidelines for Book Longevity of the Council of Library Resources.

Cover and Jacket Design by Scott W. Taylor
Photos provided by Richard M. Sabb
Book Design by Cheryl M. Johnson

*I would like to dedicate this book to the
one person who stood strong and silent,
promoting my dignity,
and nursing me back to
life:*
My best friend, sweetheart, and soul mate

Cathryn Sabb

In Memory of
and Inspired
by

"Kenny"
July 9, 1962 to June 15, 1991

The world brings us into contact with many people, but few touch our lives like special friends. I miss "Kenny" and will carry him forever in my heart.

Acknowledgments

My Parents – Dot and Bob Sabb

How do you thank people who give you life and support you through its triumphs and trials? Although I couldn't possibly understand my parent's turmoil caused by facing the potential death of their child, I do know the appreciation I hold in my heart for their sacrifices to help Cathi and I live. Without their help and support, I would not be able to bring you this story of *"triumph and life."*

Acknowledgments

My Doctors

I do not want to ignore any of the fine physicians and interns who worked with me, but the list is extremely lengthy and I surely would forget someone's name. I would therefore, like to use the three primary doctors in this acknowledgement, and hope that all others know they are included.

Drs. Lambert, Gochfeld, and "Ricky" for me define the term "*respected world renowned research scientist.*" They use their medical expertise and ability to evaluate medical information as it pertains to the patient's circumstances and condition, regardless of outcome or payment.

Dr. W. Clark Lambert treated me like a son. I truly felt that we developed more than a patient/doctor relationship; rather, it was one of family love. I know that, through his daily work, "*he kept me alive.*" Through scientific scrutiny of my case, he discovered that I am the living model of his "*Thymus-Bypass Theory,*" which was accepted by NATO's Advanced Studies Workshop on "*Basic Mechanisms of Physiologic and Aberrant Lymphoproliferation in the Skin*" in 1994.

Dr. Michael Gochfeld didn't look at me as a study participant, but more as an individual, a person whose feelings and need for understanding were of major importance. His research and analysis not only assisted me in my legal battles, but supplied Drs. Lambert and "Ricky" with information to support my "*battle for life.*"

Dr. "Ricky" also viewed me as a person and family. He had the uncanny ability to recognize the emotional and psychological turmoil that both Cathi and I faced. He evaluated the treatments, the alternatives to

Acknowledgments

medications, and the emotional reactions, to be sure that the entire microcosm of my life was treated appropriately. Without his assistance, the psychological stability necessary to survive *"the war"* would not have been possible for Cathi and me.

Together, these fine scientists battled with Cancer and gave me the opportunity to *"Live With Cancer."*

Acknowledgments

Makita Power Tools
of New Jersey

During the long battle for my life, Makita Power Tools, through Karen, compassionately allowed Cathi to provide the emotional and physical support for my healing. They worked with us to allow her to have a flexible schedule to be with me when I needed her. Very few corporations promote this feeling of family, and I truly appreciate Makita's understanding and compassion.

Foreword

This book is a True Story based on my life as an active Cancer patient. All of the events have been described as I recalled them or interpreted them after they happened. Therefore all the information contained herein is based on my opinion and/or interpretation of what was happening in my life at that time. Any similarities to actual people or places not directly involved are purely coincidental.

Many names have been changed because this is not intended to be vindictive or spiteful, but rather a learning experience.

It is important to understand that my purpose in writing this book is solely the reader's enlightenment as to how complex Legal, Medical, and Family situations can evolve into glory or disaster.

All of the Doctors and Medical Facilities referenced herein are depicted as the actual situation presented itself to me. It should be further understood that, regardless of their position on this topic, they conducted themselves within the parameters of the law and their individual years of specialized study. The doctors and scientists referenced in the following chapters are actually some of the finest in this country, with most being recognized as leaders in the global medical community, regardless of how they appeared to me or evaluated my life situation.

Foreword

My legal trials and the manifestations that precluded them have been kept to their simplest form. This is due to the vast amounts of files and rhetoric that is inherent to legal confrontations.

Ironically, I too must state that I was considerably fortunate in that my legal representation was substantially above average. The attorneys and law firms knew that they were getting involved in a precedent setting case that would require the most prudent due-diligence to surpass a seemingly insurmountable challenge.

As with all families, my relationships were filled with emotional charges that led to misunderstandings, misinterpretations, and manipulation. Adding the complexities of continuous participation in legal and medical procedures only caused exaggeration of this form of behavior. Emotional pain was caused with the "best of intentions." I use the context of family very broadly here to include relationships with persons whom I have emotionally adopted.

Please do not judge any of the participants harshly, for this is told from my point of view, and their view may be totally opposite to mine.

I found the journey down this memory lane painful and enlightening. I hope that because you chose to share my journey as a learning experience, your path in life will have considerably less pain and overwhelmingly more joy. Thank you for accompanying me.

Richard M. Sabb

Table of Contents

Table of contents

1
The Enemy's Strike Force

June 18, 1986—Hayward Pool Products claims that the eyewitness account that I am about to describe Never Happened and the machine that failed, Never Existed.

I gave a nod to Harold, letting him know it was okay to go. Harold pushed the "start" button and the toggle arm began to push the female portion of the mold toward the male, causing it to close. I leaned my right arm on the safety door and relaxed against it as I watched the mechanical action.

"In a few minutes," I shouted, "we should know if all our work is going to pay off."

The basketball mold looked like some kind of Frankenstein experiment. We added heating rods to the mold and there were at least thirty-two wires coming from the heating elements and from all sides of the mold. It was our hope that this additional heat would help the mold stay warm, thus giving us more control of the fiberglass resin mixes. Hydraulic hoses were connected to ball valves, controlling the pressure in and out of the basketball itself. Other pipes with release valves extended from the top of the mold. The toggle arm slowly—with its 200 tons of pressure—clamped the mold into place. Harold waited for a couple of minutes to make sure the temperature reached the 400-degree operating level.

Conversation was almost impossible over the roar of the machine and hydraulics. Harold glanced at his watch and then hit the "run" button. The hopper released the injection mixture into the five- to six-foot length of the corkscrew shaped lead screw. Heating coils maintained the 400-degree temperature along the way to the mold.

As noisy as the machine was, there was a comfort in the sounds of the pneumatic pumps and the familiar whining as the material progressed through the lead screw. All we could do now was wait until the process was complete. Harold stood about four feet to my right at the control panel, and Henry was still on my left, about six feet away, watching the workings of the machine.

I will never forget that surrealistic moment when I knew something was desperately wrong, and yet my mind could not translate the messages it was receiving and therefore could not react. The sound of the machine changed from the familiar whine to a harsh grinding and shearing of metal. There was a deafening bang and a cloud of yellow-brown fumes billowed out of the machine. I was conscious of a swishing sound as the hydraulic clamp released. Even with the safety door closed, the injection mixture, now heated to 400-degrees and the consistency of a thick milk shake, gushed out around the gates as though the machine was regurgitating it. The mixture spewed out around the door. More was launched into the air and fell in splats. Totally disoriented by the thick toxic fumes and severely nauseous, I was aware of a burning sensation on my right hip and other parts of my body. I could hear Henry roaring, "What the hell?" as the mixture fell on him. I looked toward Harold, and could see that the man was still coherent enough to hit the emergency shut off. My right hip and thigh continued to burn and was becoming more and more painful. When I looked down, it finally registered that I was covered with the heated resins. I started to loosen my blue jeans in an attempt to keep the resin from continuing to burn my skin. Simultaneously, Henry and I stumbled down the long aisle toward the shop door. Harold was close behind us.

Mike, the shop supervisor, alerted by the intense bang, opened the metal doors to the shop as the three of us approached them. "What the hell are you guys screwing up now?" he began. But, it took only an instant for him to realize that something was very wrong. The acrid fumes filled the huge molding room and other operators began to leave the building. Henry and I cursed as we rushed from the room, loosening our splattered clothing as we went. Mike could see only a few spots of the resin on Harold, although he could tell the fumes had greatly affected him. More of the mixture landed on Henry, who was still quite disoriented from the blast of fumes he inhaled. My right side from my hip down was covered with the thick mess and I was sick to my stomach.

"Get over to the bathroom," Mike ordered. "Rodwell," he yelled to the man across the room, "get some rags and help these guys get that shit off."

By the time we reached the bathroom area we regained more of our senses. We were each trying to wipe the splotches of mixture off our bodies. Rodwell, whose area was close by, handed us dry rags. "Get some Triclean," Harold snapped. "That's the only thing that's going to get this stuff off. And, hurry! If it hardens, it will take the skin with it."

I took off my boots and socks, which were soaked through. I stripped off my jeans. Someone handed me a rag soaked with Triclean, and I began to rub the hardening substance off my body with the strong solvent. Still suffering from the affects of the fumes, the nausea overtook me and I began to vomit. My head ached, I was sick and the burns were becoming extremely painful. Rodwell offered me a 7-Up to help settle my stomach.

"Goddamn it, Harold," I croaked, "what happened out there?"

"I don't know. It all just went to hell." Harold was still wiping his arms with the solvent-soaked rags. It would be days later that we would find out that a metal pin about two inches thick on the toggle arm had sheared in two. This had caused the hydraulic pressure to release, allowing the mold to slightly open and the pressurized, heated resin and fumes to be released in an explosion.

While Henry, Harold and I were cleaning the hardening mixture off our clothing and bodies, Mike went into the molding department and ordered everyone still there to evacuate. All the employees in the building were given the remainder of the day off and were allowed to see the nurse or the company doctor if they thought it was necessary. Two of the machine operators fifty feet across from the explosion area were so overcome by the fumes they became sick while seeking attention from the company nurse.

The three of us surrounding the machine had no idea that this single event would so dramatically change our lives. Henry and Harold would succumb to Death's roll call. I, a 24-year-old power-lifter, would live, but would fight a 14-year War. The first six years, I wouldn't even know I was battling as the chemicals insinuated themselves into my body and began the undercover operations that resulted in the cellular transformation into Cancer.

My battles would include enemies of an insidious disease, corrupt judges, high-priced insurance and corporate law teams, depression, pain, and emotions—mine and others'.

My troops would include a daredevil spirit, a devoted spouse, a strong family, several caring doctors, hardworking lawyers, and an army of the most renowned and incredible scientists and their teams.

My arsenal would include radiation, chemicals, vitamins, exercise, humor, love, and multiple intelligent minds.

I would have triumphs and defeats in my War for Survival, but I never gave up. Meet me, Richard Sabb, as I share my story of *"SURVIVING CANCER & AMERICA'S FAILING JUSTICE SYSTEM."*

2
Training of the Spirit

1962–1978—I could not do justice to my childhood, so my mother shared some of her memories about my rambunctious, daredevil, "Never Say Die" spirit with me.

It is not unusual for a parent to believe her child is special, and my mom believed all four of her children possessed unique qualities. But there was something more that set me apart from my siblings. In retrospect, she could identify three distinct details surrounding my birth that seemed to prophesy the character of Richard Michael Sabb.

My mom was a devout Catholic. She attended mass regularly, was involved in many church activities, and made sure that her children were schooled properly in the ways of her faith. Like many women, she had a special relationship with the Blessed Mother. When she needed solace, it was the Blessed Virgin Mary that she would pray to. When she rejoiced, it was the Mother of God she thanked. Just before I was born, she told my father, "You know how I feel about the Blessed Mother. I've always wanted a statue of the Blessed Mother. Would you get me one for when the baby is born?"

Respecting his wife's wishes (and being a good Catholic himself), my dad bought a statue he was sure she would like. But rather than a Blessed

5

Mother, what he brought to the hospital was a statue of "The Infant of Prague." "Bob," she explained, "this is not the Blessed Mother."

"I know," he responded. "But there was something about this statue that just made me think that you would like it. I can exchange it if you want."

My mom hesitated, because she understood the uniqueness of the statue. "No, you're right. I really do like it. Thank you."

When she got home from the hospital, she wanted to find out more about the statue. She remembered hearing about "The Miraculous Infant Jesus of Prague" and knew that somehow the gift was remarkable. She found this passage about the original statue and, in years to come, she realized just how remarkable it was:

All who approach the miraculous statue and pray there with confidence receive assistance in danger, consolation in sorrows, aid in poverty, comfort in anxiety, light in spiritual darkness, streams of grace in dryness of soul, health in sickness, and hope in despair.

The second indication of the exceptional nature I was to develop was in the birthmark I bore. My mom noticed it when they brought me to her in the hospital. The birthmark was on my upper chest. It didn't seem unusual at the time. In fact, it was not until several years later, when the family took a trip to Manassas, Virginia, that she realized how special it was.

In Manassas, the tour guide was expertly delivering his narrative about the historic area and the personalities involved. When he began telling about General James Longstreet of the Confederate Army, my family paid particular interest. My mom had shared stories with us about the famous Civil War general who was her great-great-uncle. Longstreet was considered a great warrior and a skilled leader to his men. He is said to have had an intense fighting spirit and determination. His best tactical moment was at the Battle of the Wilderness. Prior to the tour, she told the guide about her family connection with the general. As the tour guide described the wound to the upper chest which nearly took the life of General Longstreet, I stepped up and said, "Was it like this?" and pulled back my t-shirt to expose the birthmark.

"Why, yes," the guide stuttered. He realized the connection between the famous general and the young boy. "That is exactly where the wound was."

My mom was astounded, too. She had never realized the strategic position of the birthmark and marveled at the connection with the wound of her ancestor. "Your great-great-uncle was an extraordinary man," the guide stated. "You must have a special relationship to him, because you bear that mark."

The third harbinger was in the naming of the new baby. So often, children are named after relatives, but my mother had already selected the two names she wanted, and they had nothing to do with family names. Several months before I was born she told my dad, "I've been giving some thought to a name for the baby. I don't know why, but if it's a boy, I want to name him after Richard the Lion-hearted and Michael the Archangel."

"Richard Michael," my dad said. "Sounds like a good name to me, if that's what you want, then okay."

As I was growing up, I became intrigued with the stories my mother would tell me of my namesakes. When playing with friends, I pretended I was General Longstreet or King Richard the Lion-hearted, of England, out to conquer evil and fight battles for justice. I especially liked the legendary exploits of Michael the Archangel. During those developmental childhood years, Mom often reminded me of the story from the Bible when Satan, at the death of Moses, claimed the body of Moses because of his involvement with the murder of the Egyptians. God sent Michael to fight the angel of darkness and, of course, Michael conquered Satan. Influenced by my Catholic upbringing and parochial education, my childhood games included imaginary battles where I would shout, "Bring it on, God. I'll take care of Satan for you."

Whether these three circumstances influenced my future or were instrumental in building character is hard to say. But, I enjoyed a typical childhood, mischievous at times, and definitely all boy. My friends and I would often concoct practical jokes and pranks to play on each other. We never meant to be malicious, but sometimes things backfired.

Once, while attending a Boy Scout Camp in the mountains of Pennsylvania, my friends and I devised an elaborate prank on a fellow scout mate. It took three of us to orchestrate the plan. First, we altered the boy's cot so that he was able to lie on it but, unbeknownst to the victim, it was barely supporting him. We planned it so that he would roll to the right once the bed toppled. We also rigged the side of the tent to collapse when the boy fell on it. That night, when the boy was finally asleep, we pulled the triggering string. The scout fell to his right onto the collapsing side of the tent, just as planned. The one flaw in our plan was the attention to complete detail. Our victim rolled out of the tent and, oblivious to what was happening to him, continued to roll down the hill until he came to an abrupt stop against a tree, causing his wrist to break.

Our den leader was not happy. Fortunately for us, he realized it was an innocent, boyish prank that had gotten out of control. He let us go with a warning.

Scouting was not the only activity that my parents used to develop my life. When I was seven years old, my grandfather gave me my first electric toy train. Gramp was an avid train collector and at one time worked as a security guard at the Lionel train factory. Through the years, he gathered quite a collection and wanted to share it with me, his youngest grandson. The first set he handed down was a 1934 Lionel O gauge, which had belonged to my father when he was a boy. The set consisted of a steam engine, a Babe Ruth boxcar, a gondola and a caboose. My grandfather saw how much I loved that train and soon gave me another, similar set from 1938, which had been discarded by my uncle.

The train sets quickly became a permanent part of my family's holiday decorations and would often stay up for months afterward. By the time I was eleven, it became evident to my parents that I was interested in expanding my small collection. They would watch the newspapers for ads and check out any sets that were advertised. When I was twelve, my parents allowed me to set up a small train table in the basement. The layout started off as a simple four-foot circle and continued to grow into an eight- by twelve-foot complex, which included a village and an industrial park.

This expansion was initially influenced by my mom, for it was about this time that she started taking me to my first local train shows. I was in awe of the many local collections; my young eyes were wide with excitement. I had the bug for collecting already, but these events fueled my fascination with trains even further. Through my grandfather, I met many of the founders of the Train Collectors Association. Occasionally Gramp would take me to visit the men and see their massive collections and operating layouts. Through my young imagination, these collections and layouts were an endless mass of play and creativity. I was lucky to spend countless hours in the "old timers" basements, listening to stories about finding rare and desirable items in the garbage or items disposed of by the Lionel Train factory. With each passing story, I learned more about the intricacies of the hobby, thus allowing me to develop a general expertise as the years went on. Through the mutual interest of trains, we developed a bond that still lives long after my grandfather has passed.

3
Training of the Body

1978–1986—I was never a great student in school, but I excelled in sports. At age 13, and now in public school, it was obvious that baseball was my game. My father and I would practice throwing the ball every day. And each day, he pressed me to throw the ball a little harder or just a little farther, but was cautious to keep it fun. Often, he would move his glove to a fixed position and shout back at me, "Bet you couldn't hit the center of the glove without me moving it." I was up for the challenge, but never realized he was "fine tuning" my pitching skills.

By age 15, it was not unusual for the coach to clock my pitches at 85 miles per hour or for me to strike out 16 of 21 batters per game. Because of my speed and precise throwing ability, the rules were changed during the summer Babe Ruth league playoff games. Now, no player could pitch more than four innings per game.

My sports career continued and, as coaches sometimes assume that if you can throw a baseball, you can throw a football, I was made the quarterback of the town team. Despite my athletic prowess, football was not my game. In my three years as quarterback I had only one win—a less than illustrious record. Unfortunately, that game was won by default when the opposing team didn't show up.

But what I lacked on the gridiron, I certainly made up for on the pitcher's mound. My natural ability brought me the MVP for every season I played. Professional scouts were soon alerted to my talent and, at age 15 at the end of my junior year, I was invited to attend the Pro training camp in Florida.

That summer before the baseball camp, my parents and I visited my older brother in San Diego, California. The afternoon before we were scheduled to leave, Ricky, a local friend I had back in New Jersey and who subsequently had moved within blocks of my brother's new home, and I sneaked off to a nude beach. I knew that my parents would not approve, but hey, this was the chance of a lifetime.

At the beach, we found some low cliffs, perfect for inexperienced divers. Before long, some girls down on the beach noticed us and began flirting with us, daring us to dive off the higher cliffs. Up to the challenge, and showing off as young men will do, I climbed to the higher cliffs. On that one dive, I arched my back too quickly as I entered the water. I knew I had done something wrong when I heard and felt a "pop" in my back. As I pulled myself up onto the rocks, it was obvious that Ricky had heard something snap.

"Are you okay, Rich?" he asked, frightened by the sound.

"I don't know," I groaned. "My back really hurts and my legs don't feel right."

I was in excruciating pain as he helped me out of the water. Also, I was having a hard time walking and forced myself not to show any signs of pain or injury, especially in front of the topless girls.

"Hey, Rich," Ricky suggested, suspecting I was hurt, "we better get out of here. Maybe if we go back to the house and relax in the hot tub, you'll feel better."

As we two daredevils walked away from the girls, I was struggling not to show the pain I felt. I finally managed to speak. "Yeah, let's give that a try."

Not willing to tell my parents the truth about where we were and what happened, I kept my injury to myself. Even during the long and very painful six-hour flight home, I never mentioned a word. The family arrived back in New Jersey late the next day. At home, I immediately went to bed.

By morning, I was still in a great deal of pain, so I devised a plan. I would ride my bike the mile and a half to a friend's house, tell him about the diving accident and the girls, then go back home and tell my parents that we were out riding in the woods on the motorcycle and I crashed.

What I hadn't counted on was the amount of suffering my injury would cause me as I attempted to ride my bike. I was only able to ride half way before I succumbed to the pain and turned back home.

Even after making my way very slowly, I could no longer tolerate the pain riding the bicycle caused me. I got off the bike and used it as a "crutch" to walk the remaining mile to my home. More than an hour later, I stumbled through the side garage door. My legs were unable to support me any longer, and I collapsed in the doorway.

My parents were sitting in the kitchen eating lunch and looked over to greet me. Instead, they watched me crumple to the floor. Both my parents lunged from the table and down the steps to come to my aid. I lay on the floor squirming in pain.

"I can't feel my left leg," I moaned, "and my back hurts really bad."

Carefully, my father helped me to my feet, being cautious to move my back as little as possible. "Let's get you in the back seat of the car and to the hospital," He said to me. "We need to get you to a doctor."

Gently, he helped me lie down in the back seat of the car. Once situated, both my parents jumped in the front seat and rushed me to the hospital.

During the ride to Perth Amboy Emergency Medical Center, they drilled me for information about what happened. Still worried to tell the truth about the nude beach, I opted for the motorcycle accident without my friend's knowledge.

After numerous x-rays and tests, the doctors informed us that I had snapped my lower back's fifth lumbar vertebra. They recommended we first try to pull it into place by using traction, thus allowing the bone to naturally fuse. If this did not work, or if I continued to lose feeling in my legs, they would have to operate. One thing the doctors were certain of, my chances of playing pro baseball were over.

In the meantime, my friend Dave, the scapegoat, was punished for being so careless. He visited me in the hospital only once, the day before I was to be released. Still in a lot of trouble over my lie, he didn't have much to say. Finally, he awkwardly managed, "Boy, you have more cables than my compound bow."

"Yeah, I know," I replied. "You okay with your parents?"

"Yeah, it will be okay." Dave looked down, scuffing his shoe on the floor. "I changed the story a little. I told them I was not riding with you; that you went out on your own."

"No problem." My story to my parents was still somewhat intact. "Did you hear I've been having some fun in here?"

"Yeah, I heard. You better be careful though," Dave chastised. "This one is serious. You may end up paralyzed." The fear was obvious on Dave's face.

"Hey, don't sweat it," I said confidently, trying to cheer up my friend. "The doctors said in about a year I'd be good as new."

"Well, I gotta go. My mom is downstairs waiting for me." Dave's face could not conceal his relief. He was going to be able to make his getaway. "Give me a call when you get out."

"Sure will," I told him, "and, like I said, don't sweat this. I'll be okay." I watched as he left the room.

While in the hospital, in full traction with cables and weights connected all over my lower body, I was still able to find ways to have some fun, and get into trouble. My visitors, and there were many, all brought gifts and toys. The semi-solid rubber ball my brother gave me to exercise my fingers and arms, as the doctors had ordered, soon began to be bounced off the wall and ceiling. And, of course, the inevitable happened—the ball went through the television screen.

When my Uncle Al, from the boatyard, came to visit, he was intrigued by the electronics and numerous gadgets attached to my bed and to me. "What do you say we find out how some of this stuff works?" Uncle Al suggested.

"Sounds good to me," I eagerly agreed, ready for some diversion. "This bed looks supercharged. Let's see what it can do."

The two of us began to fiddle with all the gadgets beside the bed. When the bed started to lift from both ends, I knew I was in trouble.

"Oh shit, stop this thing! It's really hurting me," I shouted, as I began to form a "V," head and feet moving closer together, weights pulling on my body.

"I'll pull the plugs," Uncle Al responded excitedly.

Just as he pulled the many plugs, and the bed stopped moving, the nurses arrived. "What are you doing to him?" one nurse demanded.

"Just seeing how this stuff works," Al answered innocently.

"Richard, do you still have feeling in your legs?" the nurse inquired as she leveled the bed back into position.

"Yeah, I'm okay," I responded, thankful that the pain was receding. "We were just trying to adjust the bed when something went wrong with it. It must be broken," I added, in defense of my uncle.

"Yeah, I think something's wrong with the bed," Al added.

But the nurse would not be duped. "I don't think so, boys," she said, still angry about the near catastrophe. "You really could have hurt him. Now, how about leaving while I get a doctor to check him." It was much more of a command than a request.

As Al headed for the door, I called to him. "Uncle Al, don't worry, I'm okay. I'll see you in a day or two."

"No problem, Rich," Al responded. "I'll see you soon."

Two days later, I gave the nursing staff a real scare. I was experiencing a lot of pain but, in an effort to stay off pain pills, I was up all night. Frustrated and bored, I began examining the wires to the control box for my bed. As I removed and replaced wires, one came loose from the terminal. When I attempted to push it back in, the wire sparked and caused the tissues on my bedside table to smolder. As I swatted them into my tin garbage pail, I grabbed my bedside emergency baton and pushed the button several times. Within seconds, four nurses or order-lies rushed in. There was now a small fire in my garbage pail. One of the orderlies grabbed a fire extinguisher and quickly extinguished it before the main hospital alarms sounded.

Shortly after that incident, I was released from the hospital in a full metal back brace. I had been in traction for three weeks.

During my stay, I celebrated my 16th birthday. Not exactly the way I wanted to spend it.

As my parents drove me home, I was unwilling to verbally express my thoughts. My mind was full of doubts and fear. Barely able to stand on my own and still in severe pain, I couldn't help but be fright-ened by the thought of: "Will I be able to walk and function normal-ly again?"

As we pulled into the driveway, I saw many of the neighbors there to greet me. To everyone's dismay, and against doctor's orders, I very slowly forced myself out of the back seat of the car and into a standing position. My mom rushed to my side to help.

"Leave me alone, Mom. I can do this," I insisted.

"What the hell you think you're doing, Rich?" Dad exclaimed in disbelief.

"Well, I plan on walking over to see Skipper," I responded as I made my way across the lawn. "Then, I'll walk back, and then we'll get to the therapy those dumb doctors think I need."

The walk to the fenced yard to see Skipper, the neighbor's black and white spotted Labrador mix, was a good seventy-five feet. It took me a while, but once I made it, I relaxed against the fence to recoup my strength for the long walk back. Skipper was excited to see me. With his paws on top of the fence, the dog waited anxiously to be petted and greeted me with a wet lick to the face.

The walk back proved to be more difficult and painful. I realized that doctors might not be so dumb after all. With the pain mounting, I struggled toward the house. The onlookers began to cheer me on. "You're gonna make it, Rich." "What do those doctors know anyway?"

"You'll be okay!" "Hey, let me know when you're ready to pitch again. I'll catch for you."

Although well meaning, it was the last encouragement that hurt. There would be no possibility of pro baseball, and at age 16, baseball was still my primary focus. I would not even be able to participate in high school gym class. In fact, the recuperation process would take well over a year.

During the course of my extensive therapy, which included repairing my motor coordination, balance, and relearning how to walk, I was introduced to weight lifting. It began with small weights to help me rebuild the muscles that had suffered due to the accident. Gradually, I was able to add more weight and regain full control of my body.

By high school graduation, my back brace was permanently off, my body weight had increased and there was much more definition to my physique than ever before. My friends noticed how muscular I was becoming, and the girls were treating me differently. I started going to the gym on a daily basis. It didn't take long for the regulars to notice me.

It also didn't take long for me to develop another group of friends at the gym. This new group offered a great deal of inspiration to my new interest, and this added attention spurred me on to greater intensity and focus. I would push myself and continually added more weight to my workout. Soon I was bench-pressing over 350 pounds.

One day, Rossi, the gym owner and ex-pro power-lifter and bodybuilder, was watching me. "Hey Rich, how much do you weigh?"

"About 180," I puffed, as I expelled my breath, lifting the weights.

Rossi looked closely at the weights. Three hundred and seventy-five pounds was pretty impressive for someone at 180, and the kid seemed to have a lot of drive. Rossi always had his eye out for someone to train. "There just might be some potential with this one," he thought.

"Hey Ros," I called, as I set the barbells on the stand, "I got the notice about the rate increase for the gym. I'm going to have to quit. It's more than I want to spend."

Rossi hesitated only momentarily. "Tell you what kid, if you'll come work out with me both morning and evening, we'll just waive the fee."

"Great, no problem," I happily responded. I knew that Rossi was formerly a national contender and I figured I would be able to learn a lot from him while we trained.

It didn't take long for me to realize that we were doing more then just working out together. He was training me for competition and initially would not admit it. He put me on a strict diet and supplements, which included free-form and peptide amino acids. Unknowingly, Rossi used the same tactics for my weight training as my father used for baseball training. Every morning, Rossi had a protein or carbohydrate drink ready for me. And, every day, he spoke to me about what foods to eat and vitamins and other supplements I should be taking throughout the day. Rossi preached the importance of changing my workout regimen, and he constantly challenged me to lift more weight in different positions. The excuse was that we were building up my back so I would never injure it again.

I was a good student, and we developed a good relationship. Finally, after four months, Rossi confessed that he was training me for competition. He started me in some small meets with other gyms. But after two years of serious training, Rossi developed me into an "almost" national contender. He worked my body weight to a solid 190 pounds, but my lifting ability—425-pound bench press, 600-pound leg squat, and 235-pound military press—was not good enough to qualify for any of the divisional or national meets.

My gym buddies occasionally invented pranks of strength for us to perform. One such incident was played on a girl who refused to go out with a fellow power-lifter. We took, or rather lifted, her Toyota Celica and placed it between two trees, thus, completely preventing it from any forward or reverse movement. The girl didn't think it was so funny, but after some convincing, and a confirmed date, we removed the car from between the trees.

As much as I enjoyed being with my friends at the gym and competing in the smaller power lifting meets, it was evident this could only be a hobby, more serious than most, but just a hobby. Besides, there were more things in my life that I enjoyed.

4
Recruiting 1st Lieutenant of My Soul

It was on a hot August afternoon that my friends, Gary and John, and I were out in the garage lifting weights. I had converted my parent's small garage into a perfect workout area. The refurbished garage/gym allowed an area for us to get a full body workout and still provided garage space at night for my parents' car. We stored the weights under the workbench and pulled them out each day to exercise. The garage door was kept open while we exercised, just in case one of the local girls came by.

That hot summer day, while going through our routine, we saw a pretty blonde girl ride past on her bicycle. She was new to the neighborhood. Her parents had built a home at the end of the street. Gary and I had heard of this "new blonde" but this was the first time either of us had seen her up close. "Hey Rich," Gary called out. "I think that's the girl; the one whose house we got all the wood from."

"Yeah, I know," I responded.

Disgruntled because the new house was being built right over our favorite fishing hole, we had been "requisitioning" lumber from the construction site. We were building a clubhouse that would serve as a base camp for deer hunting during the winter. As unhappy as we were about the house replacing our fishing hole, the addition of an attractive blonde made up for it, especially in my eyes.

"Man, she's gorgeous," Gary, said, as he stared at her riding down the street. Gary, impressed by her looks, was acting like a dog in heat, pacing up and down the driveway, all excited with a big smile.

"Yeah, whatever," I said, keeping a close, but inconspicuous eye on her.

"She sure is, and I've got to figure out a way to meet her," Gary determined.

"Don't count on it," I said. "I plan on taking her out this weekend."

"Shit, you haven't even met her yet," John scoffed.

"Well, I guess we should stop her on the way back," I told him confidently.

John and I were not too concerned about meeting the girl right away. John already had a girlfriend and was not so anxious. I wanted to meet her, but figured I could just take a walk up to her house later this evening and introduce myself. After all, I knew that she usually sat outside with her parents in the early evenings. But Gary wanted something to happen now. He was the one who initiated the idea. "I got it," Gary announced. "We can act like we're washing Rich's car, and when she comes riding by, we can, like, accidentally, on purpose, throw a bucket of water on her. She'll have to talk to us then, or at least she'll try and beat the shit out of us. Either way, we meet her."

"Who you kidding, you just want to see her in a wet t-shirt," I laughed.

"And, man, that's just a cheap thrill, Gary," John added.

"Well, you come up with a better idea, then," Gary taunted.

Neither of us cared for Gary's idea, but we thought it might be nice to see her "kick Gary's ass" in a wet t-shirt. "Okay, Gary. I'll go get the buckets and stuff, you keep a watch out for her." I instructed.

There was more to Gary's plan, though. "Hey, John," Gary whispered as I went into the house. "Forget throwing the water on the girl.

When she comes back, we'll throw the water on Rich and then see what happens."

More interested in the plot with this new twist, John snickered, "Great, but if he gets mad, I'm blaming it all on you, and you throw the water. I'm not gonna get Rich mad at me."

I returned with the buckets and polishing cloths. At the very least, I figured my car would be clean again. It took some time for the new girl to come back, and when she did, we had the car completely clean. Gary saved a bucket of soapy water, and a bucket of clean water that we used to chamois the car to a high gloss.

As the blonde approached on her bike, I stepped out to the side of the street. I thought I would just stop her, and introduce my friends and myself, and forget about throwing the water on her. I didn't expect that my friends would challenge my change of plan. But Gary was true to his plan. As the girl approached, I walked out to greet her. Gary splashed me with the soapy water, and immediately after, John hit me with the bucket of clean water. It was a sort of "wash and rinse" for me.

Although stunned by the sudden turn of events, I took it gracefully. Instead of getting mad at my friends, we all burst out laughing. Even the girl stopped and laughed with us.

"Hey, I'm Rich," I said, laughing and extending my wet hand to her. "I guess you know that was meant for you."

"Hi, I'm Cathi," she said as she smiled, gently accepting my hand. "Who are your bum friends?" she asked.

Gary and John cautiously approached, unsure whether I might still try to take a swing at one of them.

"Well, this idiot is Gary. He's the one whose idea this was. But I was told he wanted to see you in a wet t-shirt," I told her, embarrassing Gary with my candor.

"Well, keep dreaming, Gary," she laughed.

"And, this is John," I continued. "He's okay, not like Gary here. Hey, you gonna be out on the porch tonight with your parents?" I asked, taking advantage of my knowledge of her habits.

"You know I am every night. I see you go by. You stopping over this time?" Cathi asked in a daring voice.

"Yeah, I think I will. I'll come and hang out for a while tonight. Could be fun," I said casually, but with confidence.

Once our new friend, Cathi, had left, the three of us continued to horse around. They teased me, asking if I was going to be the first to ask her on a date, threatening that one of them would beat me to it. But I didn't really care what happened. I was happy just annoying Gary, who was still panting after the girl. He kept telling me that if I didn't go to her house that night he would.

That evening, after returning from the gym, I took a walk up the street to see if Cathi was there. I took some time to think about her during my workout. She had impressed me during our childish meeting. I started to get a little nervous. She might be pretty nice to go out with, not like one of the "throw-away" dates that most of my friends went on after weight lifting competitions. As I got closer to her home, I noticed she was on the porch alone. The porch light illuminated her long, curly blonde hair in the darkness. As I approached, I saw her warm, glowing smile. "Good to see you," she smiled. "How'd it go after I left?"

I felt myself returning her smile. Well, I guess she's interested, I thought to myself.

I found Cathi easy to talk to. She responded to my positive manner and good humor. I told her about my back injury, and that I worked in tool and die making. We talked about the high school, about my college plans and about our families. Cathi was the oldest of three children. She often took care of her younger brother and sister, Scott and Kim. I found Cathi and I had a lot in common. We both liked outdoor activities, hiking and biking. Cathi's family had a boat and they often spent time during the weekends out on the water.

I soon became a regular around their household. I would come by three or four times a week. Sometimes we would go over to the mall, but mostly we stayed at her house. Cathi's father was not real happy about all the attention I was giving his daughter. One day while I was waiting for Cathi to get ready to go out, Cathi's father made a comment to me. "You know, I don't play baseball," he said menacingly, "but I do have a bat."

I got the message loud and clear. Despite this attitude, there were many times that I went with the family on weekend boat outings. Her parents were fun to be around, and they became more relaxed with me. They even started letting Cathi go to the movies or on day hikes with me to Pennsylvania.

5
Training of the Mind to Create

In September, I enrolled at Middlesex County College. My parents had encouraged me to further my education. Although I dreaded having to take English 101 and some other core classes, I anxiously anticipated the mechanical engineering course I had enrolled in. That was where my heart was, so I enjoyed it and did well. But English was a different story—that I hated the class showed in my attitude. It only took me one semester to figure out that college was not for me. I dropped all of my classes except for the engineering course, and began looking for a job.

During high school I had spent a good deal of time in the machine shop. It was my favorite class and I excelled at it. My parents, realizing that I was not interested in college, began pushing the idea of a trade school, "maybe something in the machining field." Knowing that I would be more open to something that I enjoyed, my dad began checking the help wanted ads in the newspaper.

One evening, Dad was relaxing in front of the television, reading the evening paper. I walked in, returning from my workout at the gym. "Hey Rich, why don't you check this out?" he called out. "A shop called WebbTool is looking for help. Why don't you give them a call?"

I took the paper and read the ad. "Sure, Dad," I nodded, handing the paper back to Dad. "Tear out the ad and I'll call tomorrow."

WebbTool was advertising for an apprentice toolmaker. It was an ideal position for me, and a good place for me to learn and get some experience. It was a small, family-owned job shop that did sub-contract work for some of the aerospace industry big boys. They built parts for airplanes, rockets and missiles. Bendix was their principal contractor, although occasionally they would do work for Lockheed and Boeing.

My interview with the owner, Ed Sr., went well. He was a huge man at 6'2," thick boned, well over 400 pounds. I liked him, and he liked me. I brought along a brass cannon I had made in my high school metal shop and he was impressed with the work. He was always looking for young talent. He had hired Kenny, another talented young man, only a month before. Ed could see that pitting two competitive young men against one another would be to his benefit. What he really liked about the situation was that he would not have to pay us as well as he would have to pay someone with more experience. I was hired.

On my first day at WebbTool, Ed Sr. introduced me to his sons. Fred was the oldest and the shop foreman, Ed Jr. ran the office with his father, and Eric worked in the shop. All three of the sons were well-educated and tall but, unlike their father, they were all very slender.

Here I met Kenny, in a "sweat shop." Kenny was my age, a little shorter and stockier than I. We shared the same curly brown hair; he had a brown moustache and mine was blonde. We could have been brothers, and most people thought we were. Instantly, we established a rapport with one another.

My first duties were on the production line. For someone with my skills, it was grunt work; basic, repetitive functions and none of the creative work I longed for. But, I was satisfied for the time being, and settled into the position with the ease of someone who had done the job for years. I progressed into more complicated and detailed work. Kenny and I were a good team. Both of us shared an enthusiasm for the work we did and it didn't take long for our friendship to deepen.

One day, about a month into my employment, Kenny casually mentioned, "I'm going to take some classes over at Union County College starting next semester. Why don't you come with me?"

"Well, I didn't have much luck at Middlesex," I responded. "I mean, I really enjoyed the engineering class I took. It's just all that other stuff they want you to take that I don't like."

"Union County College has a program where you can just take the classes in your field. You can get your certification in mechanical engineering and take some tool and die courses," Kenny encouraged. "Besides, we can take the same classes and study together. Think about it. It could be fun."

It took Kenny two weeks to convince me to enroll with him. But the two of us signed up and started the same classes at the beginning of the next semester. We quickly developed a routine and became inseparable, at least during working hours. Each morning, we would meet at the shop about 6:30 or 7 A.M. and work until 8:30. We would then leave for the nearby campus and an occasional breakfast. From 9 until noon, we would attend our classes in engineering or tool making. During lunch we would study and then return to work about 1 in the afternoon. Often, we would continue working until 7 or 8 at night.

We became very good at our craft. We were both competitive by nature, but it was a friendly competition between us. We challenged each other to produce the best product. Many of the projects we worked on required close tolerances of the metals. Because the parts were for the aerospace industry, precision was vital to the final product. We were perfectionists, because we understood the critical nature of what we produced.

We shared an attitude when it came to coworkers. Both of us knew the value of learning the trade from older, more experienced craftsmen, men who owned the knowledge but because of age and arthritis, were unable to handle the intricate nature of many jobs. Kenny and I would spend our breaks talking with the older men and often consulted with them on aspects of the difficult projects.

It didn't take long for our talent to be recognized. By the end of the first year, our peers viewed us as the best in the shop. And Ed Sr. quickly saw an opportunity to make a big profit off of our talents. He began seeking more contracts that required a high degree of precision, confident that the two of us could accomplish the more difficult tasks. And, we never disappointed him.

One morning, as we were arriving for our class at Union College, the instructor, Mr. Dewire, stopped us. He had been our instructor in shop, mathematics and computer programming classes during the past two years and the three of us enjoyed a good relationship. This morning, however, the teacher was distraught.

"I had an accident last night with my Corvette, and was wondering if you guys could come help me repair it?" The 1963 candy-apple red split-window Corvette was his pride and joy. "I live close by and with the three of us working on it, we could get it finished pretty quick."

Kenny was experienced working on cars and really enjoyed it. "What's the damage?" he asked, already planning on skipping the rest of the morning's classes.

As we gathered our belongings and walked toward our cars, Mr. Dewire described the crack on the nose that the pristine fiberglass body sustained. Kenny and I followed the teacher to his house a few blocks away. The car was already up on the portable ramp. After a quick examination, the three of us began preparations for the repairs. Because Kenny was more adept at bodywork, he took the lead. As I heated the fiberglass resin, Kenny and Mr. Dewire set the crack in the body. Once the resin was heated, Kenny set it on the engine and crawled underneath the car. He began to expertly apply the heated mixture to the underneath side of the damage. "Someone hand me that other brush," he called out to us. Mr. Dewire reached for the brush and as he did, he bumped the side of the car, knocking the can of resin over. The thick liquid spilled down the engine and onto Kenny's shoulder and back. "Shit," Kenny cursed as he scrambled out from under the car, "that crap is hot." He stripped off his t-shirt began wiping the resin off his skin. Mr. Dewire got a cloth and began wiping Kenny's back.

"You okay, Kenny?" I asked as I grabbed a nearby cloth, too.

"Yeah, just a little burn," Kenny nodded, "but some spilled on the engine. We need to get it off of there before it hardens."

I quickly found the spill. Within minutes, the mess was cleaned up. Mr. Dewire went into his home and brought out some Vaseline cream for Kenny to put on his burn. Then, Kenny put on the extra t-shirt that he always carried in the back of his car. The three of us went back to work repairing the classic car as if nothing happened.

That day, we were late arriving back to the shop. Tim, a big red-headed helper, was already heating up two coffee cans of cutting oil that we would be using to cut the slots on aircraft gyros. "Ed Sr. was in here a minute ago, yelling," Tim reported. "He's all bent out of shape about the deadline and . . ."

Ed Sr. just then walked back into the work area. "Where have you two been? We've got to get these things out of here, and . . ."

"We had a class project we needed to finish. We need to get this going now," Kenny dismissed the older man as he made himself busy preparing the milling machine to begin cutting. Ed Sr. left in a huff.

The cramped working quarters made it difficult for the four of us to work, but with direction from Kenny and I, the two inexperienced helpers usually managed to stay out of the way. Today though, possibly because of the pressure from the boss, we were all pushing ourselves to work a little faster. Tim moved one of the cans of heated cutting oil to the hot plate close to the machine. He picked up the second can and was turning to place it with the other, when he bumped into Kenny, who had moved to reposition himself at the milling machine. Startled by the heated oil now spilling down his lower back, Kenny lurched forward, knocking the first can of oil over, spilling it onto his abdomen and thighs.

"Jesus Christ," cursed Kenny, "I should have just stayed home today. Nothing is going right!"

"Sorry, Kenny," Tim apologized, "I didn't see you move over here."

"Let's just get this mess cleaned up and get back to work," Kenny said, wiping his clothes off for the second time that day. "We don't want Ed back in here yelling at us." The incident was quickly forgotten as the four of us returned our concentration to the job at hand. Kenny left the confined area to clean the oils off himself with chemical solvents. Later I would remember this day vividly.

In June, 1983, Kenny and I graduated from Union County College with certifications in mechanical engineering, Class A tool and die, and drafting. Kenny took the top honors in the class and I graduated second.

With school behind us, it was obvious to both of us that they did not need two full time employees with our abilities and talents. We used WebbTool as a learning situation, but Ed Sr. took advantage of our skills, too. He stopped giving us raises, and it didn't take us long to figure out that it was because he wanted one of us to quit. Both of us started looking for new work, and made a pact that whoever found another job first, the other would remain at WebbTool.

I was the first to find another position. I was hired by Parkway-Kew to work with large wire dies. The evening after my first day on the new job, the phone rang. It was Kenny. "How was your first day?" he inquired.

"It was okay. It's pretty simple work, but the pay is much better than Eddie gave us," I responded.

"Well, guess what?" Kenny broke in. "It's just what we thought. The old man gave me a three-dollar-an-hour raise today. I guess both of us are better off now."

"Congratulations. We both know you deserve it. Of course, you owe me dinner now," I teased. "We'll have to get together soon and bring the girls."

"Sounds like a good idea, but you should pay," Kenny teased. "You're the one with the hot new job."

But, as often happens, we were busy with our separate lives and we drifted apart.

My new job turned out to be too easy. Although I liked my employers and my coworkers, the work did not challenge me and within three months, I was out looking for something that would hold my interest.

Dad heard that Bendix was looking for someone with my experience. It was an ideal position, but there were lots of applicants. Bendix was the type of company where someone could work for the rest of their life. It is well known as a good stable company that pays well and has great benefits. He made a phone call to his friend, Ron, the president of Bendix, and managed to get me an interview. Impressed, as supervisors often were, but cautious because of my youth, Frank Myers hired me, with conditions. If I made any mistakes during the first 90 days of my employment, I would be out on the streets looking for another job. Up to the challenge, I zealously accepted the terms and began work on the graveyard shift the following week.

I excelled in my work at Bendix and, within the first month, was being considered for a promotion. Frank was discussing the new position with me when he casually asked, "How did you manage to get an interview here? Bendix usually goes for older, more experienced guys."

"Well, I earned my certifications at school while I was at WebbTool and I guess they figured I was qualified. My Dad called the president, who's a friend, and got me the interview, and you hired me."

I noticed Frank's expression visibly change and harden. Frank just looked at me and then walked away. I cursed myself for mentioning my father's friendship with the president. It was obvious that Frank, already insecure and underqualified for the position he held, was threatened by this connection.

My speculation was proved to be correct. His attitude changed entirely overnight. I did not receive the promotion and Frank began finding fault with everything I did. He initiated a rubber stamp program where each employee was required to stamp the parts they produced. Frank made sure that I got the stamp that previously was used on defective parts. Once he was able to unfairly blame me, he called me into his office and terminated me after only two months. I was back in the job market. I wasn't worried, though. I knew I was good at what I did and I figured I would take some time off to fish and hang out with Cathi before I began looking for another job.

6
Engineering the Future

Hayward Pool Products was an international company and a large employer in New Jersey; 400 employees worked in the local plant alone. When Hayward advertised for someone to work in the tool room, I responded. Floyd Harris, the plant manager, interviewed me. He liked my background and was impressed with my attitude. Aware of the personalities involved, Floyd found humor in the story about what happened at Bendix. "You've got the job," he told me, "but under the same hiring conditions as your previous employer. You screw up in the next 90 days and you're out on the street. Now, let's go meet your new supervisor, Henry."

When I first went to work at Hayward I was assigned to the tool shop, where Henry was my supervisor. Henry took an instant dislike to me. Whether it was Henry's distaste for my cheerfulness—I was friendly and easygoing, and made friends quickly—or whether Henry felt I was a threat to his job, I was not quite sure. Maybe it was jealousy. Arthritis had begun to plague Henry's hands and I, young, strong, nimble-fingered, and just out of college with substantial experience behind me, posed a definite risk to Henry's position, or at least his ego.

Henry made it clear from our first meeting that he wanted me fired. Arguments were a daily occurrence. Henry cursed at me and often assigned me to demeaning tasks which were beneath my abilities. The conflict between the two of us was humorous to some of the employees. They knew it would take only one blow from me to deck Henry, but I would never dream of touching the older man. If Henry were to ever take a swing at me, I would merely have to sidestep it. Verbally, I could take whatever Henry could dish out, and I could give back as good as I could take.

About six months into my employment with Hayward, a fatal accident occurred at one of the injection molding machines. A hopper, into which raw plastic pellet-like material was placed, broke loose due to the vibration of the machine. It fell on a female employee who was working near the machine, removing sharp edges, or "burrs," from the parts that were being produced. I was told she died instantly. Word spread quickly throughout the plant and everyone was in an uproar. Laborers were frightened that their machines might be faulty, also. Supervisors and managers were concerned that they might somehow be blamed. All struggled to contend with the tragedy of a lost life.

I left my workstation in the tool shop and inconspicuously made my way to the area of the accident. Paramedics were still there, attending to the body. Floyd, an ex-marine paratrooper and a brute of a man at 6'5" and 375 pounds, was furiously berating the group of engineers. "How did this happen?" he shouted. I never saw anyone purple with rage, but that was the only way I could describe him. "And, how do we correct this so that it will never happen again?" Floyd continued screaming at the engineers and supervisors, when he spied me. "What the hell are you doing here?" he boomed. "I suppose you think you can fix this Goddamn problem."

Unthreatened by the man who I now knew well, I stood calmly, examining the machine for a few minutes. "Well, it wouldn't take much," I said, thoughtfully. "If we craft a tapered male and female support flange with four vertical ribs cut on a 45-degree angle, that should supply enough support for the hopper against the vibration. We can just fit it to the machine like a support clamp."

Floyd paused for a moment, glaring hard at me in disbelief. He looked at the machine and back at me. Slowly, he turned to the maintenance manager and barked, "Do whatever he wants, and get this damned thing fixed." He turned to go, then stopped, and turned back. Obviously still livid, he glowered at the men standing around. "I find it amazing that you staff engineers couldn't figure out how to solve this simple mechanical problem, when a tool shop employee took one look and at least had an idea for a solution." With that he did an about face and stormed off, still cursing profusely.

It took the maintenance manager, four other workers and myself only three hours to clean up the area, construct and install the device. Once completed, we performed numerous tests, intentionally causing excessive vibration to the machine. This proved the effectiveness of the device. The hopper was secured and supplied perfect support. As an added safety precaution, management considered it for use on all the machines, until it was discovered later that the original hopper failure was caused by an improper connection to the machine. My clamping device was never instituted.

Within the week after this incident, Floyd came to me. "You did a good job with that hopper. And, I know that you and Henry don't get along very well. In fact, he came to me a few days ago demanding that I fire you. But, you are one of my best men. I hired you and I'm not about to fire you just because of some bullshit between you two. What do you think about transferring to the model shop? I've already talked to the supervisor there, and he would like to meet you. What do you think?"

It didn't take me a second to think about it. "That would be great!" I responded. "When can I go?"

"How's right now?" Floyd asked.

"I'm right behind you," I said, eager to go.

We went straight to the Model Shop and Floyd introduced me to Jerald.

"Nice to meet you," I said, shaking the slender black man's hand. "I've got to say," I said, joking, "I'm really grateful to be out from under Henry's verbal abuse. But most of all, I'm excited about the prospect of working on some new and more challenging projects."

"Good to meet you, too," Jerald replied, returning the handshake and the smile. "I've heard some good things about you. I think you'll do great here."

Thus began my nine-year stint in the model shop and my introduction to the basketball project. But I wasn't through with Henry yet.

Three months after I was transferred, Floyd came to me again.

"I've got to do something about Henry," Floyd began. "I'm still having problems with him in the Tool Shop and a lot of the guys didn't like the way he treated you. I know you all usually joked about it, but some others went to the union rep about it. They want me to fire him, and you know I can't do that, even if I wanted to. At one time, he was a good worker, and of course, it helps that he's a close friend with the owner." Floyd paused for a moment, unsure of how I might take his suggestion, and then plowed ahead. "Listen, Rich, he knows his stuff and he's getting close to retirement. I want to move him here to the model shop, but I want to make sure that you can work with him. I've talked to him, and he knows it's either this, or I'm going straight to Nash and letting him solve the problem."

I knew that Oscar Nash, president and owner of Hayward, would not take kindly to the predicament Floyd found himself in. I liked Floyd, and didn't want to see him put in that kind of position.

"Floyd, I never had a problem with Henry, other than the way he treated me," I told him with a laugh. "I can get along with anyone. If it's what you have to do, don't worry, I'll deal with it."

But, Henry, although somewhat subdued, didn't deal with it well at all. Upon arriving in the model shop, cigarette hanging out of his mouth, Henry's first comment was "I gotta work with this fucking asshole again?" Henry's workstation was set up right next to mine. What Henry didn't know was that earlier, Floyd and I moved and set up all his tools for him.

"'Fraid so, Henry," I responded cheerfully, not expecting any acknowledgement of our kindness. "I guess you'd better get used to it. I don't think I'm going anywhere. Are you?"

Henry ignored me, and turned to walk away as if nothing had been said.

The bickering, or small talk as I considered it, continued, day after day. But undaunted, I continued to force my positive nature on Henry and never really reacted to the verbal attacks.

Finally, one day, Henry managed a tenuous "good morning."

Well, I thought to myself, it only took two months for him to work his way from "fuck you, asshole" to "good morning." Maybe before he's dead, we'll actually talk.

And, shortly after that, much to the dismay of coworkers, we began to develop a lasting friendship. The daily comedy show, as most of the others thought of it, came to an end.

Henry was an accomplished chef, and it was not long before he was teaching me how to make my favorite dessert, chocolate mousse. He opened up to me and talked about his time in Nazi Germany, Hitler's Third Reich, and even his time in prison. Henry shared stories with me that family members did not know. I felt more than a little privileged that Henry was confiding to me.

7
Entrance into the Battle Field

June 18, 1986—This project was significant. We had been working on the process for over a year, and I was anxious to start the day. Today's test would go a long way in proving the viability of the procedure. After all the other unsuccessful attempts, my hopes were that we had finally devised a workable plan.

It was all I could think of as I sat up in bed. I must have been dreaming about it all night. I stretched my solid, muscular 6-foot frame, as I yawned and lumbered to the bathroom. It was a typical New Jersey June morning; the beginnings of what I knew would be a hazy, hot and humid day. I could hear my mom in the kitchen making coffee—the "morning mud," as Dad often called it. But as usual, Mom was up and catering to our every need, never taking to heart any of the morning comments. I assumed Dad was there too, sitting at the table already eating his bowl of corn flakes with sliced banana and perusing the morning paper. This had been his usual morning routine for the last five years. He was also most likely dressed in his suit, prepared to leave for the University of Medicine in Newark, where he held a powerful position as Assistant Facilities Manager. My parents, who had been high school sweethearts, were happily married (for the most part) and had been for 35 years. Despite the ups and downs of any marriage, they were still close. Of their four children, I was the youngest. At 24, I was still at home enjoying the rent-free, responsibility-free life that many of my friends envied. Mom took care of everything: cooking the food, making lunches, doing the laundry, and making the beds. It was any young man's dream-come-true.

I went through my morning exercise regime; squats for my leg muscles, bench presses for my chest, and a few arm curls. I considered this just my morning warm up. The serious workouts were done at the local gym in the evening. Although I no longer competed in power-lifting events, I was still capable of squatting 600 pounds and bench pressing 400. Outside my upstairs bedroom window, I could see the idyllic Sayreville neighborhood. I often thought it the character of the perfect neighborhood: manicured lawns; perfect flower gardens; groomed trees; picket fences; freshly painted houses. It was like a scene out of "Leave it to Beaver."

As I exercised, I mentally ticked off the steps I would take when I reached the plant. I had been a member on this project team almost from the time I was hired by Hayward 18 months ago. Hayward's business was the engineering and manufacturing, via plastic injection-molding, of industrial pumps, pool filters, heaters, strainers, valves and all aspects of filtering systems. Harold Duncan, one of the executive vice presidents of the company, and my immediate supervisor on this project, visualized a design of a new pool filter housing, including the manufacturing process. We had been working on the prototype and process for over a year. Nothing worked so far, but today we were going to get to use the injection-molding machine for the first time and finally explore the project's possibilities.

Harold was a good boss. He was easy-going and got along with all the employees. I enjoyed working with him. Always the professional, Harold would often come into the model shop and work in his suit and tie. He would just push up his sleeves and dig in, typically getting in our way and slowing progress. He was nearing retirement age and was the moving force behind this project, which everyone referred to as the "basketball project." It was his baby, his "brainchild," as Harold called it. He dealt with serious opposition from Sam, the other executive vice president. Sam didn't like the project and was vocal about it. He felt all along that it was too dangerous and didn't believe it would ever work. But, Sam was considered a chronic worrier, and a whiner to some, so no one took his comments too seriously.

In the shower, I checked my foot. There was still some redness and irritation from the previous day, when Harold had accidentally bumped a container with heated liquid styrene, and it had spilt on my leg and down into my boot. I had cleaned the thick molasses-like substance off my jeans as best I could with a solvent that was kept nearby for such mishaps. My sock had been soaked with the liquid styrene, so I had thrown it out. My boot had been a mess, but the solvent had gotten most of it off. After I had washed my foot with soap and water and had applied some alcohol and hydrocortisone cream, I had gone to work on the project. It was no big deal, just an inconvenience. I simply hoped my boot wouldn't aggravate the area too much as I worked today.

Now dressed and having eaten breakfast, I stepped into my pearl white 1980 Pontiac Firebird for the 45-minute drive in the infamous New Jersey Turnpike traffic to the plant. I could still smell Cathi's perfume in my car from the night before. I had been dating this intelligent, pretty blonde since high school. We were even engaged at one point, but decided to call it off. Neither of us was quite ready for marriage yet. Or, maybe in reality I was spoiled, too used to the good life at home. Either way, we had an enduring friendship. Often on weekends we traveled to places like the Delaware Water Gap or the mountains of Vermont. Sometimes it was just out to the movies.

Last night was different. We went out to dinner with Henry and his wife, Angela. Once Henry and I had developed a friendship, we often double dated, and dined at some of the better restaurants in the Newark area. Cathi and I both enjoyed the older couple's company, and were eager to hear stories from their "homeland."

I was also glad that Henry was assigned to the basketball project with me. We had developed a good rhythm in our work.

The only glitch in the project had been on February 11, 1986, when Henry and I were running a test procedure using a mixture made with fiberglass resins, liquid styrene and some other chemicals. We heated the chemical slurry (mixture), and it gave off fumes. The fumes overcame us, and we experienced extreme nausea, severe muscle cramping, headaches, and heaviness in our chests. Disoriented, we stumbled out of the area to the door for fresh air, trying to regain our composure. When we were able, we both went home ill.

As unpleasant as the experience was, after taking a long three-day weekend away from work I was ready to get back to work on the project. Still suffering from headaches, the determination to "make it work" prevailed, and both of us were back at work on the following Monday.

Henry was already at his desk as I walked into the shop. "Why don't you come and hang out while I cut these strands?" I invited. Both of us knew we were going to have to wait for Harold and there wasn't much for us to do until he arrived. We became experts at looking busy and killing time.

"Good food last night, yah?" Henry commented.

"It was great food. We should go there again soon," I said, as I pulled out some of the fine diameter, 40-inch strands of fiberglass. Holding a dozen or so, I began cutting them into 1-fi inch pieces. "I don't get why Harold wants us to put these pieces into the resin," I commented as I cut. "Hell, we have fiberglass resin with fine strands pre-mixed in already. As far as I'm concerned, this is just a useless duplication, another waste of time."

"Yah, but it is Harold's project. We just do what he tells us," Henry replied.

Sam walked by while we were preparing the mixture. "What the hell are you doing, Rich?" he barked.

Henry and I glanced at each other. It was no secret how much Sam disapproved of the project. "Just doing our jobs, Sam," I responded, and turned back to concentrate on the mixture, hoping Sam would let me off easy.

"Well, this is stupid," Sam grumbled, as he walked off. "And, it's a waste of time and money, I don't know where Harold gets these dumb ideas."

Once we were sure Sam was not coming back and, the mix being completed, I went out onto the floor where all the injection-molding machines were. It was important to start the machine's hydraulic pumps and heaters to allow the machine to heat up to the proper operating temperature. The molding machine room was easily 200 feet long and about 100 feet wide. The machine we were to use was considered small by our standards. It was called a Cincinnati 200-ton toggle press. This meant it had the capability of 200 tons of clamping pressure. The "toggle" was comprised of the fulcrum-style metal arms that closed the moveable, or female side of the clamp, also known as the movable platen. The machine stood about 8 feet tall at its highest point, 6 to 8 feet wide and about 20 feet long. The hopper brought the height to about 11 feet. This particular machine was located to the far-left end of the building, perpendicular to two large 500-ton presses. This made a large horseshoe-like work area.

I pushed the button to start the warm-up. It usually took about an hour for the huge machine to warm up, and I wanted to make sure everything was up to speed when Harold arrived. Dwight, from the maintenance department, had installed the mold the night before. It was ready to go.

Once the machine warmed up sufficiently, I climbed up on a stool and poured the injection mixture into the bottom connection flange. This was where the hopper would be when the machine was in normal operation. I positioned a six-foot wooden table close to the machine, knowing we would need a place to work. By the time I returned to the model shop, Henry had the "test basketball" fitted onto the metal flange that would eventually be installed in the mold.

It wasn't until 10 o'clock that Harold finally arrived. By that time,

Henry and I had completed the injection mixture, a rather thick mixture that consisted of a factory-mix fiberglass resin with extremely fine fiberglass fibers in it, polyester resin, liquid styrene, Methylene Chloride and Methyl Ethyl Ketone, (MEK). There was about two gallons of the mixture. Despite the Methylene Chloride that was added to thin or "melt" the mixture together, it was still thick, but we expected the heating process in the machine would thin it out further.

As Harold strode into the shop, he declared, "Today's the day. It's going to get done right today. It feels right." He set his notes on the table and continued, "Okay, let's get that fiberglass soaking mixture ready. Here are the ingredients." I had been careful to keep written measurements and detailed procedures, so that we could duplicate the experiment later on. The problem was that Harold was constantly changing amounts, adding a little of this and a little of that, destroying my accurate records.

The three of us worked together, preparing the soaking mixture. I stirred in the liquid styrene, polyester resin and Methyl Ethyl Ketone. Harold added Methylene Chloride, closely watching the consistency so as not to make it too thin. He was like a chef, worrying over his prize-winning sauce. Henry was cutting long woven fiberglass strips that were to be soaked in the mixture. These strips were to be used to wrap around the basketball. They were fine industrial basket-woven fiberglass strands that made up the "strip" or cloth-like material. Each strip was about two inches wide, one-eighth inch thick and 6 to 12 inches long.

When Harold was finally satisfied with the liquid creation, we dumped the fiberglass strips into it.

I picked up the basketball, Henry took the tray with the soaking strips, and the three of us hurried from the shop to the machine.

"Now comes the fun part," I said, as I set the ball and flange on the table. Henry carefully set the tray next to it. We both began hurriedly taking the soaking strips out of the tray and placing them on and around the ball. It was messy work and the two of us managed to get as much of the thick, viscous mixture on ourselves as on the basketball.

The procedure was, "get it on, get it in and get the machine closed" as quickly as possible. I took the basketball and mounted it to the male side of the mold. The metal flange that held the basketball was a tight fit to the mold, and with all the sticky resin mix, it stayed in tight once I let go. Henry scrambled around to the back of the machine and continued to add the strips and the thick resin mix. There was little for Harold to do at this point but, despite that, he still managed to get in the way more than once. Well, it is his brainchild, I thought to myself, as I picked up a brush to paint on more liquid styrene. I guess he's allowed.

"Richard, what do you think?" Henry called out, gesturing to the material on the ball.

"Yeah, Henry, I think it's ready," I responded. "I'm closing the safety door now." Only after the door was secure could the machine be activated. I gave a nod to Harold, letting him know it was okay to go. Harold pushed the "start" button and the toggle arm began to push the female portion of the mold toward the male, causing it to close.

I leaned my right arm on the safety door and relaxed against it, watching the mechanical action. Henry and I attempted a conversation over the noise of the hydraulics.

"In two minutes," I shouted, "we should know if all our work is going to pay off."

The basketball mold looked like some kind of Frankenstein experiment. We had added heating rods to the mold and there were at least 32 wires coming from the heating elements and from all sides of the mold. It was our hope that this additional heat would help the mold stay warm, thus giving us more control of the fiberglass resin mixes. Hydraulic hoses were connected to ball valves, controlling the pressure in and out of the basketball itself. Other pipes with release valves extended from the top of the mold. The toggle arm slowly—with its 200 tons of pressure—clamped the mold into place. Harold waited for a couple of minutes to make sure the temperature reached the 400-degree operating level. Conversation was almost impossible over the roar of the machine and hydraulics. Harold glanced at his watch and then hit the "run" button. The hopper released the injection mixture into the 5- to 6-foot length of the corkscrew shaped lead screw. Heating coils maintained the 400-degree temperature along the way to the mold.

As noisy as the machine was, there was a comfort in the sounds of the pneumatic pumps and the familiar whining as the material progressed through the lead screw. All we could do now was wait until the process was complete. Harold stood four feet to my right at the control panel, and Henry was still on my left, about six feet away, watching the workings of the machine.

In that surrealistic moment when I knew something was definitely wrong, and yet my mind could not translate the messages it was receiving, and therefore could not react, the sound of the machine changed from the familiar whine to a harsh grinding and shearing of metal. There was a deafening bang and a cloud of yellowish-brown fumes billowed out of the machine. I was conscious of a swishing sound as the hydraulic clamp released. Even with the safety door closed, the injection mixture, now heated to 400 degrees and the consistency of a thick milk shake, gushed out around the gates, as though the machine was regurgitating it. The mixture spewed out around the door. More was launched into the air and fell in splats. Totally disoriented by the thick toxic fumes, and severely nauseous, I was aware of a burning sensation on my right hip and other parts of my body. I could hear Henry roaring, "What the hell?" as the mixture fell on him. I looked toward Harold, and could see that the man was still coherent enough to hit the emergency shut off. My right hip and thigh continued to burn and were becoming more and more painful. I looked down and it finally registered that I was covered with the heated resins. I started to loosen my blue jeans in an attempt to keep the resin from continuing to burn my skin. Simultaneously, Henry and I stumbled down the long aisle toward the shop door. Harold was close behind us.

Mike, the shop supervisor, alerted by the intense bang, opened the metal doors to the shop as the three of us approached them. "What the hell are you guys screwing up now?" But it took only an instant for him to realize that something was very wrong. The acrid fumes filled the huge molding room and other operators began to leave the building. Henry and I were cursing as we rushed from the room, loosening our splattered clothing as we went. Mike could see only a few spots of the resin on Harold, although he could tell Harold was greatly affected by the fumes. More of the mixture was on Henry, and he was still quite disoriented from the blast of fumes. My right side from my hip down was covered with the thick mess and I was sick to my stomach. "Get over to the bathroom," Mike ordered. "Rodwell," he yelled to the man across the room, "get some rags and help these guys get that shit off."

By the time we reached the bathroom area we had regained more of our senses. We were each trying to wipe the splotches of mixture off our bodies. Rodwell, whose area was close by, handed us dry rags. "Get some Triclean," Harold snapped. "That's the only thing that's going to get this stuff off. And hurry! If it hardens, it will take the skin with it."

I took off my boots and socks, which were soaked through. I stripped off my jeans. Someone handed me a rag soaked with Triclean, and I began to rub the hardening substance off my body with the strong solvent. Still suffering from the affects of the fumes, the nausea overtook me and I began to vomit. My head ached, I was sick and the burns were becoming extremely painful. Rodwell offered me a 7-Up to help settle my stomach.

"Goddamn it, Harold," I croaked, "What happened out there?"

"I don't know. It all just went to hell." Harold was still wiping his arms with the solvent-soaked rags. It would be days later that we would find out it was a metal pin, about two inches thick, on the toggle arm that had sheared in two. This had caused the hydraulic pressure to release, allowing the mold to open and the pressurized, heated resin and fumes to be released in an explosion.

While Henry, Harold and I were cleaning the hardening mixture off our clothing and bodies, Mike went into the molding department and ordered anyone inside to evacuate. All the employees in the building were given the remainder of the day off and allowed to see the nurse or the company doctor if they thought it was necessary. Two of the machine operators 50 feet across from the explosion area had been so overcome by the fumes they became sick while seeking attention from the company nurse.

Harold and Henry were cleaned up quickly and offered to assist me with my clothing. Reluctantly, I accepted Henry's offer. "How about cleaning my boots and pants so I have something to wear home, Henry."

"Can I do anything for you, Rich?" Harold asked cautiously, knowing that I was becoming much more coherent, but was quite angry from all the burns and the vomiting.

"Yeah, I'm going to need some time off," I demanded. "I'm not feeling so good."

"Don't worry," Harold assured me. "Take as much time as you need, and call the doctor. Go see him when you can . . . or, I could take you now." Harold noticed the burns on my hip. "It really looks like we should go now and get those burns checked out."

"Don't worry," I responded curtly, "I'll see the doctor, but now I just want to go home and relax."

Harold just turned away, not looking to argue, and left the room.

I was as clean as I could get and Henry had my pants and boots clean enough to wear home. My socks were a disaster. Henry just threw them out. They were not worth the effort.

Still somewhat disoriented, I dressed with Henry's assistance. Mike walked up, carrying a completed accident report. "Hey, guys," Mike said, "I filled out a preliminary accident report. Just sign here." Mike placed the form on the table next to us. "Add anything you like," Mike continued, keeping his tone light. "Oh, by the way, Harold said to take your time in coming back. So, will I at least see you guys in the next two weeks or so? Rich, please go see a doctor. Looks like you took quite a hit to me."

"Yeah, Mike, I know," I said, still angry. "I'll just take a few days, and I'll see the doctor. I'll be back after the weekend."

"Hey, Mike, look at this guy," Henry added as he pointed to me. "I think he should get the month off and a raise. Shit, look at him! He's lucky to be alive. He was right in front of that piece of shit when it blew."

"Listen, Henry," Mike said in a concerned voice as he started to walk away, "I'm just repeating what Harold said to me. So, call me and let me know when you guys are coming back. And Rich," Mike yelled, "Go to the Goddamned doctor."

Thirty minutes later, at three o'clock, Henry and I prepared to leave. Henry could have left much earlier, but he wanted to stay with me until he was sure I was capable of driving. As the two of us left the building, Henry offered, "Hey, Rich, how about letting me take you to the doctor. You still don't look too good. Shit, that was some hit you took back there."

"No, I'll be alright," I assured him. "I just want to go home and get cleaned off. And, maybe sleep a day or two."

"Well, listen, Rich, call me if you need me," Henry instructed me, "and don't come back on Monday. Take the week off. Harold won't mind. I'll go in on Monday and let them know."

"We'll see you, Henry." I was in no shape to argue. "You have a need to rest, too. I'll talk to you over the weekend."

"See you, Rich," Henry said, as we parted.

As I drove home, I kept all the windows down, and would occasionally stick my head out, trying to get more fresh air. I was still nauseous, my muscles were cramping and my head was killing me. The hydrocortisone cream helped some with the burns, but the area on my right hip at my waistline was really bothering me. I just wanted to get home and get the jeans off, stiff from the remains of the hardened mixture. As I drove, I never considered that I had just experienced a life-altering event.

Mom pulled into the driveway at 5:30 and wondered why my car was already parked there. It was unusual for me to beat her home from work. I generally didn't arrive home until after 8 P.M.

"You're home early," she called as she entered the house from the side garage door. "Anything wrong?"

I was stretched out on the sofa, dressed only in a pair of shorts, watching television. "Oh, hi, Mom. Nah, we just had a little problem at work today, and they sent us home. Nothing major. I do have a headache though, and my stomach is a little upset. I think I'll go take a nap."

When I stood up unsteadily, Mom noticed the top of a bandage above the waistband of my shorts on my right side. She wanted to ask about it, but I was already making my way slowly up the stairs. I rarely discussed my job with my parents, and I didn't want to go into detail now. She shook her head as she watched me make my way unsteadily up the stairs. He obviously didn't want to talk about it, she thought to herself as she went into the kitchen to start dinner.

About an hour later, Dad walked in from work. "Richard came home early today," Mom said to him, the concern showing on her face. "He said there was some problem at the plant. Would you go up and check on him?"

"Sure," Dad said, as he pecked her on the cheek. He remembered the accident last February that had also sent me home early. He hoped it wasn't something like that again. "Richard," he called as he quietly knocked on the bedroom door, "are you awake?"

"Yeah, come on in." I mumbled sleepily.

"What happened? Your mother told me there was some problem at work." Dad noticed the bandage immediately. "Were you hurt?"

"No, Dad, I'm fine. Some stuff spilled on me, and I put some cream on it," I responded, aware that he was eyeing the bandage. "This is just so I won't get the cream all over me. They sent a bunch of us home, until they get the stuff cleaned up."

"Was it like the accident in February?" Dad asked, aware that I did not look like I felt good.

"Naw, it was different, but there were some fumes. That's why I've got this headache. I just need to get some rest and I'll be fine," I assured him. "They told us to stay home for awhile."

"You want some dinner? Your mother almost has it ready."

"Not right now, Dad. I just want to rest. I'll be down later," I muttered, lying back down.

Dad closed the door softly behind him as he left. He was worried about his youngest son. The incident in February had made me sick for several days. Upset by what he felt had to be negligence on the part of my employer, he called Hayward, demanding to know what had happened. Someone gave him the runaround and a lame explanation.

When I discovered that he called, I confronted him. "Dad, it's embarrassing to have you call to check up on me. It's bad enough that I'm one of the youngest guys there, now the guys are going to give me a hard time because my Daddy called. I'm fine, I just need some rest from the fumes; you know, like the last time." After that he respected my privacy for the evening, but was still concerned about my health.

8
The Aftermath & Death's Roll Call

June 1986–February 1987—The next morning, Dad checked on me again. "Feeling any better?" he asked as he poked his head into my bedroom.

"A little, Dad, thanks. My head still hurts, but I'll be okay. "

"You might consider going to the doctor to get checked out. Your mother and I are concerned."

"Well, maybe, but I think some rest is all I need." I did not care for doctors or doctors' offices. The last thing I wanted to do was sit in some waiting room for an hour just so some doctor could tell me that I needed some rest. "Don't worry Dad, I feel better than yesterday. I'm sure I'll be fine."

But by Saturday, I was still suffering from the headache. The muscle fatigue and occasional nausea kept me from doing much. I briefly talked to Cathi that morning and told her I wasn't feeling well. We agreed to cancel our customary weekend outing. When the phone rang that afternoon, it was Henry. "You doing okay, Richie?" he asked with his familiar thick accent. He sounded tired.

"Not great," I confessed. "My head still hurts and I haven't done anything in three days."

"Those sons a bitches better have some explanation about what happened." Henry was interrupted by a deep cough. "I still feel bad, too," he continued, once he regained his voice, "but I'm going back on Monday, just so I can yell at those bastards."

Despite the pain in my head, I had to smile. I could imagine the well-deserved hell Henry was going to give everyone at work for the accident. We both knew that we did everything correctly. Whatever caused the accident, we knew it was not our fault. We had good reason to be angry. "Yeah, I figure I'll be okay by Monday. I'm going stir crazy just sitting around, and I'd like to give them some hell myself. I guess we can double team them."

By Monday morning, the nausea and muscle fatigue were mostly gone. I still had a slight headache, but after four days I was ready to get out of the house and back to work. Besides, it was time for some explanations.

Everyone was concerned about my well-being when I arrived at work. "How are you feeling?" "You doing okay?" "That was some mess last week." Several people told me that they missed at least one day of work due to the accident. "I know how shitty I felt the next day," one of the guys commented to me. "You had to be a hundred times worse. You feeling okay now?"

In spite of the continuing headache, I responded to the inquiries with, "Yeah, I'm okay. Thanks for asking."

Henry arrived shortly after me. It was obvious he didn't feel well and he was still coughing regularly. "I still feel like hell and I haven't smoked a cigarette all weekend," Henry complained. "This cough is killing me and this rash," he said showing me his hands and arms, "is really irritated. I hope they don't expect much work out of us."

There was very little for us to do except for some minor cleanup from the experiment. Most everything was already washed down and cleared away. Only a few items needed to be put in storage. And, as if management overheard Henry's comment, no one expected us to do much. Mike stopped by to let us know that the accident report was filed with the office and with the union. He told us what they discovered about the machine that caused the accident. "Eddie tells me that the toggle pin holding the mold closed snapped," Mike explained, "and we're getting it fixed now."

"That doesn't help the way I feel," Henry growled. "The goddamned machine should have been checked out before anyone used it."

Mike interrupted before Henry could go into a tirade. "From what we could tell, the machine failed, Henry. We really can't point the finger at anyone here for the problem." It was obvious that Mike was absolving Hayward of any of the blame. "You guys just need to take it easy and if you need more time off, take it."

Later in the day, Henry and I spent some time with Harold. He looked worse than Henry. He had a gray cast to his skin and was coughing also. His cough, unlike Henry's deep chest cough, was harsh and raspy. It was obvious that he was still suffering from the effects of the accident. "It was a two-inch pin that snapped," Harold told us, "that caused the hydraulics to release. I think we all know that it was nothing that we did. The experiment was actually working perfectly. The accident was the fault of the machine." He was stopped by a cough. "How are you guys feeling, anyway?"

"I feel like shit," Henry barked, absent-mindedly reaching for a cigarette and discovering none, "and it's those bastards' fault because of that crappy machine." He, too, was interrupted by a coughing spasm.

"I still have a headache," I took over, "but I'll be okay. Mike told us earlier about the pin." I paused for a moment. "So, what are we supposed to work on now?"

Harold shook his head slowly. "I'm not sure. I think Sam may have something that he's going to talk to you about, but in the meantime, take it easy. Keep cream on any rash, and if you're not feeling well, go home. You need to get back up to 100 percent."

During the next few weeks, Henry and I had very little workload. When a job was given to us, there was never a time frame attached.

"Just get to it when you can," was generally the comment that was made, and the two of us took our time in producing anything.

Henry was the most vocal and continually complained about the accident. "The doctor told me to quit smoking," Henry shared with me, "but with this damned cough, I haven't smoked since the accident. I haven't felt the same since then, either. And, I can't seem to get rid of this frigging rash. Those bastards just don't seem to care. How are you doing?"

"Pretty good," I responded. In fact, I no longer had any symptoms from the accident. The rash had disappeared after a couple of weeks and the headaches had subsided after about three.

But I was concerned about Henry and Harold both. Henry, who had always been an energetic and vigorous man, had really slowed down. He was still coughing a lot. He often missed work. I also noticed the rash on Henry's hands and arms had persisted. It became a ritual for Henry every afternoon, just prior to leaving work, to apply cream to his arms. He continued to be vocal in his criticisms of management. "I'm still not feeling good," he would tell me, "and it's because of these assholes here. I'm going to take tomorrow off." Since June, it seemed like Henry missed work at least once a week, but no one dared say anything about it.

It was Harold that I was most worried about. I would often find him resting in his office late in the afternoon. And he just did not look well. On the first Friday in August, only seven weeks after the accident, I went by Harold's office. It was almost quitting time and Harold was sitting at his desk, not quite asleep. "'Bout time to go home," I said quietly, not wanting to startle the older man.

"Oh, thanks, Rich." He stood up slowly and stepped toward the coat stand that held his jacket. "I wish I could get rid of this rash," he said as he showed me his arms. "Maybe the doctor can give me something next week that will make it go away." Harold tediously put on his jacket. "By the way," he said as he turned back to his desk and pulled out the top drawer, "how do you like my new business card holder?"

"Very nice," I commented as I admired the dark leather case. The initials "H. P." were embossed in gold in the lower right corner.

"Well, if you would like it, you can have it," Harold offered. "I wanted my middle initial on it and they have ordered me a new one. I don't need two and it's too nice to throw away."

"Thanks, Harold," I said gratefully. "It really is nice and I can use it. I'll see you Monday. Have a good weekend."

The older man was very special to me. Harold taught me a lot and had been a good friend as well. I hoped that the doctor could do something to help Harold. He hadn't been himself since June.

As I was driving home in the heavy afternoon traffic, my thoughts switched to the upcoming weekend. Cathi and I had a busy two days planned. We had just closed on a piece of property and we were going to work on it all weekend. Each of us had been dabbling in the real estate market since our teens, and this foreclosure was just one more step in my plan for financial security.

We had our first experience in real estate together when I was 19 and Cathi was 17.

On the way up to the Poconos one weekend, we stopped at an IHOP for breakfast. We were always talking about the future. I had done a lot of reading and realized that the majority of the richest people in the world made their fortunes in real estate.

"We gotta get a piece of land or a house. We gotta get something going," I asserted.

Although I was at an age when most young men were out partying, I felt the pressure to succeed financially. I was anxious to start laying the groundwork for our future.

An older couple was sitting behind us and overheard the conversation. Impressed and intrigued by the two of us, they interrupted. "Forgive us, but we couldn't help but overhear you. We have some property we want to sell that is located on Camelback Mountain. Would you be interested in looking at it?"

I looked at Cathi for confirmation. "Sure," I said. "We'll take a look at it."

The older man wrote out the directions on a napkin. We knew the area well. "We're asking $2000 for the lot. We own this restaurant and we'll be here the rest of the day. If you are interested, come back and we'll discuss terms."

The property was perfect and by the end of the weekend, the older man and I had come to an agreement. Within two days, I signed a contract with a builder, and within three months, I owned a house and a $62,000 mortgage.

It was when the first bill arrived that the trouble began. My parents were astounded and not just a little upset. "What do you think you are doing, Richard?" my father boomed. "You're only 19 years old and you just started a job; now you buy a house in the woods. What if you aren't able to make the payments? You cannot risk your credit with this foolhardy plan. $529 for the next 30 years is a commitment you cannot handle."

"Dad, I can handle . . ."

"Richard, I don't want to hear it. I know a lot more about this sort of thing than you, and I won't see you ruin yourself this early in your life. I don't care how you do it, but get rid of that mortgage."

There was no convincing my father that I knew what I was doing. The property was close to the ski resort but I knew that as long as I kept the mortgage there would be tension in the household. As embarrassing as it was, I made the phone call to the builder. Thankfully, the builder was very understanding. He had children of his own and understood the concerns of my parents. Besides, I was only asking the value of the mortgage and it was a very good investment. He even offered to pay any legal fees, and as quickly as I entered the project, I was out of it.

Three months later, I learned that the builder had turned around and sold the property for $180,000. That was a confirmation to me that I was on the right track and that real estate was where the money was.

Now, five years later, I was back on track. I found property that was in foreclosure and purchased it for a song. It needed a lot of work, but neither one of us were afraid of a little hard work. And, we worked well together. I had taught Cathi about plumbing, carpentry and electrical work, and between the two of us, we could do almost any kind of repair around a house. This weekend we would be repairing and painting to get the house ready for resale. We were both excited, because we knew we were working on our future.

The weekend flew by and both of us were happy with our progress. It wouldn't take long before the house was ready to go back on the market, and we knew our efforts would be rewarded.

The shop seemed subdued when I returned to work on Monday morning. Everyone must be recuperating from the weekend, I thought as I put away my things in my locker.

Mike walked up. "Sam needs to see you, Richard. He's in his office."

"Sure," I responded. "I'll be through here in a second."

When I reached the office, Sam was sitting behind his desk. "Oh, Richard, come on in. Close the door behind you and have a seat."

I thought, Sam is sure being nice; shit, I must be in trouble for something. But I did as I was told.

When I was seated, Sam began. "Richard, I'm sorry to have to tell you this, but Harold died over the weekend." He hesitated, waiting for the information to sink in. Stunned, I just sat and looked at him. He continued, "Harold was getting up in years and had not been feeling well. The funeral is Wednesday. Unfortunately, we can only allow upper management to attend. I wanted to tell you, because I know you and Harold were close. But, please understand that if I let you go to the funeral, I would have to let everyone go and we can't afford to shut down the shop. If you want to go pay your respects to the family after work, I'm sure that would be fine."

I just sat, looking at Sam. Had I heard him right? Harold was dead? How could that be? We just talked Friday afternoon. But, Sam had just said that Harold was dead. I was numb. I could tell that he was through talking, so I got up to leave. "I'm sorry, Richard," he said as I left his office.

Harold hadn't looked well on Friday, but he was going to the doctor during the week. The doctor might have been able to do something, but now he was gone. I found myself standing in front of my locker again. I wasn't sure why I was back there, but I opened it anyway. There on the shelf in front of me was the leather business card case Harold given me just two days before. The initials "H. P." jumped out at me. Harold was dead. I just couldn't believe it. The older man was special to me: a friend, a teacher, and a mentor. I would miss him.

Henry, too, was visibly upset. "It happened so quickly. It was that damned accident that killed him. I know it was. It's probably going to kill me, too." It was true that Henry still did not look healthy. He still coughed a lot and complained about the rash on his arms almost daily.

I hadn't given much thought to what caused Harold's death. I just assumed it was Harold's age. Harold was old . . . had been old. The accident didn't help, but I doubted that it killed him. Henry just tended to overreact to things. I recovered from the accident within three weeks. It was probably just Harold's age.

Work fell into a regular pattern. I still enjoyed the projects I was involved in. Henry and I continued as a team, but I would often take the lead on the projects because Henry still wasn't feeling well and was missing a lot of work. When he was there, Henry would complain about his health. He was still coughing a lot and the rash on his arms would come and go.

It was the following February when Henry told me that he was going to take some time off. "I'm just going to rest and try to get my strength back. Ever since that Goddamned accident, I have felt like shit. Whatever was in that shit, it did something to me. I quit smoking and I still cough. I put tons of cream on my arms, and the rash remains."

I had to admit that Henry did not look healthy. Although Henry was not liked by many of the people at the plant, I had grown close to him. It was not good seeing the once robust man in this shape. Besides the cough and the rash, there was a certain weakness in him that wasn't there before. Maybe a vacation would do him some good. "That's probably a good idea, Henry. When are you taking off?"

"I told them that I would be gone the next two weeks. Maybe it will do me some good to get away from this frigging place for a while."

But only a week later, Sam hurried over to my work area. His face was drawn and he looked harassed. "I just got a call from Henry's wife. It was very hard to understand her accent, but she said that Henry died two days ago, and the funeral is today. I'm on my way to the funeral home right now, but I wanted you to know before I went."

"What?" I was confused by the announcement. "Henry is dead? But, how? Wh . . . .?"

"You know as much as I do at this point," Sam interrupted. "The funeral is in a couple of hours, so I'll probably just stay there. I'll talk to you when I get back."

I watched as Sam left. First Harold and now Henry, I thought. Damn. Maybe it was that goddamned accident. But I felt fine. I hadn't had any side effects since then. Oh, maybe an occasional rash, but that was typical of everyone who worked with the materials we worked with. Of course, Henry was old too. Maybe it was just their time.

The news spread rapidly through the shop. Henry was certainly not as beloved as Harold had been, but everyone was still shaken. Losing two coworkers within five months was disconcerting.

"'Ya think that accident last year had something to do with him dying?" Billy, a coworker asked. He had been working on a machine just across the aisle at the time of the accident and had seen everything. "I know it made me sick for a few weeks, and Henry was sure always bitching about how it killed Harold and was killing him."

"Damn straight, that accident had something to do with it," chimed in a guy named Tyrone. "I got sick too. That was some powerful shit, everyone in the fucking building got sick for a couple days."

"Hey, Rich, you got the brunt of the accident. Have you been feeling okay?" The question came from Eddie. Eddie and I had developed a friendship and often did things together. I could see the concern in his face.

"Yeah, I'm fine," I reassured him, "but, the accident seemed to affect Harold and Henry much worse than it did me. Maybe it was their age, too." But, in my mind, I couldn't help but have some doubts. As much as I hated doctors, maybe I should get checked out. But then again, I felt fine and it was obvious that before they died, neither Harold nor Henry was in good health, but I did not know if it was from the accident or just because of their age.

9
Drafted as MP for Safety

1988–1992—"Rich, I want to talk to you about something." Tony Haye walked over to my work area and I could see that he had something on his mind.

"Yeah, Tony, what's up?"

It was late 1988, and since Harold and Henry's death over a year before, Tony spent more time with me. Tony was always very outspoken. He certainly never pulled any punches in his opinions, so there was rarely any doubt where you stood with him. If you were having a problem with something he would be first to call you a dumb ass but, conversely, he would be the first one to explain things from start to finish. Despite his age, Tony was in good physical health. Only his gray hair gave away the fact that he was nearing retirement age. He had served as the union shop steward for years and had been instrumental in getting some things changed around the plant to make it safer for the employees. Recently, I had heard some rumors that Tony was talking about retirement.

"I don't know if you've heard, but I'm going to be retiring in a couple of months." Tony pulled up a stool and sat down close to me. "I've been the safety director and shop steward for a long time, but someone is going to have to take over once I'm gone. I like the way you handle yourself with management and with the other employees. You've got some college background and you've got a knack for handling almost any situation. You keep your head even when someone else is going nuts. I would like for you to take over my position. I don't want your answer right now, but I want you to give it some thought and we'll talk about it some more. I think you are the right person for the job, and I'll let everyone know that, too. Let's talk again tomorrow."

Just like Tony to do all the talking, I thought. I thought to myself, as Tony walked away, that it might not be too bad of a job. The proposal intrigued me. There were a lot of things that needed to be changed that would make a better working environment. The only drawback was that I didn't feel that it was fair for me to be the shop steward, too. My job at Hayward in research and development was much different than most of the employees. I was not expected to punch a clock and I had freedoms that the others didn't enjoy. The shop steward needed to be more closely associated to the regular guys.

I didn't think about it throughout the rest of the day. My friend, John, and I were meeting Gary and Frank after work to look over a new property. Over the past two years I had formed my own company, Innovative Financial Services. John, who owned Atlantic Contracting, and I had paired up to renovate foreclosure homes we purchased, and build additions to existing homes. My specialty was decks, and the work was lucrative. It kept me very busy. The up side was that my assets were growing and I was beginning to realize my financial dreams.

I had met Gary and Frank completely by accident. I heard about some real estate auctions and attended a Sheriff's auction one weekend. I noticed Gary and Frank standing together. I went over to them and, as I so easily and often did, struck up a conversation with them.

The two were an interesting pair and proof that opposites attract. Frank had lots of connections, but he was just released from prison and was starting over. He had gotten caught in some less than legal deals in Atlantic City. This had forced him into bankruptcy and, with the FBI watching him closely, starting over happened slowly.

Gary was the complete opposite. An ultra-religious, conservative Christian, he could quote the bible, and would never swear or raise his voice. The problem was the back end of what they were doing. They were both businessmen; Gary had the money and Frank had the contacts. Neither possessed the knowledge or skill to complete the projects they wanted to take on. They were aware they needed someone for the repair and construction, but they both knew it had to be someone competent.

During their conversation at the auction Gary mentioned he owned a property, located by the water, that he was anxious to sell. I was familiar with the neighborhood and knew the value of real estate in that area. I made up my mind quickly not to bid on anything at the auction and told Gary I was interested in looking at the house. After setting up a time immediately after the auction, I called John to meet us. The two of us were impressed with the potential of the two bedroom Cape Cod. We struck a deal that day and John and I were soon the owners of the house.

Gary liked the way I worked. He considered me a talented young man with a head for business. Gary checked into some of the work John and I had done and was impressed with it. He needed someone with our expertise to help with other projects.

It had been two years now, and we had worked on several houses together. Frank would locate them through his connections. I would buy them, using Gary's money. Then John and I would make them livable. More often than not, I would find tenants before we were through with the renovations. The business arrangement was a win-win situation for all of us.

I knew that a few years down the road I would be ready to quit Hayward and focus strictly on the real estate. But that was at least four, maybe five, years away. In the meantime, Tony's suggestion to make me safety director appealed to me. I would be able to make some positive changes at the plant that could help everyone. The only drawback was the shop steward position. I would have to talk to Tony about it. Although the two jobs had never been split, maybe they could arrange something. And, my arrangement with Gary was an issue I had to take into consideration when I was making plans for my future. I knew quite clearly that I was going to make more money on my own than I ever could at Hayward. But a few years was plenty of time to make a difference at the plant.

True to his word, Tony was sitting at my desk the next day, ready to discuss his proposal. "Well, what do you think? I believe you're the best person to take over and I'll start talking to people to get things in place."

"I thought about it a lot last night," I started, "and the safety director sounds good to me. The one problem I've got is that I don't believe I'm the best person for the shop steward. Being in Research and Development, I don't have the day to day contact with the majority of the guys in the plant to really be able to represent them well." I paused momentarily. "What's the possibility of splitting the two jobs, and finding someone else to handle shop steward?"

"Hmmm," Tony mused, thinking about the proposition. "The two have always been together, but I can't think of any reason why they couldn't be split. And, you're right, it does need to be someone who knows most of the people and gets around the plant. Any ideas?"

I in fact, had thought of someone who would be perfect. "Well, what do you think about Eddie?"

Eddie worked in maintenance, was all over the plant, and was well-liked. He was also one of my very good friends. We were both weight lifters. He was several inches shorter than me, but he had a powerful build. He looked like a short version of the professional wrestler, "The Rock."

I could almost see the wheels in Tony's head turning and knew exactly when the idea caught on. "Not a bad choice," Tony agreed. "Let me go talk to him. I'll get back to you later."

During the next two months, Tony talked to almost everyone in the plant about Eddie and I. True to his word, by the time the employees voted it was a foregone conclusion that Eddie would be the new shop steward and I would take over as safety representative. Tony had done well and, by the time he left for retirement, he knew he left the respon-sibilities in capable hands.

It didn't take long for me to realize that the safety committee meet-ings were a joke. The plant nurse, Barbara, who reminded me of the maid on the Brady Bunch, and an assistant plant manager, Bill, were the only others who were consistent in their attendance. Upper man-agement would often send a representative, but it was seldom the same person twice. Time was wasted in backtracking on the decisions made in previous meetings. The committee would generally meet once a month, except when there was an accident. During one period, they met almost weekly in response to a rash of small, unrelated accidents.

I was also quick to realize that management would approve almost anything we proposed, as long as it didn't involve spending money. The only time they were willing to shell out anything was in response to an accident. As usual, management was reactive. I wanted to be proactive.

The committee concentrated on developing some safety guidelines and creating safety awareness. Most accidents were minor; cuts from boxes or metal stripping, strains from lifting something too heavy or dropping something. Because the nature of the work at Hayward involved electricity and water, the more critical safety issues centered on preventing spills, and keeping fluids from getting close to or on electri-cal outlets and extension cords. The committee was able to issue guide-lines for handling some of the chemicals, but that too was a tedious process. Management would often drag their feet in approving the pub-lication and distribution of the chemical guidelines. As unhappy as I was with the slow progress, the employees were satisfied with the job I was doing, or at least attempting to do.

10
Alliance of the Souls

February 24, 1990—Even though work was going well, I was dealing with other things in my life that were troubling me. My relationship with Cathi was faltering. It wasn't really between the two of us; we had always been good friends. It was more the influence of our families that affected our relationship. Both sets of parents wanted us to wait to get married. I was getting pressure from my parents, Cathi from hers. We had been planning a weekend trip for almost three months, and I was leaving work early on Friday in preparation for the long-awaited getaway. But the last couple of weeks had been strained between the two of us.

The weekend didn't get any better. The trip that was supposed to be enjoyable for Cathi and I turned into a lot of bickering. The two of us were engaged for the second time. The wedding was planned for later that year, but by the time we returned to the city, we had called off the wedding and the engagement.

For the next two months, I tried to keep as busy as possible. But anytime I had a free minute, my thoughts were of Cathi. I knew I had to do something to get her back. Her parents didn't want me anywhere near their daughter, so I had to come up with a way to talk to her.

Cathi always drove home from work on the turnpike at about the same time. It was a sunny May afternoon when Cathi saw someone standing on the side of the road with a rose. Astonished, she realized it was me. As she pulled over, she yelled at me, "Are you crazy? You could get killed out here!"

"Can you meet me someplace?" I asked, ignoring her outburst.

Cathi was flabbergasted. "Well, yes, I guess. But I've got to go to the house first. Maybe in about an hour."

"Good. I'll meet you at the coffee shop close to the house in an hour." I handed her the rose and walked away toward my parked car.

It didn't take much convincing for the two of us to get back together. We had always had a good relationship. We enjoyed doing things together. We would often go hiking or biking. And, we were good friends. I figured if we could withstand two broken engagements, we could make a marriage work, too.

"Cathi, I want to marry you. We've got to make our families understand that we are going to be together despite them. I'll work on my parents, if you'll work on yours."

"Richie, I want to marry you, too. I know we can make it work." Cathi felt empowered by my dedication to her.

It took both of us talking to our parents, but we held our ground and the wedding date was set for February 24, 1990. I gave Cathi a third engagement ring. Each time, the ring had gotten bigger and more elaborate. I joked with Cathi, telling her that we had to get married this time. I couldn't afford to buy a larger ring.

The next eight months flew by. When Cathi would get stressed with the wedding plans, I would tell her, "We could just elope if you want to."

"No," she would say, "I want a nice church wedding." But she would laugh, because she knew we were finally going to get to have a wedding.

I was kept busy with work at Hayward, and fixing up and building additions on houses in the evenings and on weekends. I had put

Harold's and Henry's deaths behind me, and I wasn't letting the snail's pace progress of the safety committee affect me as much.

Knowing that I appreciated fun and weird things, the guys threw me a bachelor party that was very different. Instead of the typical strippers, Billy, a dead ringer for Jeff Bridges, and Mike, a blonde Arnold Schwarzenegger look-alike, hired a woman who billed herself as the "Fattest Go-go Dancer on the East Coast." They did hire a couple of other gorgeous strippers, but Billy, Mike, Eddie, and I spent the evening entertained by the very large stripper. While Cathi's brother and a few of the other guys drooled over the two attractive strippers, my group and I had a blast with the big woman.

She began her dance with her clothes on, and proceeded to perform a striptease that was awesome. When her dance was complete she was stripped down to her teddy. The guys wanted her to slide down the pole, but she laughed, "I don't know. I might rip this out of the wall." Instead, she treated her audience to an incredible rendition of the splits, considering her enormous bulk.

When posing for pictures, the dancer pulled my head between her breasts. Buried in the mounds of flesh, and almost suffocating, I yelled, "Get me out of here." The entire evening was hilarious, and memorable for the entire group.

The fun at the bachelor party set the tone for the wedding. And everything cooperated, except the weather. On the day of the wedding, it rained, snowed, sleeted, and rained again. But the weather did nothing to dampen the merriment of the wedding party.

Before the ceremony, the party went to a local park for pictures. Cathi and I did the traditional poses but, aided by the effects of more than one bottle of champagne, the groomsmen and I decided that it was time to lighten up the proceedings. When we donned ski boots and sunglasses and went through our bodybuilder routines, everyone was laughing and relaxed. The mood was set for the remainder of the day.

The ceremony went off without a hitch. Afterwards, back in the limousine, the group celebrated by toasting the bride and groom with champagne out of one of the girls' shoes. We were having so much fun we almost didn't make it to the reception. We had the driver take a tour around town. It was quite a sight to see when the girls had to stop for a bathroom break. The only restroom the driver could find was at a gas station. A bride and three bridesmaids, all in their formal gowns, piled out of the car and crowded into the small restroom.

Our parents were less than pleased when the wedding party finally arrived at the reception, but nothing could dampen our spirits.

Cathi and I were happy, and we knew our marriage was going to be a good one. We were good friends and cared deeply for one another.

Our honeymoon was in New Hampshire. Cheryl, my sister, had made reservations for us at a resort called "Disaster Valley." The weather had worsened and it was snowing heavily by the time we left for the resort the next day. I inched my pickup through blizzard conditions up Route 95 in nearly a foot of snow. It was obvious the plows hadn't been through. At one point, I could tell that the truck was not handling right. I got out to check the wheels and found that they were completely encased in ice and snow. Cathi got out to help and the two of us managed to chip away enough to continue.

When we finally arrived at the resort, we were welcomed by the news that the honeymoon suite was still occupied. The previous guests were unable to leave due to the now major storm. The only room available was small and not in the best condition. While we stood in disbelief of the dilapidated room that was now going to be fixed in memory as the "honeymoon suite," the phone rang.

"Good news, Mr. Sabb," a young, female voice responded to my "Hello." "We have a guest cottage available. It is considerably larger so go check it out and call me back." Cathi and I were relieved that we would not have to sleep in a dump. So we packed up our luggage and trekked through the two feet of snow to the new room. As we approached the beautifully appointed exterior of the home we could not believe this was actually going to be ours. Cathi was in awe and the long treacherous drive and continuing snow was no longer a bother. I dropped the luggage and said: "Let me carry you."

I picked up Cathi and opened the door. It was unbelievable, a totally trashed party house. Beer bottles, cans, whiskey bottles, old clothing, foodstuff and debris all over, it even had a pungent smell of vomit. I stood in disbelief, still holding Cathi. Cathi, tired and emotionally drained, began to cry.

I was really "pissed off" now but gently I set Cathi down. I calmly walked into the home, grabbed the phone, and pushed the "O" for the front office. Before the young lady could respond, I exploded. "This place is trashed. Give me a decent room now; tell the manager it's my honeymoon and if he doesn't find me decent room I'm going to rip his fucking head off."

Fortunately for me, it was the manager, not the young lady. "Sir, I am really sorry," the man responded, quite terrorized by my robust threat. "I have one other room, it was just cleaned, it's yours and there is no charge. Go back to the main building, it's room 226, a corner unit."

"It better be clean," I threatened as I slammed the phone down.

"Honey, don't cry," I coaxed Cathi. "It's going to be okay. We'll go to the new room, have a nice meal and things will be better tomorrow."

We again trekked through the snow to the new room. Thankfully, it was clean. I was calm now and realized I was wrong for threatening the manager the way I did. I figured I would apologize when we ordered room service. I reached for the phone and dialed the front desk. It was a completely different voice. "Would you connect me with room service."

"Sorry. The kitchen is already closed." The voice on the other end was unconcerned.

I was again getting upset but consciously relaxed, not wanting to make the same mistake twice in one evening, "Well, is there a restaurant someplace close by?"

"Don't think so. Everything is probably closed now that the storm is really bad."

I slammed down the phone. "Let's get back in the truck and try to find something on our own."

So back out into the freezing weather we went, both of us miserable. But luck smiled and we quickly found a small, elegant restaurant nearby. The two of us were seated quickly, but it was obvious that Cathi had been crying. The waitress, concerned, asked what was wrong. I explained that this was our honeymoon, and as great as the ceremony and celebration had been, nothing had gone right since we left.

The waitress was sympathetic and went back into the kitchen. In a few minutes, the manager came to our table and told the newlyweds that everything was "on the house" as a sort of wedding gift to help make up for the troublesome evening. Cathi started crying again, but this time they were tears of happiness.

We enjoyed an exquisite dinner in the warmth of the friendly restaurant, while outside the storm continued to rage. When we were through, I thanked both the waitress and the manager for making the evening so special, plus I left a large tip that more than covered the price of the meal, in appreciation of their goodwill.

Overnight, the temperature outside dropped to 60 degrees below zero. But by morning, the storm had passed and the sky was clear and blue. It had been one of the coldest nights on record. Cathi and I left the hotel at ten the next morning to explore the quaint, little town. As we drove down the street where we enjoyed our honeymoon dinner, all we saw were the ashen remains of the restaurant. Like a scene out of a cartoon, all that was left of the building was pipe, tall and straight, extending to the second floor.

"Oh, my god," Cathi cried. "The restaurant burned down! I don't believe it."

"We must have brought our bad luck to them," I remarked, also amazed to see the results of the overnight fire.

"No," Cathi announced, determinedly. "Yesterday was just a fluke, and I refuse to think of it as any kind of omen. We have good luck, and you were right last night. Everything is going to be great."

And, she was right. Life settled down to normal quickly. Cathi's job with Makita Tools was going well. I was involved in challenging projects at Hayward and the side business with Gary and Frank was thriving.

Soon after our wedding, Cathi and I moved into a three-family house that we were refurbishing. Within a couple of months, both apartments were redone and rented. Our bank account was growing and as a couple we were enjoying the comfort of financial security, but we both worked long and hard to achieve it. It was nice not to have to worry about money. I would often tease Cathi that I didn't mind her spending money on clothes as long as she wrote it down in the checkbook. Cathi would return the banter by accusing me of spending too much money on all of my antique trains. The two of us were living well.

11
Cancer's Death Squad Claims Another

June 1991—In June of 1991, I received a phone call that disturbed my idyllic existence. It was from a guy I had worked with at WebbTool. I was ready to leave work in anticipation of a long weekend away from work. Vermont was going to be a wonderful escape from the frenetic pace we had been keeping for months.

"Richard? This is Chuck from Webb."

It took a couple of seconds for the name to register with me. "Chuck! What's going on?"

"Richard, I just called to let you know that Kenny died over the weekend and the funeral is going to be tomorrow. They said it was some kind of cancer, but I thought you might want to know." Chuck rushed through the explanation so quickly that I didn't have time to react.

I seldom saw Kenny, my college friend and old work partner from WebbTool. It was usually only by accident when I would run into Kenny and his wife, Debbie, at Mr. Goodbuy's or Kmart and I did not know that they had just had their second baby about six months before.

"Chuck," I managed to get out. "When did he die? Had he been sick?"

"He died on Saturday, Rich. He was only diagnosed about a month ago and went through some chemotherapy. It was some rare type of cancer, M.F. or something. I just know that they just didn't catch it in time. It all happened very quickly." Chuck gave me the location and time for the funeral and said goodbye.

I was stunned. I wondered why Debbie had not called me immediately; why Kenny hadn't called when he found out he was sick. Kenny was 29, the same age as me. He had a wife and two small children, and he died from cancer. I was heartsick that I was not going to be able to go to the funeral because of the trip. I wanted to talk to Debbie to find out what had happened, but when I called there was no answer.

The weekend was marred by the news. I thought about the relationship Kenny and I enjoyed while we were going to school. I regretted not having kept in closer contact but, philosophically, I knew that people went their own way and lived separate lives. The most difficult emotion I had to work through was the tragic loss of such a young man that I cared about, and the surviving widow and two young children. I would try to call Debbie again when we returned home, maybe even go see her, if my schedule would allow.

But when Cathi and I returned to the city, I was swamped with the responsibilities of my job at Hayward and my own business. Time slipped by quickly, and the rhythm of my life centered on Cathi and our life together. I would think of my friend occasionally, but could never bring myself to call Kenny's widow.

Some days I would think about the day we fixed the Corvette and wonder if those accidents had anything to do with Kenny's death. This would usually be when I would think of Harold or Henry and wonder about the relationship of our accident and their deaths.

12
A Bunker for Recovery

October 1991—I had gotten up early on a Saturday to go in to work. It was October 1991 and we had enjoyed over a year and a half of marriage. As Cathi kissed me goodbye, she told me, "I'm waiting on a phone call from Bob Freeman. He's looking for some other properties, and he said he would call if he had something for me to look at. I'll probably go shopping, too."

"Just write it down," I teased, and gave her another peck on the cheek as I rushed out the door to dodge the swat she was about to give me.

"See you later. Love you," Cathi said with a smile.

The phone call from Bob came at about eight o'clock. Bob was a real estate agent who we had worked with on several properties. He was always on the lookout for new ones. He knew that we were looking for more two- and three-family dwellings, so he had called Cathi earlier in the week to let her know that he might have something to look at on the weekend. Now, on Saturday morning, he had some different news.

"Cathi, I know we're looking for multi-families, but a property just came on the market and there isn't even a sign up yet. I think you'll really like it. With a little sweat equity invested, this could be a great house."

They made arrangements to meet and within an hour Cathi was following Bob to the house. As they turned the corner, Cathi could not believe her eyes. The beautiful, two-story blue colonial stood next to some wetlands and had a park behind it. The long L-shaped drive led to a two-car garage in the back. There was a cherry tree next to a garden, two big pine trees in front and a huge three-masted oak tree to the right of the house. The tour of the inside of the house only served to convince Cathi that this was her dream home. The family was still living in it, but had to raise some money quickly, so they would be moving out very soon.

"Well, do you want it?" Bob asked, as they stood by their cars.

"Yes." There was no doubt in Cathi's mind that she and I had to have this house. "What do I do?"

"We need to make and offer and you should probably put a little down to hold it."

Cathi reached for her checkbook. "Will $500 be enough?"

"That should work fine. When do you want to show it to Richard? You want me to . . ."

"No. No," Cathi interrupted. "I'll tell him and bring him by this evening. I'll need to find a way to tell him I bought a house." Cathi felt a twinge of guilt, but she knew that I would love the house, too. And, the amount was in their price range. It was too good of a deal to pass up.

I returned home from work later that afternoon. As I stretched out on the sofa to enjoy a beer, I asked, "Well, what did you do today?"

Expecting her to bring out clothing she had bought, I was stunned when she said, "I went shopping and I bought a house."

I momentarily gagged on a swallow of beer. "You what? What was it, a 'blue light special' or something?"

"Well," Cathi continued, "we didn't go see the kind of property we were looking for, but Richie, you'll love this house. Promise me you'll keep an open mind until you see it."

"Okay," I responded hesitantly. "When can I see it?"

"We can go right now, if you want."

"It's further for you to drive to work," I said, as I looked at the two-story house. I was very impressed by what I saw from the outside. With the park in the back and the wetlands to one side, no one would be building too close to us. "And, are you sure this is in our price range?"

"Yes, I'm sure," Cathi said, seeing that I liked what I saw. "And, Bob told me about a back road that would make the travel time less." In fact, when we mapped it out, it was only an additional ten or fifteen minutes.

"You could put your trains in the basement or in the den. If you like we can add sliding doors and build a deck off the den. It will need some work on the inside, but it's great, don't you think?" Cathi held her breath for my answer.

"Well," I mused thoughtfully, dragging out my response, "let's go sign the papers."

Cathi grinned and gave me a big kiss. "Okay, let's go!"

When we went to sign the papers, Bob was able to give us more information about the house. "It seems that one of the kids ended up in jail, that's why they need to sell so fast, to raise some bond money. It's a foreclosure and there are some back taxes, but it is still a good deal."

"When can they be out of the house?" I asked. I could tell that Cathi wanted to move in as soon as possible.

"The mother said they would be out by the Friday before Thanksgiving, and we can close on the following Monday."

Concern crossed my face. "Cathi, I'm going to be in Colorado on that ski trip with Cheryl over Thanksgiving."

"I can be getting it ready to move into while you are gone. It will give me time to clean everything." Cathi was not going to let ski trips and holidays slow her down. "Let's go show him the inside, Bob."

On the Monday of the closing, the woman told us that she was not able to find any storage and wanted to know if it was okay for her to leave some things in the garage for a while. "I still have to finish some laundry and clean up some things, but you can have it later today."

Cathi agreed to the storage and took the keys. "I'll be back about 4:30, so you need everything out of the house by then."

When Cathi and I returned later that afternoon, we could not believe what we saw. The inside of the house was a wreck. It had been trashed. Food was thrown everywhere. There was a jar with human waste sitting on the bar in the basement. Carpet had been ripped up and there was a large burned spot in the living room floor. The more of the house we saw, the more upset we became. The bedroom that belonged to the daughter had pictures of naked women covering the walls.

"Interesting life style," was the only thing I could say. As I looked closer throughout the house, I found more and more things that had been covered up when we originally saw the house. The worst was the upstairs bathroom floor. It was almost rotted through.

"I'm going over to the neighbors to find out when trash pick up is," Cathi announced, close to tears. "We've got to get this stuff out of here."

When we rang the doorbell at the house across the street, a small woman with dark, short-cropped hair answered the door.

"Hi," I began, "we just bought the house across the street and . . ."

That was as far as the woman let me get. "I am Lillian Perros." The woman had a foreign accent. "The entire neighborhood is so glad to see those people go. They were 'dirt bags.'" The slang sounded funny with her accent. "They had loud parties all the time and cars were always coming and going. The police will also be happy to see them go, too. Come in. Come in."

"Thank you," I said sincerely, "but we just wanted to see if you could tell us when trash pick up is. We're going to have a lot, because they left the house in a mess."

"Yes, certainly. I have the list in the kitchen. Please come in." We stepped inside and waited as Lillian went to the kitchen. She returned quickly with the list. "Here, take this. I do not need it. Would you like something to drink?"

Cathi was grateful to the woman for her hospitality, but wanted to get back over to our house. "Thank you, but we have a lot of work to do."

"I will come help. Just let me tell my sons I will be across the street." Before we could respond, Lillian had walked into the den. She returned and said, "Okay, let us go see what mess these people have left."

We learned that Lillian was from Croatia, and she and her husband, Bernard, had two sons, Daniel and Boris. We both liked this small woman who was full of energy and would obviously be a good neighbor. As she looked through the house, all she could say was, "I cannot believe this. They are such pigs."

I felt guilty about leaving Cathi with such a daunting task, but Cathi would not hear of me canceling the ski trip. "I can get my family and your parents over here to help me," she insisted. She also did not want to put up with any grief from my sister for ruining our vacation. My sister and I were close, but Cathi never cared for Cheryl. She had never appreciated my sister referring to her as "jail bait" when we first started dating, and there was little love loss between them since.

So while Cathi and her family carried garbage bags of trash and useless appliances out to the fence, Cheryl and I skied at Copper Mountain in Colorado. On our last night at the ski resort, we were enjoying the huge hot tub. Ten or twelve others joined us and my sister made sure that everyone's drink was never empty. It was our own private farewell to an awesome ski week. I had gotten out of the tub for a moment and Cheryl noticed a rash above the waistband of my swimsuit.

"Rich, what's that?" she slurred, pointing to the rash.

"Don't know. Must be allergic to something. Doesn't hurt though." Soon I was back in the water with a fresh drink in my hand, joking with her and our new friends. The rash was instantly forgotten and replaced with "tales from the slopes."

When I returned from the ski trip, I couldn't believe my eyes. The amount of trash Cathi and the two families had cleared out of the house filled more than two city garbage trucks. Cathi even had to call the township for a special series of pickups. The home had been virtually gutted, and almost everything needed replacing.

The plumbing, electrical and heating systems all required major work, if not full replacement. Most of the major appliances, windows, and even the garage door, were useless. But Cathi had already replaced the necessary appliances and made the house somewhat habitable. She was ready to move in, and we agreed to finish the work one room at a time while we lived there.

During the next few months, every spare minute was filled with repairing, replacing and repainting. Cathi decorated each room as it was finished.Cathi's brother Scott, and I were in charge of the heavier work.

One weekend, Scott and I were installing a new tub in the second floor bathroom. As we were preparing to put the tub in place, my foot almost went through the waterlogged rotting floorboards and into the kitchen ceiling below. Laughing, I commented, "This house reminds me of the house in that Tom Hanks movie, 'Money Pit'."

"Hey, you know, you look a little like Tom with that hair of yours" Scott added.

"I don't know about that" I said, "but Cathi is much better looking than that Shelly Long character".

The huge basement had been converted, with relative ease, into a massive train and weight room. It was the perfect place for my buddies and I to play and not get in Cathi's way. The back corner, still quite large, made a perfect utility and laundry room. Although Cathi normally did the laundry, I often tried to lend a helpful hand. Cathi would soon kick me out when I failed to separate the clothes properly and mixed the colored laundry with the whites.

I converted the built-in bar and surrounding alcove into a repair station for my train collection. My hobby had evolved into the restoration and repair of the antique train sets. Even with all this going on I still made time every day for weight lifting and physical conditioning

Cathi set aside one room especially for a nursery. We both wanted kids, and had gone shopping together for decorations. When Cathi began contemplating on a room for the nursery, she gave me strict orders that I was not to enter until she said it was okay.

I was in the midst of some renovation work a week later when Cathi grabbed me by the arm. "It's ready for you to see," she beamed and hurried me up the stairwell. "What do you think?" She flashed a big smile as she opened the door.

The room had all her concepts and patterns tacked to the paneled walls, but gave a clear rendition of what her plans were. "Winnie the Pooh" trim outlined the ceiling. The curtains and trim added a softness to the light. Cathi had done an incredible job. "Wow," was all that I could express. The profound impact of having children hit me. But as I continued to look at Cathi's creation, I knew that we were both ready. It just seemed right.

13
Man's Best Friend

1992—There was one more thing, besides children, that Cathi believed would make her life complete. She wanted a dog. I was not as excited about the idea. I had had a variety of small pets as a child—pets like fish and gerbils—but as an adult, I believed that animals should remain free and not be held as property.

Not to be deterred, Cathi presented me with an idea. "Well, if you are really interested in animal welfare, why can't we help an animal in distress, like one at an animal shelter?"

Not totally convinced, I finally agreed to go to the Old Bridge Animal Shelter "just to look."

Cathi was like a child in a candy store. She talked the entire way to the shelter about what kind of dog we should have. "The dog needs to have a happy-go-lucky disposition, don't you think, one that would fit us?"

Having arrived just at feeding time, we could hear barking as we entered the well-kept shelter. There were dogs of every size and shape, from mixed sheperds to purebred collies. There were so many to pick from, and although we would have liked to save them all, we knew we were looking for the one dog that stood out and would fit for us.

Near the end of the stretch of cages, Cathi and I noticed an excited black Lab mix, jumping and barking for his dinner. He knew the attendant was making the suppertime rounds and he was ready to be fed. He was jumping as high as the 6 1/2-foot wire grating would allow him. Cathi could swear he had a smile on his face.

"He's the one. I want him!" Cathi indicated to me.

I watched the dog for a moment. "Okay, but let's just wait a couple of days and think about it."

I could see that Cathi was disappointed, but I wanted to wait. We both rode home in silence.

The following afternoon, I took off from work a couple of hours early. I had an errand I needed to run and I had to do it before Cathi got home. By the time Cathi drove up the driveway, I was ready. As she opened the door, there stood the black Lab, smiling, and wearing a red bandanna around his neck.

"Meet Maximilian Sabb," I grinned.

Cathi didn't know who to hug first, Max, as he was soon called, or me. But Max won out, running to Cathi and jumping up, expecting to be petted and hugged.

"I can't believe you did this," Cathi said excitedly. "And he is so clean now."

It was a good thing I left work early. Max needed the "works;" bath, nails clipped, flea dipping, and, most of all, food. The dog was very underweight. He had been abandoned and tied to a tree behind the pound. The pound steward figured Max might have been tied back there for three days with no food or water before anyone noticed. When I fed him for the first time at home, Max gobbled down three bowls of food.

The newest member of the family had full privileges, jogging in the park with his new "parents," eating at the same time, and even sleeping in the same room with us. Max was quickly integrated into our lives, and as most animal lovers know, our lives changed according to Max's whims.

14
The Battle Moves to the Surface

September 1992—Soon after acquiring Max, the rash reappeared on my hip. "You don't suppose you are allergic to Max, do you?" Cathi asked.

"I've never been allergic to dogs before. Besides, why would the rash just be in that one area?" I surmised. "Maybe I'm allergic to some of the cleaning products or soaps. I'll put some cream on it."

And, within a couple of days, the rash disappeared.

In the spring, however, it came back again, and this time there was evidence of the rash on my foot, also. "Richie, we need to find out what you are allergic to."

"It's probably just something in the soap," I passed it off, as I applied some cream to it. "Why don't you try a different detergent, and see if that helps."

Once again, with the change of soap, the rash went away. We were satisfied that we solved the problem.

The rash reappeared briefly during the summer, again on my hip and foot. But with the application of cream, the rash was soon gone. Life was good and I was much too busy to worry about an irritating little rash to be concerned.

Cathi and I enjoyed vacations and were preparing to leave for ten days to Maine beginning with the Labor Day weekend. Cathi bought all new clothes for the both of us and she teased me about how "hot" I looked as I modeled them for her.

But by the time we arrived in Maine, it was obvious that I had lost weight. The new clothes were hanging on me, and Cathi noticed that the rash was back.

"Richard, you've got to go see a doctor about that rash. I've changed soaps and cleaning products, but it keeps coming back. You've got to be allergic to something."

"Okay," I agreed reluctantly. "As soon as we get back, I'll make an appointment." As much as I hated doctors, and refused to sit in waiting rooms, I knew I would have to see one, if for no other reason than to satisfy my wife. "Now, let's enjoy our vacation."

We returned home from our vacation on Friday night. Cathi's cousin was getting married on Saturday, and Cathi was getting ready to leave for the hairdresser when she noticed that I was sitting at the table with a phone book spread out in front of me

"What are you doing?" she asked.

"I'm getting ready to start calling dermatologists to make an appointment."

"Good for you," Cathi said as she kissed me. "I'm on my way to the beauty shop. I'll see you later."

It was mid-September, the days were beautiful, and I wanted to get this over with so I could go out and enjoy the weekend. I set two criteria; first, who would see me immediately, and, second, who would not make me wait anymore than ten minutes once I had arrived at the doctor's office. It was my belief that since I was paying, I shouldn't have to wait. I started with the A's under dermatologists. Dr. Arthur Birnkrant was the first doctor to meet both of the criteria. The doctor was at his office and he could see me just as soon as I could get there. I told him I was on my way.

Dr. Birnkrant was a small, wiry man. He talked easily with me, asking me questions as he examined the rash. "It looks like a fungus combined with something akin to athlete's foot. You most likely contracted it when you and your wife were in the park. That is a perfect breeding ground for all types of fungus. I'm going to give you a prescription for some fungal cream that should make it disappear."

"Thanks. I was sure it was something simple."

The doctor handed me the prescription. "You can go ahead and get dressed. Let me know if for any reason it persists, but this should take care of it."

I was dressed and getting ready to walk out, when Dr. Birnkrant reappeared. "Richard, would you mind if I did a quick punch biopsy just to be sure about this? It will only take a couple of minutes."

"Well, okay. Any particular reason?"

"No," the doctor responded, "just as a precautionary measure. It would just make me feel like I had earned my fee," he joked.

I smiled and indulged the doctor with the biopsy. Within ten minutes I was on my way back home happy with the results of the visit.

15
My Enemy Has A Name

October 2, 1992—I stood next to the large water filter tank, checking some last minute details for the explosion test we were about to run. The test room was large and was made of reinforced concrete block walls with a steel ceiling. The 10- x 18-foot stainless steel test pool sat in the middle of the room, surrounded by ultraviolet test systems, a small 5-foot hot tub and other miscellaneous electrical and mechanical gadgets to test newly created products. I had just completed fastening the water tank's "hold-down" straps to the large steel grating that was built into the floor's "flood area." It was then I noticed that several men, including a couple of the "big wigs" from the front office, had already gathered in Mike's office where they could watch from behind a large Plexiglas safety window.

They're like a bunch of little boys, I thought to myself. They love to see things blow up. I checked the last figures and stress analysis wires and walked into Mike's office. "Looks like we're about ready," I announced to the group.

The phone rang and, because I was standing right next to it, I picked it up. "Mike's office."

"I need to speak with Richard Sabb, please." It was an unfamiliar female voice.

"This is Richard."

"Mr. Sabb, I'm from Dr. Birnkrant's office. The doctor wanted me to call and ask if you could come into the office right away? He said it was important."

"Well, I'm right in the middle of something, and I can't come in today. Tell him I'll try to come in sometime next week."

The nurse would not be deterred. "Mr. Sabb, the doctor did ask me to tell you that it was important that he saw you today."

"Another call from your stockbroker, Sabb?" Mike teased. Everyone was aware that my sister worked for Tek Investors and often called me at work with "stock tips" that really amounted to just small talk. This was not the first time I received some good-natured ribbing about my "stockbroker."

The others in the group laughed and took the opportunity to razz me some more. They were not about to let up; even Sam jumped in. "Any tips for me Rich?" he said jokingly.

I grinned at the remark, but continued my conversation with the nurse. "I'm sorry, but it's just not possible. I've got my bosses here right now waiting on me. I was about to throw the switch on an explosion test when you called."

"May I speak to your manager, then, Mr. Sabb?" This nurse was not going to give up.

I thought the request was odd, but I said, "Sure. Hold on. Mike, she wants to talk to you."

"Guess she wants my opinion on some stock," Mike chuckled, as did the rest of the men. He took the phone from me. "Mike here. May I help you?"

I picked up my clipboard and began checking some numbers. Two of the other men had begun talking to each other, and no one paid much attention to Mike as he spoke to the nurse. I looked up from my notes as Mike hung up the phone.

"Richard, we're not going to do the test right now. We'll do it later. Take the rest of the day off. You need to go see the doctor. It may be important." Mike's entire demeanor had changed. He was no longer smiling. Instead, his face was very somber. Everyone in the room could tell that the atmosphere had changed.

Sam, surprised by the sudden change in Mike, looked at him and knew something was wrong. "Sure, we can do it Monday," Sam assured me. "Go on to the doctor. This can wait."

I was a little confused by all this, especially when I thought the test results for this new product would be needed for Monday's board meeting, but I said, "Okay. I guess we'll do it on Monday."

The last thing I wanted to do was to make the hour drive to Dr. Birnkrant's office. But since Mike said to take the rest of the day off, I figured that when I got through at the doctor's, I would call John and we would get an early start for our trip to Vermont.

The two of us were going up to paint a house for a friend, and this would give us some extra time to work on it. Our payment for painting the house was the use of it for a week during the summer and one in the winter.

The girls weren't going with us, although I really wanted Cathi to go. She was a good worker. On the other hand, I was sort of glad that John's wife, Susan, wasn't going. She had a successful party balloon business and was really not interested in taking time off from her work. Realistically, I was very happy for her and wanted to see my buddy's wife succeed.

The traffic was thinned out and the drive to the doctor's office was not quite as bad as I had thought it would be. It was a nice day, still warm with just the hint of fall in the air. I was a little curious about why the doctor needed to see me that day. It was Friday. Maybe the doc was just being a nice guy and getting me out of work early. He just better not make me wait long, I thought to myself as I opened the office door. To my surprise, the waiting room was empty.

The nurse slid the small glass window open. "Mr. Sabb?"

I nodded. "Yes"

"Come on in. I'll show you to the doctor's office. He's waiting for you." She walked over to the door and opened it.

I followed her past the examination rooms to the large office at the end of the hall. Dr. Birnkrant was sitting behind a beautifully polished antique cherry wood desk.

"Richard." Dr. Birnkrant stood and walked around his desk, with his hand extended. "Please sit down." He motioned to a large comfortable chair next to the desk. As I sat, Dr. Birnkrant pulled another chair close to me and sat in it.

The doctor looked at me and began in a soothing voice. "We're going to need to talk today to educate you about what is going on with your body and let you know what your options are."

I did not understand what the doctor was saying. "What do you mean? Is there a problem? I thought I just had a rash."

"Well, you don't really have a rash. Listen, I'm going to be straight with you. I'm afraid I have some bad news. From the biopsy that I took at your last visit, we found large amounts of cancerous cells. *It is a very rare form of cancer*, so rare that I had the lab do the tests over." Dr. Birnkrant paused for a moment, allowing me to absorb the devastating news, but I did not react. My face held a blank expression.

The doctor continued. "There are actually two names used for this type of cancer. The common name, and what it was first known by, is '*Mycosis Fungoides*.' They called it that because, back in 1806 when it was discovered or first named by a Dr. Alibert. Some believed it to have been caused by a fungus. It actually formed a skin irritation or eruption that progressed into a mushroom-like tumor, hence the name "Mycosis Fungoides." More recently, Mycosis Fungoides has come to be classified as a type of '*Cutaneous T-cell Lymphoma*,' or *CTCL*, and is known by that name, also. This cancer is so rare that I only learned of it a few weeks ago when I attended a seminar in Philadelphia given by a Dr. Eric Yang."

I sat very still, listening intently to the doctor's soft, kindly voice. I thought that I should react, but could not think how.

"This type of cancer usually travels on the surface of the skin and is treatable with chemotherapy and radiation treatments. The problem is that when it spreads or works its way into the bloodstream, it is fatal. Unfortunately, Richard, I fear that it may be doing that now. That's why it is imperative that you get some expert help immediately."

I marveled at how comfortable Dr. Birnkrant made me feel. I knew the information I was hearing was a death sentence, but the doctor's calm, caring voice was like a tranquilizer. Somehow, I felt very close to Dr. Birnkrant.

"There are only two doctors I know of who might be able to help you. Dr. Yang is one. The other is Lambert. I have both of their phone numbers and contact information that I will give you. In fact, if you would prefer that I call them for you, I will be happy to do that. If you contact them, make sure you give them my name and tell them that I made the diagnosis. They will also need to see the lab reports. I'll give you a copy of both reports."

I nodded my head.

"I must be very straight with you, Richard. When this type of cancer is diagnosed, most people don't make it six months. There is really no such thing as a survival rate. I don't know any patient who has had this cancer that is still living. Your biopsy looked bad. You look to be in the dying stage, what is called "*large cell syndrome*." I am not sure if the doctors will be able to do anything for you. At best, they may be able to prolong your life one or two years.

"Richard, there is nothing wrong with accepting death. It would be a perfectly normal reaction, and no one would blame you, if you went out and had as much fun and did as many things as you could in the time you have left. The treatments will not be easy. You may or may not need surgeries. As is very often true, the cure, which, as I said would most likely be a form of chemotherapy, is harder to endure than the disease. They will be painful. Most people take the attitude that, 'I'm going to die anyway, so why put myself through all the pain and agony.' But the decision will be up to you. Take the weekend to think about it and call those two doctors and get their opinion, this one is really new to me and I am no expert on this. I only know your test results do not look good."

The doctor continued in a now more somber voice, "Listen Rich, as a dermatologist I never had to say anything like this to a patient. You never know, you might make it—it's just that when I saw the photos of what happens to patients that advance to large cell syndrome—it made me think. I just don't know what to say . . ."

I felt like my body and my brain were immobilized. One thought wandered sluggishly through my consciousness. He has just told me that I am going to die, and I am just sitting here listening, looking at the clock to leave for the mountains. It's 11:07.

My attention slowly swung back to Dr. Birnkrant. He was asking me a question. " . . . planning to do for the weekend?"

"I was planning on going to Vermont with a friend." I was amazed that I had been able to put a sentence together.

"That sounds like a very good idea. I would suggest you do that. In fact, you might consider taking more time. It's up to you." The doctor paused for a moment. "I am really not qualified for this kind of disease. I know that sometimes these things can be related to the workplace environment, but you must talk to an expert in the field. Dr. Yang is at Hahneman University in Philadelphia. Professor Lambert is here in New Jersey. I'm just not sure where."

Again, I could only manage a nod.

"I would like to examine you again, if that would be alright. If you have any questions, I'll try to answer them as best I can."

"Okay," I responded mechanically. I stood to follow the doctor into an examination room. As I undressed, the doctor asked me questions about my work, home life and financial situation. I found that I could respond to direct questions, probably because it required no thought. What I found that I could not do was formulate any questions. My mind simply was not functioning.

When the examination was over and I was back in Dr. Birnkrant's private office, the doctor handed me a folder. "These are the lab reports and the phone numbers. Take the weekend to think about it, and if you want me to call for you, I'll be here in the office Monday morning. I've also given you my personal number in case you need to reach me over the weekend about anything. Please, Richard, don't hesitate to call."

I took the folder and stared at it. "Thank you, doctor," was all that I could manage.

"Will you be alright driving home?" Dr. Birnkrant could tell that I was still stunned by the news.

"I'll be okay," I assured him. I turned and walked out of the office. Everything I did seemed very mechanical. Turn the knob, walk out the door, open the truck door, start the truck. Ordinary tasks I could manage. It was my thought processes that were paralyzed. I tried to think through the information I had just received, but my mind would not follow through.

I do not remember the drive home, but I was pulling into my driveway. I got out of the truck and was walking toward the house, when I heard my name being called.

"Rich, what are you doing home so early? Does this mean we can leave for Vermont?" It was my partner, John. He had pulled in behind my truck and was getting out, walking toward me. "That was me that honked at you at the intersection. "

Somewhere in my subconscious I heard a horn, but it had not registered either.

"What's going on?" John wasn't sure, but he thought I looked a little strange.

"I had a doctor's appointment."

John was confused. "Didn't you do that a couple of weeks ago?"

"Yeah, but the test results came back." I stopped my explanation.

"Well . . . how were they?"

"Not good." I knew I was going to have to tell John, but I stopped. It was as though, by speaking the words out loud, it was going to make it true. And, I didn't want it to be true. Despite that, I continued, "I have cancer." The truth slammed into my consciousness. *I had cancer and I was going to die.* I sat down on the steps.

"Cancer?" John was stunned and unbelieving. "What the hell are you talking about? What kind of cancer?"

In a rush of emotion, I relayed the events of the morning to John. By the time I finished, both of us were sitting on the steps, tears streaming down our faces. I realized I didn't know much about what was going to happen, other than the weekend trip to Vermont, and I needed to make some phone calls.

I had to call my dad. I had to tell him the news, but maybe Dad could help locate the doctors, too. Dad, being an assistant manager at the University Medical Center, would certainly be in more of a position to get information about the doctors that were recommended.

I needed to call work, and I needed to call Cathi. This was going to be the most difficult phone call. How was I going to tell my young wife that I was going to die?

"I've got to call Cathi and tell her, but I don't know how." I did not want her in any danger as she drove home. "We've got to come up with some story to get her home, so I can tell her face to face."

John wasn't thinking very clearly, either. He, too, was trying to understand the news his partner and friend had just given him. "Why don't you call your dad and work first, and maybe we can come up with something to tell her in the meantime."

Dad's secretary answered the phone. "Mr. Sabb's office."

"Is he in? This is Richard, his son."

"Yes, Richard, just a moment."

Within seconds, Dad answered the phone. "Richard, what's going on? Why aren't you at work?"

"I just got back from the doctor's office. How's your day going?" I could hear the stress in my father's voice, but I could not say the words that I knew I had to say.

"Rich I don't have time for your bullshit today. Get to the point. Is there something important going on or not, 'cause I got to go." Dad, obviously having a bad day, had no time to chat.

"Well, kind of. Do me a favor, Dad. There are two guys I need for you to try to find for me. Their names are Yang and Lambert."

My father was becoming more irritated with me. "What the hell happened today at the doctor's? Stop wasting my time and get to the point," he demanded.

"Can you just try to find those two doctors for me?"

"Rich. No! What are we doing here? Is there a problem or are you okay?"

I did not want to say it. I knew he had high blood pressure and this wasn't going to help it, but I knew I couldn't stall any longer. "Okay." I took a deep breath. "No I'm not okay, I have a very rare form of cancer and I'm gonna' die, unless one of these two doctors can help me. So when we leave this weekend for Vermont, and we're leaving early, we may not be coming back. We're just going to go out and have fun."

The phone line was completely quiet. I could tell that he was trying to digest the information. "Wait, Richard, what do you mean you're going to die? What kind of cancer?"

For the second time that day, I had to repeat what the doctor told me and my plans were for the weekend.

"What do you mean, you're going to Vermont? You're not just giving up, are you? You've got to do something about this." Dad knew I was a fighter. He could not understand this attitude he was hearing from me. It sounded like I was just going to quit.

"Dad, I'm not giving up, but it's Friday. There is no way I could get in to see a doctor this late in the day. Besides, Dr. Birnkrant suggested that I take the weekend off, or more time if I need to." I was a little exasperated with Dad's pushiness, but I managed to stay calm. "Dr. Birnkrant gave me the names of those two doctors who might be able to help. Can you see if you can find out anything about them?"

"Of course. Give me their names again."

I gave him the information Dr. Birnkrant had supplied me with.

"I'll start calling right away," he assured me. "How soon are you leaving for Vermont?"

"I have some other calls to make, and I haven't told Cathi yet." Again, a sense of dread swept over me, but I forced myself to go on. "We're going to have the girls go with us to Vermont. It should be a couple of hours yet before we can leave."

"I'll call when I find out something. Do you want to come by and pickup some money and my credit card in case you decide to stay longer?"

"Thanks, Dad, but we'll be okay. I just don't know what I'm going to do yet."

"You've got to promise me one thing." Dad's voice and attitude had changed. I could tell that he recognized that I had to make my own decisions. "If I find these doctors, you've got to promise that you will come back for a second opinion. If it doesn't pan out, then go and have fun. Hell, your mother and I will even pay for it!"

"Okay, Dad."

I sat down next to the table that held the phone. John sat on the sofa watching me. That was a difficult call to make, but it was one hurdle completed. Next, I needed to call work.

By the time I heard Sam's voice on the phone, I had decided to give him only a little information. "Sam, I guess by now you know that I had to go to the doctor. The diagnosis was not very good. I'm going to have to take some time with the doctors. I don't even know if I'll be able to come back. It appears to be serious. I'll call you next week when I know more about what is going on."

"Is there anything we can do?" Sam was concerned about me. I had been a very good employee for almost nine years, plus I was well liked by most everyone in the plant, including Sam.

"No, but thanks, Sam. There's not much that I know yet. I'll talk to you next week."

I sighed as I hung up. That one was easier. I could feel myself calming down. But now, I knew I had to call Cathi. "I can't tell her over the phone." I spoke to John as I was formulating a plan. "How does this sound? I'll call Cathi's supervisor and tell her that she has to send Cathi home, because Max got out and bit a kid."

John thought for a moment. "That should work," he responded. "Max is like her baby. She'll be upset, but at least that will get her home so you can talk to her."

I picked up the phone once more and dialed. When I heard Cathi's voice answer, I immediately hung up. My next call was through the main switchboard at Makita. "Would you please page Karen for me?" I requested. Within a few minutes, Karen answered.

"Karen, this is Richard. I need for you to send Cathi home as soon as you can. We've got a situation here."

"Richard, what do you mean a situation? Is everything okay?" Karen was not only Cathi's supervisor, but also a good friend. She wanted to know what was going on.

"Just tell her that Max got out and bit a kid." My voice quavered. It was obvious to Karen that there was something that I was not telling her.

"Richard, what is really going on?"

Not able to continue the charade, I responded, "Karen, I've been diagnosed with a rare type of cancer. I'm just afraid if I tell Cathi over the phone, she will be too upset to drive home. I came up with the story about Max just to get her home. Can you just tell her that Max bit someone?"

"Oh, Richard, I am so sorry." Karen's voice was full of tears. "Of course, I'll tell her whatever you want me to. Richard . . . ?"

"Thanks, Karen. I just want to tell her face to face."

What was normally an hour drive, took Cathi only 35 minutes.

In the meantime, John called Susan, his wife, and told her about the diagnosis. "It's a terrible situation, but we are all going to go to Vermont and try to have a good weekend. Go to the house and pack some clothes as quickly as you can. I'll pick you up there and we'll come back over to Richard's."

When Cathi walked into the den, she saw Max sitting on the floor next to me. "How bad is the kid? Is his arm gone? What did he do?"

"No, no, no. Sit down." I tried to emulate the soothing voice that Dr. Birnkrant had used, but it was obvious that I had been crying.

Cathi looked at John and could tell that he, too, had been crying. Even more alarmed, she demanded, "What did he do?"

"No, Cathi, just sit down." I had to tell her quickly before she lost control. "Remember when the doctor called here last night, and we missed it?"

"Yeah."

"He called again today at work. He had me go down to his office. I have cancer and they are only giving me six months or less to live."

Cathi exploded in a volcanic out burst of tears. "What? What kind of cancer?"

"It is called Mycosis Fungoides . . ."

Cathi could not hear anymore. She put her hands over her ears. Tears were pouring down her face. "No," she cried hysterically, "This can't be happening!" She turned and ran out the door and down the driveway.

John and I jumped to our feet and ran after her, fearful of what she might do. When I was able to reach her, I grabbed her and held her close.

"No, no, no," she sobbed into my shoulder, and we sank to the ground.

"Cathi, Cathi, it's going to be okay." I was crying, too. I hoped that the practice I had gotten by talking to John, Dad and work would have made this easier, but it didn't. "We're all going to go to Vermont this weekend and just relax. We can stay as long as we want. We don't have to come back right away. We can talk about it and decide what to do. There are doctors I will need to see, but that's all up in the air. Cathi, you've got to hang in there with me."

"Cathi," John said as he sat down next to us, "almost anything can happen. The diagnosis may be wrong. The doctor said it was rare.

Maybe it's just a mistake. But no matter what, you and Richard can handle it."

I held her in my arms and rocked her until her sobs subsided, all the time reassuring her that it was going to be all right. When at last she had quieted, I began to discuss the plans for the weekend. "John is going to go pick up Susan, and as soon as they get back, we'll leave."

"I don't have anyone to take care of Max." She knew that she had to calm down and think logically. "I can call my Mom and see if she or my sister can come over."

"That's a good idea," I said, thankful that she was beginning to get back to her old self. "In the meantime, I'll go get packed."

I could hear her voice downstairs talking to her mother on the phone, as I put my clothes into a small suitcase. I didn't know how much to pack. We might be gone for a while.

The phone rang and Cathi answered. It was Karen from work. I couldn't hear if Cathi was telling Karen that she was not sure when she would be back at work.

"He has cancer," Cathi said matter-of-factly, trying to stay strong. The conversation continued, but I could not make out anymore.

I finished my packing and took my bag downstairs. Cathi was standing by the phone, staring into nothingness. I could still see the tear stains on her cheeks. "Why don't you go on up and get packed. John and Susan will be back pretty soon."

"Okay," she said, coming back to reality. "Kim is going to come stay at the house and take care of Max."

Cathi went upstairs. I sat down in the big comfortable chair I claimed as my own. It had been only two hours since I left the doctor's office, but my entire world changed. The reality of it was overwhelming. I wondered what it would be like to die.

The shrill ring of the phone interrupted my thoughts. I hesitated as I reached to pick it up. The last time I answered a phone had been in Mike's office. Since that time, my life was not the same.

"Hello?"

"Rich?" It was Dad's voice. "You are not going to believe what I found out."

"What is it, Dad?"

"I called Bill, the president of the university, right after we hung up and told him what happened. He told me not to worry. Yang is affiliated with us through Hahneman University and Lambert works right here, over in the next building. I damn near had a heart attack."

I was astounded by the news. According to Birnkrant, Lambert was one of the foremost authorities on this cancer. "Yeah, go on."

"Well, I think I hung up on Bill, but I took the elevator down and found Lambert in his office. When I told him about your diagnosis, he couldn't believe that it was true. He said that Mycosis Fungoides doesn't usually happen in someone so young. But I told him that Dr. Birnkrant could confirm the diagnosis. Lambert said that if you'll be here first thing Monday morning, he'd have a whole team of doctors waiting to see you. They want to run a whole series of tests on you to make sure. He knows that things don't look so good and if you choose not to come back, he can understand that, too. But he hopes that you will. He said to have you there by 7:30 A.M."

"Well, we're going to Vermont . . ." I could tell that my dad was fighting back tears. "Okay Dad, here's the deal. I'll come back Monday and I'll give them a week. If I don't like what they come up with in a week, then we're leaving again and having fun."

"That sounds fair. I'll be there at 6:30 to pick you up." Dad was not going to allow me to miss this appointment.

"Okay, Dad. I'll see you Monday morning." I hung up. I couldn't believe that one of the foremost experts on this rare type of cancer was right in the same building complex where he worked. I felt good, too, about the way everyone was respecting my decisions; this expert doctor and even Dad.

The doorbell sounded. It was John and Susan. It only took minutes to get the truck packed. Heading out for Vermont, I shared the news. "I guess that means we'll have to come back Sunday night."

But the others didn't mind. They were encouraged by the quick response of the doctor. The mood in the vehicle lightened somewhat and we were all determined to have a good weekend.

16
Analyzing Troop Status and Battle Strategies

October 5, 1992—I was up early Monday morning, in cautious anticipation of the day. I hadn't gotten much sleep. I was not sure what to expect with this Dr. Lambert. I knew that there would be all sorts of tests. Dad had mentioned something about a full body workup, but I had no idea what all that involved. I was sure that most of it was not going to be pleasant.

The weekend had gone well. It had taken us less than a day to get the house painted. Cathi and Susan taped and papered while John and I scraped and got it prepped. We quickly painted it by using an airless power sprayer.

On the drive up, I decided that being morose would not solve anything. "Screw it," I said, "if I'm going to die anyway, I might as well have a good time." Not many people appreciated my cavalier attitude toward adversity, but this time John and Cathi were in total agreement.

Susan, however, could not handle this kind of behavior. Like most people, she had no idea of what to say and was very uncomfortable around me. Talk of the diagnosis made her become very quiet, and she would walk away.

John was the opposite and was a Godsend to both Cathi and I. As long as Susan was not around, the three of us could talk freely. Respectfully, no one in the group wanted to make Susan feel uncomfortable and we all suspected that when she walked away it was to show respect toward me by allowing us to talk, as I needed.

However, considering the circumstances, we did not dwell on the news. I was determined to have a good time and the others followed suit. We explored the area and found some great antiques. John and Cathi did the cooking, and both being great cooks, we ate well. We laughed and had fun. I appreciated their efforts, and was glad to be away from the city where I knew that reality would have been more difficult to escape.

The drive home on Sunday though, was subdued. Everyone was quiet, living through his or her own personal fears of what was to come.

I knew now that I was going to try to fight this thing. Maybe, like John said, the diagnosis was wrong. Maybe it was not as severe as Dr. Birnkrant had thought. I just knew that I was not going to give up. I was in excellent physical condition. That had to count for something. Modern medicine was pretty amazing these days and only getting better. I had myself convinced.

When we arrived home, I talked with Dad again. "I'll be there about 6 or 6:30 to pick you up, " he informed me. "Have you decided what Cathi is going to do?"

We had discussed it. Our final decision was that Cathi would go back into work on Monday and talk to her superiors about the flexibility of her schedule.

No one knew what was going to happen. The only thing that I was sure of was that the day was going to be filled with testing. "Yes. For now, she's going to go into work and let them know that she may not be coming back for a long time. We want to wait until we know more about what's going on."

Dad was there promptly at six o'clock. Despite the early hour, the drive to the university was hectic through the beginnings of rush hour traffic.

When we finally arrived, he took me up the elevator to the doctor's offices. "Lambert wanted you to see Dr. Bueller first. Then, he'll be showing up a little later."

A nurse sat behind a desk as we entered the office. "Good morning," she said pleasantly. "May I help you?"

"Yes," I took charge. "I'm here to see Dr. Bueller. I'm Richard Sabb."

"Right this way, Mr. Sabb. The doctor will be right with you."

At least there is no waiting, I thought to myself. That's encouraging. The nurse showed me into a room with a stainless steel table and instructed me to disrobe completely and lay on the table. She handed me sheet to cover myself with.

Within a few minutes, Dr. Bueller entered, followed by the nurse. The doctor was reading something on a clipboard and barely acknowledged me. He sat the clipboard down and turned to me. "Well, what can you tell me?"

"I've been diagnosed with Mycosis Fungoides, and evidently, it's pretty bad."

"Uh-hum." The doctor reached to lift the sheet. "How did you get here?" he said absent-mindedly.

I assumed the doctor was just making small talk. "Well, the traffic was really bad on the parkway . . ." I started.

"What?" The doctor had stopped. "You mean you weren't flown here?"

"No, my Dad and I drove in." I watched as the doctor's expression changed to disbelief and then anger.

"What the hell am I doing here? You're not going to make it through this, anyway. You shouldn't even be here wasting my time!" With that, he dropped the sheet back over me and walked out of the room in a huff.

I was shocked. But in an instant, a flood of fury washed over me. "That son of a bitch!" I yelled.

The nurse scurried out of the room as I jumped up and grabbed my clothes. Within seconds, I too was storming through the door and out into the hallway where Dad was waiting.

"I want that asshole fired," I raged. "He didn't even examine me. He said he was wasting his time. I was going to die anyway."

Dad could not believe what he heard. "Oh, my God, this is insane. He couldn't have done that."

"Bob, what's going on?" The question came from a large man walking up the hall. He had a shock of graying hair and thick features.

Dad turned. "Dr. Lambert, we need you to take care of this. This is my son, Richard."

Dr. Lambert looked at me. I was obviously distraught. "I'm Clark Lambert. What happened?"

Still furious, I told him about my brief encounter with Bueller. "I want that man fired," I said.

Lambert was well aware that Dad did not have the authority to fire medical personnel and, although he knew that the doctor's behavior was inexcusable, the doctor was a good staff member.

"Richard, I'll take care of this. He just doesn't know what the situation is. He doesn't know the case. Let me talk to him and I'll get this settled."

I took a deep breath and calmed down somewhat. I was able to see something in the face of Dr. Lambert and I knew that he would take care of it.

Lambert instinctively began asking me questions about what Dr. Birnkrant had told me. He knew what he was doing, he was methodical and most importantly, focused on the real problem at hand, my condition. "Oh, this is Dr. Martinez," Lambert said, as another man in a white lab coat walked up. "He specializes in hematology, oncology and pharmacology."

"You must be Richard." Dr. Martinez extended his hand to shake mine. He spoke with a very thick Spanish accent.

Lambert turned to speak to Dad. "Bob, we'll take it from here.

Why don't you go do what you have to do, and we'll give you a call when we're done with your son."

Dad turned to leave then hesitated and said, "Listen doc, keep me posted, have me paged if you need anything, take good care of him."

Professor Lambert could see the emotions overcoming him and quickly responded, "I'll take care of this Bob, you go do what you have to and we'll call to keep you posted.

The two doctors and I went to the elevators to go down to the lab area. Lambert kept the conversation casual, asking me if I was married and about my hobbies.

It was obvious to the two doctors that I took good care of myself. I looked to be in excellent shape. They were not at all surprised when I told them about my weight lifting background.

Lambert asked what I had done over the weekend, and was pleased when I told him about the trip to Vermont and that I was able to relax and forget about the diagnosis.

When we arrived in the lab, Dr. Lambert introduced Dr. "Ricky," a small man with thinning hair, plus several interns. I was swamped with names and knew I would never remember them, but they all seemed friendly and ready to start working to help me.

"I don't want you to be worried about this, Richard," Lambert reassured me. " The diagnosis could be wrong, and if not, we'll do everything we can for you."

I liked the confidence this doctor instilled, but when I glanced at Dr. Martinez, it was obvious from the look on his face that he was not as optimistic. I could see the concern and worry there.

"That's okay, Doc," I said, summoning up my bravado, "*I've got no time to die*. There's too much that I still want to do."

Lambert liked me and admired my attitude. I made it clear to the doctors that I was a fighter, but he knew that it was going to take all the fight I could muster for me to survive, even for a little while.

The first thing I had to do was strip down to nothing. Lying on a table, butt naked, it was evident that any modesty I might have had was going to disappear quickly. Lambert was giving instructions to the team and they each began to work on their assignments.

My first day consisted of numerous blood samples, the first series of x-rays, and tissue samples from all areas of my body.

Each member of the team explained to me what he or she was doing and how it would be used in the analysis. They showed me how to do the stitches on the larger biopsies. I learned that if the needle was inserted in at an angle when injecting Lidocaine, there was less pain.

The interns joked that Lambert had four Ph.D's, Martinez had three, and 'Ricky' was low man on the totem pole with only two. Because it was a teaching university and they were in a scientific laboratory, most of the tests and analysis would be done right there.

What impressed me most was that they all treated me like one of the team, despite my being the object of their research.

A Dr. Patel, who Lambert introduced as a micro-surgeon, stopped by in the afternoon. "I just wanted him to meet you," explained Lambert, "just in case we find that you need some surgeries, Dr. Patel will perform them."

By the end of the day, I was sore and exhausted. I had been poked and prodded, stuck and stitched for over six hours. As I was dressing, one of the interns handed me a candy bar. "We took a lot of blood today," she said. "This might help you."

Several members of the team were standing close by, including 'Ricky' and Martinez. "You know," I said, "it might be easier tomorrow if you just attach a valve to me. It would make it much easier to draw blood then. You wouldn't have to stick me so many times."

Everyone laughed. Dr. 'Ricky', in a perfect rendition of Boris Karloff, responded, "We want your blood."

On Tuesday, the doctors continued the series of x-rays, took more blood samples and more biopsies.

I learned more about the procedures. I felt like I was enrolled in Medicine 101. But it was better to know what was going on. I understood now that what I thought had been a rash was in fact cancerous plaques and tumors.

I also learned that the possibility of Sezary Syndrome, a more advanced form of Mycosis Fungoides, was a real concern. It would mean that large numbers of cancerous cells were in my blood. I recalled Dr. Birnkrant's warning about the cancer in the bloodstream.

Dr. 'Ricky' would perform most of the biopsies, taking them right in front of me. He showed me how to slice the skin, put it onto a slide and then under the microscope. He would point out the good cells and the bad ones. It was fascinating to see what cancer looked like, but also alarming to realize what was going on in my body.

Martinez did much the same with the blood tests. He would take the tube of blood out of centrifuge and put a sample on a slide under the microscope. "See that right in the middle of the slide," he directed. "That is what a hyper-convoluted nuclei looks like in the cell."

The cell had a dome mass of many other nuclei; it was like taking a glass of milk and using the straw to blow a dome of bubbles. The dome of bubbles would represent hyper-convoluted nuclei.

Lambert conducted a long drawn out test, called a T-cell Beta Chain Analysis. He went into detail about how the test analyzes what a cell line looks like. The explanation was way over my head, but because he took the time to explain it, I was impressed.

A pattern began to form with my doctors and each day we became more comfortable with one another. On occasion, we even had lunch together. They kept the conversation casual, asking questions about work and hobbies. I appreciated how they nurtured me, careful not to be to frightening with unknowns. I marveled at how they made me feel like I was working with them, instead of being the actual project. The doctors separated my cancer, from me, the person. I was very comfortable with that.

During lunch on Tuesday, I asked if they had any idea about what had caused the cancer to develop. Lambert responded quickly. "Let's first focus on what's wrong with you and how we're going to treat it. We need to get more tests done, and then we'll think about how it may have developed. Our primary goal is to come up with a treatment schedule that is going to work. We need to figure out a way to make sure that you live."

But test results were beginning to come in and they did not look good. I was failing them. I had CTCL, minor blood damage, and some large cell syndrome in various tissues. Luckily, large cells were not circulating in my body yet. I had internal damage, and although minor, it showed up in my liver and kidneys. It was imperative that they come up with some options for treatment quickly. Everyone knew that the cancer could kill me at anytime.

It felt strange to me when they talked about my dying. I didn't feel bad, just sore from all the needles and stitches. The Lidocaine they used to numb the areas where they would take biopsies made me tired by the end of the day, but I didn't feel like I was dying.

Cathi's mother, Loren, drove me to the hospital on Wednesday. They told me it was the day for the CAT scan. I drank the iodine liquid and waited for it to circulate through my body. Normally, CAT scans take only five to ten minutes, but that is when the doctors are looking for only one thing. Because the cancer was throughout my entire body, my scan took an hour and fifteen minutes.

When it was lunchtime, Loren and I went up to the cafeteria. It was obvious that she was concerned about me, but what showed was her impatience after a boring morning of sitting. After we were seated, Dr. Martinez walked up and asked, "May I join you?"

"Sure," I said. I really liked the intense, dedicated man.

"So, how do you think things are going?" Loren demanded, once the doctor was seated. "Are you ever going to do anything besides testing on this guy?" She was in no mood for diplomacy.

"We're being cautious," Martinez purred in his Spanish accent. "A lot of doctors misdiagnose this. We don't want to give Richard treatments he doesn't need. And, the testing doesn't do him any harm. He is sore for awhile or sick from the things we put into him, but it goes away by the end of the day." Turning the conversation to her, he continued, "Where do you live? You are Cathi's mother, yes? It is very nice that you are here with Richard, taking him to the hospital. Bob is very busy with the university."

I didn't know if it was the Spanish accent or turning the topic to her, but I admired the finesse with which Martinez handled the situation. Smooth, I thought to myself, very smooth.

Much of Thursday was taken up with liver testing. The doctors opted to use the old-fashioned green dye test, rather than just a blood test. Due to the type of cancer I had, they believed it would give them a better look at the liver as a whole and it's exact function. Every few minutes for a half hour, green dye was injected into me. Once all the dye was in me, blood samples were taken every five minutes or so to measure how much my liver was actually filtering out.

Every day began about 7:30 A.M. Every day, blood work and some sort of tissue samples were taken. There was always lots of conversation during the lulls between tests. And, every day would last until 3:30 or 4 P.M. My world was exhausting and painful, but I knew that my life was in the best hands anyone could ask for.

At night, when I got home, I was not much of a conversationalist. I would try to share with Cathi what happened during the day, but I often fell asleep on the sofa before she got home from work. I even tried exercising a couple of times, but I had so many holes and stitches in my body, I accomplished very little. I am not sure what was harder, the testing or the emotional concept of dying at such a young, vibrant age leaving behind my beloved wife?

Fortunately, the doctors gave me Friday through Monday off to rest up and heal. It had been an exhausting week and I was glad it was over.

But the time at home was unsettling. Cathi and I tried to make it a normal weekend, keeping ourselves busy with jobs around the house and shopping. But the looming future would inch its way into my consciousness, posing unanswerable questions.

What was my treatment going to be? What if it was the wrong one?

How would my body respond? Would I live? I would mentally jerk myself up and resist the questions that tumbled through my mind. All I knew was that I was a very sick man and there were crucial decisions to be made in the very near future.

On Monday, after Cathi left for work, I put in a call to Sam. "I thought I would come by the plant today and pick up my stuff, Sam. I'll stop in to talk to you when I'm there." The only person from work that I had talked to since returning from Vermont was Eddie Roman, when Eddie had called to check up on me.

Sam must have spread the word that I was going to be coming by. Everyone was waiting and interested to see me, all wanting to talk with me. My area had been cleaned and straightened up. I could tell that they were thinking in terms of my family. My first instinct was what if a brother, sister or parent had to come get my things, anything that might caused emotional trauma, like photos, had been removed. It struck me that Dr. Birnkrant must have told Mike that I was not expected to live.

So, they know, I thought. No one is saying anything, but they know. They all greeted me casually and respectfully, wishing me good luck. It's like I'm just leaving to go to another job, I thought. But my new job was to stay alive.

I stopped in to see Mike and then went to Sam's office.

"Anything you need, Richard, anything you want, you just let us know, " Sam said, when I was seated in front of the desk.

I simply nodded. I could tell that Sam was uncomfortable. Although he did not move, I knew that mentally, Sam was squirming. When, at last, Sam formulated the question to his satisfaction, he blurted out, "Should we make any plans for you coming back?"

"No." It was not much of an answer, but there was not much I could say.

"Well, anything with insurance, have them contact me. I'll make sure you get what you need."

I left the office within minutes. Sam, as hard as he tried to act as though everything was okay, unknowingly, he made me feel uncomfortable. He was my boss, the one I had to inform that I would not be back.

I went by to see the other draftsmen and designers, and then to some other departments where I wanted to talk with other coworkers. By the time I completed my rounds and returned to my old work area to pick up the boxes containing my personal belongings, one of the guys had already taken them out to my truck. This made leaving much easier for me.

Well, this is it, I thought as I got into my truck to drive home. A sense of desolation swept over me. I knew that I had just said goodbye to my former life, and my new one would be filled with uncertainty, alien medical terminology and endless tests.

Tuesday of week two, under Lambert's instruction, Dad joined Cathi, and me and we drove to Hahneman University in Philadelphia. As a professional courtesy, Lambert wanted Dr. Yang to review the progress that was being made.

As Yang reviewed the blood and tissue samples, I thought about the seminar that this doctor had hosted. It was what motivated Birnkrant to do the first biopsy. Due to the seminar, Birnkrant essentially gave me a chance to fight for my life with this rare cancer.

After checking the samples and reports, the doctor looked up at me. "I am very happy with the work they have done so far. Dr. Lambert has an excellent group of doctors and scientists. The one thing I would like to do is check the tumors you may have. And, then we will talk some."

After the brief examination, Dr. Yang brought us into his small private office.

Dad insisted on staying with me during the examination and Cathi waited outside in the waiting room.

"Dr. Lambert wanted me to talk to you about some of the possibilities for treatment," Yang began. "I realize that he explained to you that this is a *very rare* condition, especially at your age. I would guess that less than 1000 people are diagnosed with this and many are misdiagnosed and, therefore, improperly treated. You were lucky to be referred to doctors that have the means to evaluate you properly. Having said that, I want you to know that we will devise a treatment schedule cautiously and in conjunction with your body's reactions."

It was obvious that Dr. Lambert had contacted him about my case.

"Most often we like to present three alternatives to the patient. However, because of the proliferation of the cancer over your body, I believe we find ourselves limited to two."

"As you can see for yourself, you have about 32 various areas on your body that have plaques developing on your skin. And this evidently happened in a very short period of time. You also have some small nodules forming. These are tumors and may even be another form of cancer called *Lymphomatoid Papulosis* or *LyP*. We will have to test for that. But because of this I do not think that the topical forms of chemotherapy will benefit you."

"Another option is called *Total Skin Electron Beam Therapy*, or *TSE*. This type of therapy has been really perfected at Stanford University and has been used by them since about 1958. They have become expert enough where most any patient is qualified for treatment."

"The major drawbacks are no one can really predict how the patient will react until after the treatment, and due to constant research and theory as to what CTCL really is, sometimes the patient can only receive minimal treatment for their lifetime."

"I think it is best to be used as a last resort due to the *potential* severe effects it could have on the body, both internally and externally. I want you to know that you are a definite candidate for TSE, but I think we should wait on that decision. Remember, it's our job to devise a treatment schedule that kills the cancer while doing minimal damage to your body—and we always like for our patient to live," he added with a smile, relaxing the mood.

I was trying to digest all of the information that he had given me thus far. This electron beam therapy sounded like it was one of the

NO TIME TO DIE

"cures worse than the disease" that Birnkrant had mentioned. What did he mean by, *potential* severe side effects or they didn't really know how a patient could react? Did that mean that it could kill me? I felt myself becoming despondent.

"The treatment alternative that I am recommending, and in agreement with Dr. Lambert", he continued with eyes focused on me, "is to combine a low dose of chemotherapy with a low dose of a type of radiation therapy, but in an aggressive format. I will be suggesting to him that we start you at 3-4 treatments per week."

"This treatment is called *Photo chemotherapy* or *PUVA*. I must tell you that this is the option I prefer. It allows us more leeway. We could evaluate your body as you do the therapies, and increase or decrease the dosage as needed. If necessary, we can even add the topical treatments in conjunction with the PUVA. Furthermore, you will still have the option of TSE."

"Our objective is to slowly and progressively see what your body can handle as we try to kill the cancer. Most importantly, it gives us the opportunity to do as little damage as possible to you."

I comprehended all too well what the doctor was saying. "This is a cancer that we do not have a standard to treat and patients often react differently. We are not in agreement as to what it is, therefore some doctors, misdiagnosis, mistreat, and/or the patient dies during one of these many variables." Later I realized my emotionally derived thoughts, although somewhat accurate, certainly did not represent the logical meaning he intended.

"Richard," Dr. Yang resumed, "this is something which you, your wife and your family need to discuss. Don't be afraid to ask us questions or seek other opinions. There are still more tests to run, and Dr. Lambert wanted me to present you with my opinion and more information so that you can better understand. The most important thing for you to realize, is that the end decision will be yours. *We are here to educate you, and to help you make the right decision.*"

The drive back to New Jersey was *an emotional mind melt.*

Cathi was angry with my Dad for not wanting her in the examination room.

Being in a room with his daughter-in-law while his son was naked embarrassed my dad. Then Dad was upset with himself for not having Cathi there.

As my Dad and I shared every detail of the doctor's conversation and demeanor, we all realized, and subsequently became quite happy and optimistic, that Dr. Yang really handled us properly. He kept the tone positive, identified the grave problem with honesty, and focused on a solution objectively.

As the odometer clicked off the miles we began to jokingly feel sorry for Dr. Lambert. Through our evaluation of the visit we summarized a mental listing of questions for my primary doctor. He now had a patient/student to add to his interns.

On Wednesday morning I was ready for Dr. Lambert with a barrage of questions. But the professor put my interrogation on hold until after my full body MRI and more blood samples.

"Okay," Lambert stated, once they finally finished, "what do you want to know?"

I had his undivided attention and he addressed all of my concerns and questions more than once. With grace and elegance he defined medical terminology and testing procedures that I could not comprehend.

"Wait, Richard," Lambert interrupted. "At this point, I want you to understand that there are many ways to treat you and there are other test results that we are waiting on. We must determine the full extent of the cancer and we must be very cautious in our evaluations. As I am sure Dr. Yang told you, there are advantages and drawbacks with all of the proposed treatments. And I assure you that before we expect an answer from you, you will have all the information we can provide to help you with your decision."

I knew Dr. Lambert was being very careful in how he worded his explanation. He did not want to mislead me in anyway.

Deservingly, I trusted this brilliant man, literally, with my life. And, although there were many questions left unanswered for the moment, I knew as test results came in they would be answered and taught.

The testing eased up for the rest of the week and the two weeks that followed.

I would show up so that 'Ricky' and Lambert could make sure that my biopsy sites were healing properly. This also gave them the opportunity to visually observe and evaluate the growth of my cancer.

Martinez would take more blood samples, but only about every other day, rather than four and five times each day. And, they would fill in gaps in my understanding of the proposed treatments.

I learned that the radiation treatments would actually be a type of photo chemotherapy call PUVA. It stood for *"Psoralen and Ultraviolet 'A' light radiation."* The Psoralen is a photosensitizing, chemotherapeutic drug that would be taken orally. It would be digested and broken down in the stomach where it could then be circulated throughout my body. As my blood distributed the drug, it would bind only to the cancerous DNA cells. Then be radiated with the ultraviolet light, which sensitizes the body and activates the Psoralen. The drug would kill the cancer cells lying close to the surface of the skin. I was warned that this type of therapy could be dangerous due to possible radiation overexposure and alterations in the immune system.

But that was not nearly as frightening as the electron beam therapy. There were just too many questions about it. Although it might have worked faster to kill the cancerous cells, it too easily could kill me or my body may not be of the type that allows for more than one treatment schedule.

I was leaning more toward the treatment schedule with the combined chemo- and radiation therapy. There were chemicals like *Oxsoralen Ultra, Alpha-interferon* and *Methotrexate,* involved.

We talked about DNA altering topical creams called nitrogen mustard, for my skin. But my disease was progressing much too fast for the doctors to gain any control with this option.

PUVA allowed the amounts and lengths of treatments to be controlled on a day-to-day basis. The main advantage to me was that I could go home after my treatment. I would not have to be in the hospital except for the brief time I was taking the radiation.

I made it very clear to everyone that I hated hospitals. If I was going to die, I did not want it to be in the hospital. "If something goes wrong," I told Lambert one day, "and I'm at the hospital, I want you to strap my ass on that gurney," pointing to the steel table close by, "and push me out the door."

Lambert laughed, but he knew I was serious.

It was now five weeks since the diagnosis, and my world had become a whirlwind of mixed emotions and critical decisions.

Cathi and I were sitting in his cluttered office with Martinez and 'Ricky'. They were all there "*for me*" and anxiously awaited more questions or my response in deciding a treatment schedule. There were numerous medical books, research papers, and studies scattered about. Stacks of papers and folders were everywhere, but he knew exactly where and what, each one pertained to. Lambert reminded me of an absent-minded professor. He might forget where the 'proverbial light switch' was, but for him, conversation and thought about cellular structure, molecular biology, or immunopathology, was a relaxing pleasure.

"I've thought about it a lot and talked it over with Cathi, and we both agree that the low-dose chemo and radiation is the way to go. So, what do we do now?" I could tell that the three were happy with my decision.

"We will schedule you for your first treatment and educate you and Cathi on how to administer the chemo," Lambert replied. "Then we see what your body can take." Lambert paused for a moment. "Richard, we are fairly sure that something from your work environment must have caused this cancer. Do you have any ideas?"

Over the last few weeks, the doctors had been subtle in their questioning about my work. They had wanted to know about the chemicals I used and how often. They asked in detail about any accidents I might have been involved with.

It had taken several discussions with my parents to pinpoint the two incidents in 1986. I had almost forgotten about them, and was still not sure about the dates. But through thorough discussion, things were starting to fall into place—the basketball project and the injection-molding machine. The heated resin had hit me on my right hip, exactly where the rash and now cancerous tumors were developing.

"I think I might have an idea," I told them. As I related the story of the accident and my work place environment, notes were taken. Occasionally, one of the doctors would interrupt me for some clarification and more detailed questioning.

"These other two men who worked on the project with you, Henry and Harold," Dr. Martinez asked, as he referred to his notes, "what about them."

"Harold died shortly after the accident, and Henry died a few months later," I answered.

A quick glance passed between the three doctors, but I saw it.

"How old were these men?" 'Ricky' asked.

"They were both getting close to retirement age. What are you saying?" I looked at each of the doctors. "Are you suggesting they died of this same cancer?"

"There is no way to know conclusively," Dr. Lambert told me. "What we do know is that Mycosis Fungoides most often shows up in people over 50 and progresses very rapidly."

"My god," I exclaimed, suddenly remembering, "Harold showed me the rash on his arms the Friday before he died. And Henry was always complaining about his arms and putting lotion on them."

The doctors knew that, collectively, they had to be careful not to let me make assumptions that they could not prove, but this revelation confirmed questions they had in their own minds.

Lambert spoke first. "It is very important that you talk with an attorney about this. Provided that we can keep you alive, you will never go back to work. You need him to apply for Social Security and Worker's Comp benefits. Get your family to help you. Richard, you and Cathi must focus on your treatments and your health."

The treatments, I thought. "When will they start?"

"I'm going to make some calls and confer with the rest of the team," Lambert told me, "but it will be very soon, within a week, I expect."

17
Chemical Warfare Begins

November 13, 1992—I understood perfectly what the doctors had meant by "burn-in." Dr. Martinez told me that was how the first treatment was always described by the patients.

It was Friday afternoon and I had just experienced my first therapy that morning. We had set it on Friday so that I would have time to recuperate. As the 2 ccs of Alpha-Interferon blistered its way through my body, I could feel its progress. The PUVA treatment only consisted of 25 milligrams of Psoralen, and radiation, one hour later was only for two minutes. Before leaving, about four hours later that day, I joked with Dr. Martinez that I was ready to kick ass (the cancer).

So, this is what my life is going to be like, I thought miserably, as I lay on the sofa, feeling like my intestines and insides were on fire. I was nauseous and wanted to vomit, but I held it back. They told me that I was most likely going to have a reaction to the chemicals, but I felt they understated it.

From age 13, when my brother started me lifting weights and teaching me about nutrition, I had taken very good care of my body. Now, it was being intentionally bombarded with vicious poisons. I moaned as I repositioned myself, attempting to find some source of relief.

Cathi watched, helpless. It was almost time to give me the injection of Methotrexate. Earlier that day the doctors showed her how to give the shot in my thigh. Cathi's grandmother had been a nurse and all the memories of watching her and talking with her came rushing back.

The doctors were impressed with her innate skill. She was a natural, and this made the doctors more confident about their decision to let her assist in my care. They talked to her about what to expect, but hearing it and living it were two different things. Once she gave me the injection, there was nothing she could do, but wait for the chemicals to run their course.

Max sat next to the sofa, cautiously eyeing me, his master. The normally rambunctious young dog was calm and attentive. I had to believe that Max understood that something was wrong. I reached out to pat Max on the head and winced at the pain the small movement caused.

It had been a short six weeks since my diagnosis in Dr. Birnkrant's office. And, in those six weeks, the cancer transformed to a more aggressive growth and was looking a lot like stage three of a four-stage sequence. One of the interns described stage three as a "Hail Mary" situation. It was something that not many people came out of.

As the evening progressed, I was still in agony, moaning from my fetal position on the sofa. Cathi was concerned. Some of the symptoms should have receded. "I'm going to call Dr. Martinez," she told me, as she reached for the phone. "This can't be right."

"Hello." Cathi heard the rich accent through the phone.

"Dr. Martinez, this is Cathi Sabb. I'm worried. Richie is still in a lot of pain, and it doesn't seem to be getting any better."

"Can he talk to me?"

"Hold on. Let me give him the phone."

Dr. Martinez could hear the rustling of blankets and a slight moaning from me as I took the receiver. "Hi, doc." I tried to sound cheery, but knew that I had failed.

"Richard, tell me how you feel."

"It really burns and I keep wanting to vomit, but so far I've been able to hold it back."

"No, no," the doctor exclaimed. "Let it out. It is good to get sick. Relax. Take the weekend off and don't do anything. Take it very slow. Your body is adjusting to the chemicals."

I had assumed, wrongly, that by not vomiting, I was keeping the medicines in my body so that they could work longer. Now, after receiving permission from Martinez, I began what was to become a ritual after almost every treatment.

By Monday, I was much better. I taken Martinez's advice and done very little for the past two days. And, the doctors seemed pleased with the first treatment.

"We are going to switch you over to 50 mg of Oxsoralen Ultra and try increasing the PUVA by 30 seconds with each treatment," Lambert informed me. "We will do only three treatments this week, but if we find you can handle four, we will change to that next week."

"Richard," he continued, "we are really going to be pounding your body, but because you are in excellent physical shape, I believe you can withstand it. The normal dosage of Oxsoralen Ultra is 25-30 mg. Dr. Yang and I agreed on bringing you to 50 mg. PUVA is generally administered twice a week for three to seven minutes. We are starting you on three, and we will increase the time as much as you can stand without you getting radiation burns. Cathi will continue to give you injections of Methotrexate at home two times a week. If we see the need, we will add the topical medicines. We will continually monitor and evaluate your progress here in the lab."

I began the treatments at the University Medical Center, but it didn't take long to realize there was a problem. The University catered to huge numbers of patients, and timing was critical with my use of the PUVA equipment.

Dr. Martinez identified a small window of opportunity that would allow maximum penetration of the cancer cells by the ultraviolet light. Once I had taken the chemicals, I had 50 to 70 minutes. Anything over that, the treatment was much less effective and I would get sick.

The Medical Center was not equipped to accommodate my schedule. The number of patients requiring attention was high and on a "first come, first served" basis. It was obvious something had to change.

Dr. Lambert was not tolerant of this interference and made arrangements to transfer me to St. Barnabas Hospital in Westfield. It was a longer drive, but Dr. Brooks' office at the hospital was more specialized and better able to conform my time limitations. If needed, the minute I arrived at the office, I could begin the treatment.

I quickly became familiar with the side effects of the therapy. Within minutes of taking Oxsoralen Ultra, I knew something powerful was dissolving inside me. Intense nausea would follow after about 15 minutes.

I found out the hard way that food and liquids, especially hot liquids, would negate the effectiveness of the drugs. An innocent cup of soup prior to ingesting the pill caused the chemical to disperse rapidly throughout my body. I became violently ill, vomiting for the next fourteen hours.

Another side effect was an extreme sensitivity to light. I would wear sunglasses with shades on the sides of both eyes. At home, after returning from the treatments, the bedroom had to be completely dark. Cathi hung dark, heavy towels over the curtains to block out any light that might come through.

I had headaches and head noise or tints, after each treatment. My eyes were often swollen and sore. If I weren't vomiting, I would have an upset stomach and diarrhea. At times, it was both. I was very sensitive to smells, especially cigarette smoke and automobile exhaust. My skin would itch and often I felt drained and disoriented.

My schedule was simple Monday through Thursday: get up, take the medicines, my mom and mother-in-law took turns driving me to the hospital for treatment while Cathi worked, return home, get sick and sleep.

I would sometimes attempt to watch television, but even that was too much light. There was about two hours after each treatment where I could still function, but then I would become ill and sleepy. Once the force of the chemicals hit, I could not remember anything. Even after I woke up, there would be times when I could not remember what I was doing or where I was.

By the end of the second week, I was up to 10 minutes of therapy in the PUVA equipment four times a week. At the end of the second month, I was at; 20 minutes of radiation, 60 mg. of Oxsoralen Ultra, and Cathi administered 1 cc of Methotrexate at the end of the week.

The doctors were astounded at my capacity for the treatments. I rapidly surpassed the standard treatment schedule. The only reasoning they could come up with was the incredibly healthy diet I had maintained since my teenage years.

The free form and peptide amino acids had made it possible for me to withstand the battering my body was taking.

Conversely, the cancer was very deadly and persistent. The doctors main concern now was the adverse effects of the therapy. Too much could also begin to deplete my bone marrow.

Reactions to the therapy became commonplace. Cathi had to be taught how to control my body during convulsions. She learned where pressure points were and where to hit me in the neck if I was out of control. The local EMTs were on a first name basis with us. They quickly became aware of our problems and came to trust Cathi's judgment about whether I required treatment at the hospital.

Overexposure to the ultraviolet light would mean radiation burns and having to apply aloe Vera cream hourly. Max became Cathi's indicator for my well-being. If the dog met her at the door, she knew everything was all right. If he wasn't there, she instantly knew that something was wrong.

Through all of this, I was determined to live a "*normal*" life. And, although I would seem to be totally competent and lucid, I sometimes would not remember anything.

Waking up after the treatments, I would go to the train room and work on an item or go visit a neighbor. I had conversations with them that I did not recall afterwards.

I would go for walks with Max in the park next to the house and forget to bring him home with me.

Eddie visited with his wife for dinner one evening, but when Cathi later mentioned aspects of our conversations, I did not even remember their visit.

One Saturday early in December, I told Cathi that I wanted to go visit a friend and fellow train collector, Don. He lived only three miles away and I seemed to be alert and was feeling good, so Cathi agreed to let me drive over on my own. Two hours later, the phone rang. It was me.

"Cathi, did you send me out for any particular reason?"

Cathi could hear the confusion in my voice. "Richie, where are you? Are you at Don's?"

"No, I'm on the Atlantic City Expressway. I don't remember anything. I paid the toll; suddenly I came to when the toll attendant said I didn't look too good and wanted to know if I needed any help. I couldn't remember where I was going, how I got there or why?"

"Richie, that's 90 miles from here. Are you okay?" She stayed calm. During the last few weeks, she learned not to overreact.

"Yeah, I'm okay now," I reassured her, but I was embarrassed. "Just don't tell Don about this. I guess I am just on overload."

That gentleman at the tollbooth saved my life with a simple caring question. Less than five miles down the highway was a narrow bridge that I doubtfully could have crossed without causing an accident, in such a non-coherent state of mind. So, do guardian angels exist?

More than once, Cathi came home to strange things. One day, I took all the knobs off the cabinets in the kitchen and replaced them with wing nuts. Why, I had no clue. She gracefully replaced them without adding embarrassment.

Another time, she prepared marinated chicken for dinner. I was responsible for taking it out of the refrigerator one hour before she came home from work. Then putting it in the oven and turning the oven "on" to 350 degrees.

That day, my treatment seemingly went easy and I was up early from my nap.

Not wanting to let her down by not completing the simple task. I took the dinner out early and went into the basement to work on my trains.

When Cathi came home she found the dinner on the counter, the stove on 350, and a once valuable train, in the oven cooked to a crisp. Again, I admit to not remembering a thing.

Fridays I did not have treatments, but the cumulative effects of the chemicals would last into Saturday. I would try to do things around the house but often became confused with what I was doing. My body and mind still required extra sleep.

Sunday was the only day that Cathi could really count on me being totally coherent. Often, she spent this time conforming to my desires, while covering up her fear of my potential death.

While I was undergoing the treatments, Cathi and my family continually worked on gathering information. Mom had begun researching every source she could find on Mycosis Fungoides. She wrote letters to world-renowned scientists and physicians, explaining my case and asking for advice.

One day, not long after I had begun treatments, the phone rang. When I picked it up, the voice on the other end had a distinct Austrian accent.

"This is Dr. Herbert Hönigsman from Vienna. May I speak with Richard Sabb?"

"This is Richard." The doctor's name sounded familiar to me, but I could not place why.

"Ah, Mr. Sabb. I recently received information from your mother concerning your diagnosis, and called her this morning. She told me that I should speak with you directly."

I finally made the connection. "Yes, Doctor?"

"I am calling," the doctor continued in broken English, "to inquire about the treatments you are currently receiving, and to also tell you that I am very familiar with Drs. Lambert and Martinez. There are no finer doctors, particularly in the area of Mycosis Fungoides. I trust their judgment implicitly. I would be happy to offer my services, however, Dr. Lambert is more than qualified to do anything that I might do."

"Thank you, Dr. Hönigsman," I responded. "They are taking very good care of me, and I appreciate you calling to let me know that." I was in awe of this world-renowned doctor and that he had taken the time to call.

"With your permission, I would like to request blood and tissue samples so that I may study them. You have a fascinating case."

"Sure, Dr. Hönigsman, I'd welcome your input," I responded.

Hönigsman continued. "Tell me about the progress you have made with your treatments."

I spent the next 30 minutes detailing the treatments and medications I was taking. The doctor would interject questions, and I would answer each of them as best I could.

"Well, Richard," the doctor finally said, "as I told you earlier, you have the best doctors available. I agree with the approach they are taking. If you do not mind, I would like to call you occasionally to know about your progress, if it is agreeable with you."

"Certainly, Dr. Hönigsman," I told him. "I would be honored."

I could not wait to call Mom to tell her about my conversation with the Viennese doctor.

"He called you all the way from Vienna?" Mom asked, unbelieving.

"Yeah, Mom. And what a nice guy he is, too," I said proudly. "He told me that I was with some of the best doctors around, and he wants to call again, so that he can keep up with my case. He appreciated you sending him that letter."

Mom couldn't believe it. She had received written responses from almost all of the doctors and scientists she had written to, but the kindness of the foreign doctor touched her.

"You know, Mom," I continued, "it's like the bigger and more influential they are in the medical field, the nicer they are."

"Yes," she replied, "it certainly seems that way."

In the meantime, Cathi and my sister were busy interviewing attorneys to represent me. Through her work at Tek Investors, Cheryl had access to their in-house attorneys. This gave her access to some excellent outside attorneys that have won or made monetary settlements for clients. She would make the initial contact to the law firm and, if she liked what she heard, she would set up an interview.

Cathi was making inquiries of her own, either through recommendations from her friends or just out of the phone book. She, too, would set up interviews. Between the two women, several high-powered law firms were being considered. I tried to help with these interviews, but I found it difficult to remember the discussions.

The second week of December, Cathi called her friend Alex. Alex had been our attorney for some years now and handled all our Landlord/Tenant disputes and real-estate closings. He was an exceptional attorney in that he took everything seriously and told you like it was, not always what you wanted to hear. He resolved problems fast and as inexpensively as possible.

As Cathi explained the entire medical and now to be legal turmoil, Alex interrupted, somewhat flabbergasted and startled. "Cathi, please understand I can't possibly take this case for you and Richard. If I lost I couldn't live with myself. We are much too close, let me refer you to someone that I know can handle this; his name is Dennis Murray, he's known in local legal circles as 'the Shark.'"

Cathi had seen him on TV, when he was interviewed about a local case where he won his client over a million dollars. Cathi understood Alex's concerns and called Dennis as soon as they finished speaking. When she told the receptionist that Alex had referred her, she was put directly through to Dennis. When they spoke of Alex, Cathi got the impression the two were friends, the conversation was completely casual and intuitive of our relationship with Alex.

Not to Cathi's surprise, Dennis' schedule was very full, but he could fit us in on Friday the tenth of December. Cathi knew she was taking a risk with me, I would have done four treatments that week, but she wanted us to meet and talk in person. The final decision for representation had to be made by me. Fortunately, that day, I seemed clearheaded and quite lucid.

Dennis was impressive, like the doctors; he too was very thorough in questioning me. It was as if he was trying to find ways the case could fail. But with each question he became more intrigued. Finally after about an hour Dennis declared, "Well, I like what you have told me, and it appears you have really the best doctors backing you, if you want me to take the case it will have to be both the State Workman's Comp. and the Civil Action against Hayward." Cathi and I were relieved, someone serious wanted to handle the case, and we hired him on the spot.

The only thing that concerned us was that he was extremely busy. He told us it would be a minimum of two weeks before he could even look at our case, but not to worry, when he did have time he would focus on it intently.

We drove home after the appointment, satisfied with our choice. Cathi went to get the mail and was shuffling through it, when she saw a letter from Winslow and Abby, obviously a law firm. It was addressed to me. She brought it to me and asked, "What's this? Do you know who this is?"

I took the letter, ripped it open and began to read. "It's from John Reeves and he is evidently working on my case," I responded. "I don't get it."

Cathi was furious. "What does he mean he's working on your case? I'm going to call him right now."

She went to the phone and dialed the number on the letterhead. Within seconds, she had the attorney on the other end of the line. "Mr. Reeves, this is Cathi Sabb, Richard's wife. We just received your letter. I want to know who gave you the authority to begin work on our case?"

"Mrs. Sabb, Richard came to my office and hired me a couple of weeks ago." Cathi could hear him moving papers. "It was November 25th."

"Are you aware, Mr. Reeves, that Richard is undergoing intensive treatments for his cancer? How could you let someone in his condition sign legal papers?"

"No, ma'am, he did not tell me he was taking treatments. On the day we spoke, he was very articulate and straightforward about what his needs were. I had no idea."

Cathi could hear the shock in the attorney's voice. "Would you hold just a moment, Mr. Reeves?" Cathi turned to me, somewhat mollified. She knew that I could have hired this attorney, and never remembered it. "Do you remember hiring John Reeves as your attorney two weeks ago?"

"No," I was subdued.

"Could you have and not remembered it."

I thought for a moment, trying to dredge up a memory that was just not there. "I think I remember talking to him, and I remember I liked him, but I don't remember hiring him."

But Cathi knew. She returned to the phone. "Mr. Reeves, we have a little bit a problem here." She explained the situation.

Although surprised, because I had handled myself so well during our appointment, the attorney understood the predicament we were in. "Mrs. Sabb, I completely understand. Why don't you call Mr. Murray and let's see if we can work this out."

It took a day for Murray to return the call, but he too was empathetic. "Whatever your decision is," he told us, "I will respect it."

After some discussion, our final decision was to go with Reeves. He had already begun to work on the case, but more importantly, he was accessible to us. Murray was much harder to get in touch with and had already mentioned delays. And medically, time was not on my side.

Once settled, Cathi sat me down and told me, "You cannot do things like this anymore. This situation with the attorneys could have cost us a lot of money that we don't have. Do not," she commanded, "make any major decisions without me or one of your parents present."

Penitent and well aware of the potential disaster I could have caused, even with Alex's friendship, I readily agreed.

Cathi had been taking off from work a lot to be with me and to drive me to my appointments. Her employers were very understanding about the stresses and demands of her home life, but she and I both knew that she was going to have to return to work full time.

We wanted to remain independent as long as possible. Mom and Dad offered us financial help, and we knew we might have to accept the offer later, but for now we wanted to try to make it on our own.

If I could start getting some Social Security or Worker's Comp benefits soon, we might even be able to make it without outside help. Cathi knew that she would worry about me when she was at work, but she also knew it was something she had to do.

Her returning to work meant that we would need help with transportation to and from my treatments. Both mothers volunteered to drive. Mom and Loren took turns driving me to the hospital and my doctor's appointments, and they would straighten and clean the house when they brought me home. This proved to be a great help to Cathi.

I actually preferred my mother-in-law taking me. I didn't feel pressured to report everything to her like I did with Mom. Very early in the process, I had to remind the doctors that they were to speak only to Cathi or me about what was happening, and the doctors respected that confidentiality.

But Mom, curious and demanding by nature, always wanted to know exactly what was going on. I tried to respect her maternal instinct and concern, but the car was my safe haven, a place to relax without having to act like everything was okay. I typically answered her questions but never offered more information than what she needed to know. I was attempting to protect her from my own uncertainty.

I knew Mom meant well. I was beginning to understand how difficult it must be for both my parents to stand by and watch their son deteriorate from treatments and stand so close to death. Dad put it well one day, when he had told me, *"You're supposed to bury your parents, not your children."* I was not trying to withhold information from them, but rather protect them. I knew that they both worried too much and the stress was bad for their health.

18
The Enemy's Mata Hari

December 1992—On Tuesday, December 15, I received a phone call from Carolyn Fox. She introduced herself as a third-party mediator assigned to my case. "I can make myself available at anytime, Mr. Sabb, to interview you. What would be the best for your schedule?"

I thought for a moment. "Mornings would probably be best, before I take my meds." I also knew that I wanted Dad or Cathi there, and mornings would not interfere as much with work schedules.

"Would this Friday morning at 8 A.M. work for you?" she asked sincerely. "That would be the 18th."

I grabbed for a pencil and wrote the date and time down. Since the near debacle with the attorneys, I received lectures from everyone to take notes! Cathi, well she was just the first. I was not going to make that mistake again. "That should work fine," I answered and gave her directions to the house.

After I hung up, I called John Reeves. "John, I just got a call from a lady who said she was a third party mediator. She's coming over Friday for an interview."

"Yes, I knew you would probably be getting a call soon," John told me. "Just tell your story the way you told it to me. Let her know what the doctors are saying, and Richard, be sure Cathi or your Dad is there with you."

I called Dad next and gave him the information for the interview. I felt better about the way I handled this, knowing that I had done it correctly.

The doorbell rang promptly at 8 A.M. on Friday. I answered the door to an attractive, dark-haired woman, professionally dressed. She had a friendly, compelling smile. "You must be Richard," she said. "I'm Carolyn Fox."

I escorted her into the living room and introduced Dad. When we were all seated, Carolyn began. "First, let me say that I am here to help you, Richard. I am going to do everything in my power to get this settled quickly. Although I am a third party in this, and I have nothing invested in the outcome, I do know that my clients are sensitive to your needs and want this taken care of. The information I get here today is only intended as a general statement."

I felt encouraged. Carolyn seemed to really care. I liked her, and I could tell that Dad liked her, too.

She began with her list of questions, but her interview style was very casual. While I told my story of the accident and the subsequent rash, she listened compassionately. She would often interrupt her line of questioning to ask about our personal life.

I knew these were "just" because she was a caring person, because she would stop her note taking. To me, she seemed genuinely interested. She wanted to know more about Cathi, and things we liked to do.

"I hope I have a chance to meet Cathi soon," she commented. She was interested in my hobbies and things we did for fun.

When I told her about the homes I worked on, she wanted to know more about what she referred to as "very gratifying work."

She oohed and ahhed when I told her about my train collection. "My brother was interested in trains for a long time," she told me.

I took her on a tour of the house, when she told me how nice she thought it was.

She saw the hot tub on the deck, and remarked that she loved hot tubs. "This is wonderful. You and Cathi must really like the water," she said. "Is that the bay behind the trees?"

Dad filled in the information about childhood illnesses, and would occasionally correct some minor information that I would give her.

At the end of the interview, I felt that I indeed had a good person on my side and was confident that I would soon see a settlement. I believed she understood how difficult the treatments were for me to endure and how the constant threat of death affected me.

"I'm going to get this information typed up as quickly as I can," Carolyn told us as she was leaving. "We want to get this settled right away. And, in the meantime, Richard, take care of yourself. Mr. Sabb, it was a real pleasure meeting you." She shook our hands and left.

"Nice lady," Dad remarked.

"Yeah," I agreed. "I feel good about this."

On Tuesday of the next week, the doorbell rang. Cathi had just left for work and I was expecting my mother-in-law for the ride to the hospital in about five minutes. I wondered who it could be, since it was the front door. No one ever came to the front door. When I opened it, I was surprised to see Carolyn Fox standing there.

"Carolyn."

"Richard, I am glad you are home. I have the report ready for your signature and wanted to catch you before you went to the hospital. You haven't taken your medications yet, have you?"

"No," I said, a little taken back by this unannounced visit. "But my mother-in-law will be here in a little while to take me to my treatment." I showed her into the living room.

Carolyn handed me the typewritten report. "This is the report from our interview last Friday. Please read through it, and there is a place for your signature on the last page."

"I would really rather wait until my wife or my father are here and can look at it, too," I said, unwillingly taking the papers. "Besides,

whatever I sign today wouldn't be legal, would it, because of the medications I have to take?"

"But you haven't taken them yet you said," Carolyn quickly interjected. "And, I am a notary. You could sign this verifying that you have
not taken your medicine yet." She smiled warmly at me. "Because of
the holidays, it is really important that you sign them now. Why don't
we go ahead and do this." She held a pen out for me to take.

Reluctantly, I began to skim the eight-page document. I had a treatment the day before and was not sure about signing something that, in
all likelihood I was not going to remember reading.

It looked okay, but I knew that I probably shouldn't sign it. I also
knew that things would move much faster if I did. Plus, Carolyn said
that it was just a general statement. I took the pen and scratched my
name on the line. Carolyn smiled and took the report. She signed her
name, also.

"Richard, there is one more thing. My clients know that this is a
'Mercedes' case. They know they were wrong. They have authorized me
to give you $300,000 today. By the time you get home from your treat-
ment, it will be in your account. Speaking very bluntly, none of your
doctors expect you to live. Even you don't expect to live. We're just giving you this money so that you can go out and have fun in the time that
you have left. It's three days before Christmas. This could make your
holiday very enjoyable."

$300,000, I thought, could ease our financial situation tremen-
dously and make things better for Cathi when I was gone. It would be
a nice Christmas gift. But I knew that I could not make this decision
alone. I already succumbed to the pressure to sign the report. I was not
going to be forced into this. "No, Carolyn," I said firmly. "I can't make
that decision without talking it over with Cathi and my Dad." I felt
good about standing my ground.

Carolyn began gathering her papers. When she stood to go, she
looked back at me, her face was hard and cold. *"This offer will not be*

good after the holidays. They are going to fight you to the end on this." And, she left.

I didn't quite know what to think about the drastic change in attitude I had just seen in the woman. She had been so accommodating throughout the interview. I had felt pushed this morning, but had her position changed that much? I thought about it while I got ready to leave. Loren would be there shortly, and I had to focus on the treatment and the timing of my medicines.

On the drive to the hospital I summarized the mornings events to my mother-in-law with a flare of pride. I was glad I had not taken the money without first conversing with Cathi and was certain that the amount would not even cover my first month's billings.

Loren was pleased that I could not be bought for what she considered a small amount and commented that Carolyn was angered that she probably would not be receiving a large Christmas bonus this year.

Physically, Christmas Friday of 1992 was miserable for me. I had gotten slightly overexposed during my last PUVA treatment the day before. I developed a good working relationship with my doctors and convinced them to intensify the treatment in preparation for the upcoming long Christmas weekend.

My doctors were receptive; however, this time it was not because of my holiday concerns. While undergoing treatments the cancer continued to spread to my groin area. Dr. Brooks was concerned and decided to call Professor Lambert to jointly decide the increase.

Since the diagnosis I had developed 32 affected areas of my body and the aggressive treatment schedule appeared to have been depleting the disease substantially. Due to this added development of cancer in a medically and physiologically difficult area the doctors respectfully allowed me to believe the increase was my own decision.

Given my "survival" attitude of "give me more and kill this shit", I overdid it and suffered with my usual "power vomiting spree" coupled with blistering radiation burns over most of my body and a 103-degree fever.

With most of us being in the cognitive world of reality, with maybe the exception of the defense attorneys within this case and Mrs. Fox, it should be understandable that I forgot Carolyn Fox's offer and threatening remark in a haze of pain, sickness and recovery procedures.

It was Cathi's job to keep my entire body swathed in pure Aloe Vera gel, stay up all night on bathroom guard duty and make sure I didn't slam my head on the toilet or pass out of exhaustion or fall down the steps due to my disorientated and weakened state of mind.

As one can tell, Cathi had a difficult life caring for me, but somehow stood as strong as her determined husband. Yet, as stoic as I was about pain, when she gently applied the gel, it would cause me to wince, but the gel helped relieve some of my suffering and drastically enhanced the healing process.

Every inch of my body hurt. Blinking my eyes was painful, because my eyelids were burned. My fingernails and toenails turned black as a result of the overexposure. Even the loosest of clothing caused me pain, so I spent the weekend, wet with Aloe Vera, lying on towels completely nude.

The worst areas were around my nose, my nipples, and especially my groin. Three times a day I stood in the bathroom, hands cupped and full with Aloe Vera, and I soaked the family jewels. It was when large pieces of the dead skin would peel or inadvertently pull off, that I would writhe in anguish.

In the last month and a half, Cathi had seen me suffer from the treatments. I had constant headaches, debilitating fatigue, sore joints at the elbows, knees, and ankles, swollen and sore eyes from the light and the Tinnitus or annoying tone constantly sounded in my ears.

Tinnitus is usually a condition caused by years of listening to loud sounds like music or the pounding of a jackhammer. It could also be the effects of age, but in my case the auditory nerve damage was a side effect from my medicines.

Whenever I took Methotrexate I could be sure that the next day I would lose a little more hair and the tone in my ears would escalate substantially. On occasion I also experienced violent fits of vomiting that lasted from 2 to 10 hours. Praying to the porcelain "Gods" of the bathroom was commonplace, at least for the quick "one—two" clean out as I called it. But this overexposure brought a new level of agony for the two of us.

On Christmas morning, I forced myself into some sweats so that we could go over to Cathi's parent's home. It was only a short 10-minute drive and I figured I can hold back showing any pain for a while. Besides Cathi's family was close and usually quite fun to be around. We simply wanted to deliver the gifts we had purchased for her family, pick up the gifts from them and take some of the Christmas dinner Cathi's mother had prepared.

Cathi's parents noticed that I was unusually dark and not moving too well, so when Cathi casually stated that this was going to be a short visit because I needed to rest, no one complained. Cathi's father was quick to keep the mood light hearted, as he wished me merry Christmas and shook my hand, he patted me on the shoulder saying "you hang in there buddy", then laughed saying, "how about we get it dark in here so we can see you glow". They all enjoyed the humor in my mounting radiation treatments, including me, but only Cathi knew I was ready to crumble to the floor in pain from the playful swat. The visit was short and sweet, and Cathi had me back home in less than two hours.

My family was away enjoying all the grandeur that a holiday vacation had to offer at Loon Mountain in New Hampshire.

Cheryl, who the family called their own personal travel agent and director of fun, had rented a home in the resort town. She made the plans for the vacation just after my diagnosis, she too was scared of losing her younger brother and intended the ski trip as a "just in case you die soon," lets all go out and have fun.

She was very thoughtful in that there were no rules as to who could join us, the entire family was invited. Within her good heartedness it was apparent that she really wanted Cathi and I to spend time with our young niece and nephew, Sharon and Jack.

At this time the family's fear of me meeting an untimely demise was still quite a part of life's daily routine.

Secretly crushed that Cathi and I would not be able to join the family, I displayed my upbeat attitude and put on a strong front. "You guys go ahead and have a good time," I told Cheryl over the phone, knowing that my family would indeed enjoy themselves. "Cathi and I will be fine here." Cathi was listening in on the conversation and could hear the kids and my parents in the background cheering us to come out and play with them.

"Oh, come on up with us," my sister insisted. She clearly did not understand and certainly had no way of knowing the pain I was experiencing. I would not show my distress except in the privacy of my own home, or automobile and most people, including my doctors, did not realize the extent of my misery. What the outside world saw was a smiling, optimistic, determined young man.

"Well, you're going to ruin the family vacation," Cheryl pouted in one last attempt to persuade us to reconsider. "We all love you and the kids really miss you." I knew her persuasiveness was intended for the good of all but also realized that by not telling her the truth of what was happening I would allow the family to have a joyous holiday with minimal concern for my well-being.

In spite of the pain and the continuous concern that this may be the "last day," I considered it one of the best Christmases ever. Cathi had the entire house decorated with a barrage of ornaments and lights. She decorated the tree that her brother had brought in for her and even set up her favorite red Lionel passenger train set from the 1920's.

I was not of much help and most likely posed as more of a hindrance or hazard, but Cathi always conformed to the situation at hand and dealt with it. She was just happy I was there. I spent most of the days in bed or on the couch with my best friend caring for me.

We so rarely had time just to ourselves, that I cherished this time alone with her. We lay on the sofa, now made out into a bed, in front of the fireplace with the train rumbling around the meticulously decorated tree, and together we opened our gifts. Although the words were never spoken, we both knew that this could be our last Christmas, and we reveled in the moments we had with one another.

On December 28, we received a late Christmas present in the mail. Our attorney, John Reeves filed the claim petition for Worker's Compensation benefits. The legal trials were about to begin.

19
Unmasking of the Spy

January 1993—It was not until early January that Dad and I had a chance to read through Fox's report in detail. We were both quiet when we finished.

Dad was the first to speak. "What is this crap? This is not correct. She left out a lot of things that should be included, and reported other things incorrectly. Goddamn it, we didn't say half this shit!"

"And, Dad," I spoke up, "John Reeves told me that she sent a copy to him, a copy to Hayward and a copy to the insurance company. He said it was presented to him as a legal document."

Dad's face flushed with anger. "She told us that it was just a general statement so she could get an understanding of what is happening."

"Ever since she coerced me into signing this and tried to force me to take that money," I confessed, "I have been real suspicious of her motives. Her attitude changed instantly when I wouldn't accept her offer."

"We need to get this straightened out quickly," Dad responded. "You need to write out your own statement. Let's get it to John and have him send it to everyone who received one of these things." He held up the Fox report and then tossed it back on the table.

I worked furiously over the next few days putting together my own statement of facts. On January 17, I had it ready and took it to John Reeves.

After reading through it, John told me that he would have it retyped and sent to Hayward and Zurich American. "You did a good job on this," he commented, amazed that I was able to function so well with the treatment schedule I had.

The next day, Carolyn Fox telephoned. My immediate thought was that she had already gotten my rebuttal.

"Richard, I need to pick up the studies and chemical reports that Hayward furnished you. I won't be able to come by, but my husband can pick them up on Monday."

I realized that my statement had not yet reached her. I had called Hayward and talked to Mike, and had asked for any files that might be pertinent to my case. It irked me now that this woman wanted to see them. Let her do her own work, I thought to myself, but curtly responded to her request. "Fine. I'll have them here."

The more I thought about my two meetings with Carolyn, the more upset I got. I realized that what I had believed to be genuine interest was, in fact, manipulation. She obviously was working for the insurance company, Zurich American.

The questions about my hobbies and activities, so carefully posed, had been used to find out what other chemicals I might have come in contact with. Even the comment about the hot tub was made to find out how much time we spent there in what Carolyn assumed was chemically treated water. What I had not told her was that baking soda was the only thing Cathi ever put in the hot tub.

I was a little disgusted with myself, too, at my gullibility. She played me like a fiddle, I admitted to myself, but I've got her number now. She won't do that again.

The following week, Dr. Lambert set up an appointment for me with a Dr. Michael Gochfeld, a well respected and the State of New Jersey Director on occupational and environmental medicine. He conducted several studies and massive amounts of research on the causes of diseases in relation to workplace environment. "I respect his opinion," Lambert told me, "and I want to hear what he has to say about your case."

When I arrived at Gochfeld's office, Carolyn Fox was sitting in the outside office. I stared at her, but did not say a word. A middle-aged man came through the office door. "Mr. Sabb? I'm Dr. Gochfeld." He held out his hand and shook mine. "And, you must be Mrs. Fox,"

Red flags went up in my brain. "Dr. Gochfeld, could I speak to you privately?"

"Certainly. If you could wait just a moment, Mrs. Fox." The doctor showed me to an examination room.

As he did Carolyn jolted out of her chair in anger saying, "Dr. Gochfeld, my client is paying for this visit and I am allowed to participate in your evaluation of this patient."

I was quick to calmly add, "I don't think so Doc. I made this appointment through Professor Lambert and we are looking for your non-biased evaluation. My insurance is paying and this bitch is not going to manipulate documents like she has in the past".

This facade shocked the doctor, and he diligently informed Mrs. Fox that the patient's needs or request come first. Therefore she would not be allowed in.

Again, she threatened the doctor and me by saying, "Well, I will inform my superiors of your unwillingness to cooperate Doctor, and Richard you will pay for this visit."

Once in the privacy of the examination room, I asked the doctor what Carolyn was doing here? The doctor realized right from the start that he had been mislead and immediately offered an explanation. "Richard, she called and asked to be included in this appointment. She said that she had been assigned to your case. She led me to believe that she was a third-party evaluator and that she wanted to help you."

"I don't want her anywhere around me." I was adamant. "I don't trust her, and if she is going to be included, I'm leaving."

The doctor knew that I was upset and was quite experienced in the mischievous ways of the so called third party nonpartisan opinions that insurers and their attorneys practice.

During the examination, I explained in more detail my objections to Mrs. Fox and her misrepresentation and the falsified documentation that she submitted to the defense attorneys as a legal statement. "I just don't trust her. She misrepresented what I said in a interview with her, and I don't want her twisting what you have to say."

Dr. Gochfeld was not threatened or intimidated by her manipulative tactics and assured me that his findings, regardless of what they are, will be factual as they pertain to me.

Dr. Gochfeld's examination was an extensive review of all that I could remember. He started with anything that could have impacted my life as a child to every known ailment that any family member even "might" have had.

He included detailed questions about all my work place environments and personal hobbies. He also included all my personal habits, and even sent me home with a 20-page questionnaire.

It was during this three-hour plus interview I learned that Dr. Gochfeld also held PhD's in his field and that he too looked at me solely as a "case-study" patient.

When he finished his thorough examination and extensive questions, Dr. Gochfeld sat down with me. "From my preliminary findings, Richard, it certainly looks like there is a correlation between the accident and your cancer. It is a well-known fact in the medical community that the chemicals you worked with are carcinogenic and mutagenic to the human body. Needless to say it is also quite evident from this conversation that your exposures and exposure from the explosion caused a shock to your body and likely it's immune system.

It will take plenty of time for me to complete my medical research and investigations but I should be able to get a preliminary report to Lambert and your attorney within a month. *A more detailed evaluation could take many months and remember I am only going to report my find-*

ings and the possibility does exist that it may not conform to your attorney's needs."

I left, feeling quite secure in the doctor's ability and honesty, and thought that if the findings were against Hayward they would stand no chance in a court due to the very candid and blatant honesty of my entire medical team. Not to mention the unusually high level of expertise.

As I walked through the outer office, I noticed that Carolyn was no longer there. I was going to call my attorney when I got home and ask him why and how Carolyn could possibly be allowed in this appointment given her reputation. As far as I knew, she had invited herself.

"She was at the office when you got there?" Reeves questioned. He was dubious about Mrs. Fox's motives also.

"Yes, and she had evidently called Dr. Gochfeld, because he was expecting her."

John thought for a second. "It appears that Mrs. Fox, by wanting to assist in the preparation of the medical data and attending the medical evaluation by Dr. Gochfeld, is attempting to introduce a bias in favor of her client. She must have been trying to sway the report. You did the right thing by not letting her observe and I am certain the doctor realizes that also."

I smiled about the way I handled the incident. If the insurance companies were going to play hardball, so could I. Every professional who was familiar with my case, although they were careful in what they said, knew that my cancer was caused by the chemical exposure I received from the accident.

Someone also had gotten to the people at Hayward, because about this time they all quit talking to me. The insurance companies sent Carolyn Fox, an obvious hired gun, out to try to undermine the mounting evidence. I was learning the hard way about the subtle terrorism of the insurance industry.

"One more thing," Reeves interrupted my thoughts, "it might not be a bad idea to start taping conversations that are pertinent to the case, it will help you to recall things at a later date and, who knows, you might even inadvertently catch someone attempting to take advantage of you."

"Is that legal," I queried, "without the other person knowing?"

"As long as the conversation and topics you discuss concern either your own business or well-being, and provided that there is no third party involved," Reeves directed, "it is legal under federal law. I would suggest, for your own protection, that you seriously consider installing a tape recorder."

"You're right, I'll go out and get one today."

Later that evening as I was hooking the automatic recorder up to all the household phones, I was thinking about the events of the morning and the "Fox Statement" as it was now becoming known. It doesn't make sense, I thought to myself.

We pay and pay into our insurance policies; Carolyn admits that the company and their insurers know they are at fault, yet when it comes time for them to pay, it's like fighting a war.

So, if war was what Carolyn Fox wanted, she would definitely get a battle out of me. Maybe we can find a way to bring this to her home front and see how she feels. My thoughts of revenge were running wild but it only took a moment to look around and see how much more I had in life than she. Besides, she is the one manipulating information; sooner or later she'll get caught.

The day after my appointment with Gochfeld, Carolyn Fox called me at home. It was easy to tell that she was very upset. "Richard, what is this statement you had your attorney send out?"

"I wanted to correct the falsified information you had put in the 'general statement' that you distributed. Not only did you misrepresent things I said, you added your own terminology to conform to you or your client's needs, you also left out many things that I stated to you that we both know your client does not want to hear. Your conclusions were misleading and untruthful. We all know your client is running scared of the professors that are evaluating me. They know these guys are some of the best in the field and that they are not basing their findings on what a person wants to hear but on what happened to me in my specific situation. That's why your so-called caring clients want to handle this the way that they are?" I boasted in a very threatening voice.

Carolyn, was now subdued and realized that regardless of how much she attempted to convince anyone that she was working as a third party through her own company, no one would trust her.

She also understood, all too well, what her job was and she immediately composed herself and continued the conversation and procedures of gathering information in a professional manner. It was amazing how nothing that was said affected her or her train of thought. It was clear to me that her client hired the right person for the job.

Out of sheer fear of missing an opportunity of catching Carolyn in an illegal act, I started recording the phone conversation; I had pens and notepads by each phone so that I could take notes to review later, especially with this woman. I was not about to allow her to pull any fast ones. I had already been burnt once; I wasn't going to let it happen again.

My plan was to take evenings and weekends to read through my notes, when my mind was clearer, and not affected by the medicines as much. As intelligent as I was, the effects of the medicines were causing me to forget or confuse information and events.

Fortunately Mom had been at the house helping with some paperwork while this conversation was taking place. She picked up an extension of the phone to listen in.

For the next forty-five minutes, Carolyn went over her report step by step with me. This time she could not find the right questions to ask that would allow her an opportunity to manipulate my statements. I also made sure I was thorough and conclusive in my answers.

Although Carolyn's voice was calm it was clear that she was frustrated and ended the conversation with, "Let's just forget about the report and go on from here. I'll be calling you again, probably tomorrow, to review the Material Safety Data Sheets Hayward supplied us."

When we hung up, Mom walked back into the room, shaking her head. "That woman has a real knack for twisting information, doesn't she."

"Manipulation is her specialty," I agreed. "I don't like her and I certainly don't trust her and she didn't get anything this time."

"But at least now we all know what her intentions are and none of us will let our guard down around her. Remember what happened here and keep thinking, forewarned is forearmed," Mom demanded while waving her finger at me.

20
Recommended Addition to the Arsenal

About a week later I felt like a cold was coming on, and I knew it would worry my doctors. They had warned me about staying away from crowds, because my body was weakened from the treatments and could not withstand any foreign bacteria.

By the beginning of February I was suffering from all the symptoms of the flu. I took my treatment on Monday, but on Tuesday, I felt too bad to even get out of bed. I was running a fever, and slept most of time during the next couple days. I was able to drag myself out of bed on Thursday for an appointment with Dr. Martinez.

"You are a very sick young man," Martinez sympathized. "I will only take a quick blood sample and give you a prescription for some Amoxicyllin. It's a general antibiotic that you can take with your cold medicine but do not do any treatments until we get you healthy again. It should help while we wait for your results."

But it was another week before Dr. Martinez would allow me to do another treatment and this delay allowed once again, for the cancer to grow. The right hip could always be counted on to show growth first.

During that time, I received another call from Dr. Hönigsman of Vienna. "How are you feeling, Richard?"

"I've got a little cold right now," I informed him, "but, otherwise, things are okay?"

"I understand that you have seen Dr. Gochfeld," the doctor commented.

"Yeah, a week or so ago," I told him. "He seems to be a nice guy and he thinks the accident I had at work was probably the cause of the cancer."

"I have spoken with Dr. Gochfeld, and I concur with his initial thoughts. I also feel quite certain that the cancer is a result of the industrial accident, and I would like to work with Dr. Gochfeld in establishing the etiology in any way I can."

"That would be great," I said, still impressed by the interest from the renowned doctor from the other side of the world.

"One additional thought which Dr. Gochfeld and I discussed," Hönigsman interjected. "Because of the high Benzene content in the air where you live, it would be our recommendation that you consider moving away from the metropolitan area. A wooded environment would be best for you, away from the air pollutants that plague the populated cities. I would bet that just being in a clean environment would help the course of your disease. You know Dr. Gochfeld and I have checked the environmental maps of air quality for your country and the Rocky Mountains of Colorado and Montana are consistently cleaner than most areas in your country. "

Well that's fine with me I responded, my sister and I ski in Colorado often and my wife Cathi and I spend quite a bit of time in Vermont. "Vermont is fine," the doctor added, "we're just suggesting you stay out of the polluted areas."

Dr. Gochfeld had briefly mentioned this same idea to me during the examination, but I had not given it much thought. "Well, it's something to consider," I told Hönigsman. "I'll have to discuss it with my wife and family first and I also have to concentrate on my case."

Dr. Hönigsman understood the importance of my legal case and inspired me to pursue being the first patient on law record proving the *etiology* or causation of an industrial chemical exposure in the formation of a T-cell lymphoma.

He too acknowledged that that this was a medically and legally precedent setting case. The doctor ended the conversation on a more positive note by stating, "that if anyone could do it, it will be Lambert and Gochfeld, you're in the best of hands."

It felt reassuring to have medically prominent people interested in my case. And the thought of moving away from my home was something Cathi and I wanted to do anyway, but the thought of leaving my doctors was just not a consideration at this time.

21
Independent (?!) Medical Examination

On February 16 I heard from Carolyn Fox again. "Richard, I have set an appointment for you with Dr. Irwin Turner of Yale University for an independent medical examination. It is tentatively set for Tuesday, March 9th. Would you check your calendar and see if that date will work for you?"

I bristled every time I heard her voice, but remained civil while I checked my calendar book. My attitude toward her was evolving to a more professional level; furthermore, the realization of conducting myself calmly was enhancing the trust and respect of my doctors and attorneys. "That should be okay. I'll need the time and address."

She gave me the information and politely inquired, "Are you feeling okay?"

If this was her attempt at trying to keep up communication with me, it wasn't going to work. "I've been better. Goodbye, Mrs. Fox," I said, and hung up.

I called Dr. Lambert immediately. I knew I couldn't trust anything Carolyn Fox did. "What do you know about a Dr. Turner from Yale? I have an appointment with him in three weeks."

"Yes, I recommended him," the professor said, aware of the anxiety in my voice. "A woman called asking for an outside authority on Mycosis Fungoides. It's standard procedure to obtain an independent medical opinion in cases like this. Dr. Turner is a well-known expert in this field who also has written several articles about the causal relationship of chemical exposure and workplace environment regarding the development of this cancer. In fact, he and Dr. Cohen worked on one together."

I breathed a sigh of relief. If the professor recommended this guy, then he couldn't be too bad.

"Would you like to read some of his studies? I can get you copies." All the doctors knew that I wanted to learn as much as I could about my affliction. I had immersed myself in articles and studies and was able to understand what I read. Anything I didn't understand, I went straight to my doctors for an explanation. They considered me as much a student as a patient.

"That would be great professor, thanks, are you going to fax them or should I come in to your office".

"Come on in toward the end of the week, Friday should work, after your treatment. This way I can examine you, and we'll go to the medical library together. I have some studies to pick up anyway and maybe I'll have time for lunch, and then we can talk about any questions you have," the professor responded.

22
Effectiveness of the Enemy's Arsenal

The next morning at nine o'clock Loren came to the house to pick me up for my treatment "Do you mind if we make a stop on the way home?" I asked. "My fax machine has been acting up and I'd like to get it checked out. I had problems getting legible copies of some studies Dr. Gochfeld sent and now I may be receiving more from Professor Lambert. I want to be ready in case I don't get to see him on Friday".

"Certainly. No problem," Loren said.

I loaded the fax machine in the car trunk and was ready to go.

At about 8 A.M. I took my 500 mg. of Tigan, a mild anti-vomiting drug, and just as Loren pulled into the driveway, I took my first three pills of Oxsoralen-Ultra.

After about 20 minutes into the drive to the hospital I would take the second dose of three pills of Oxsoralen. By that time my mother-in-law would be keeping that "mother's watchful eye" on whether or not I was having any bad reactions. She knew it only took minutes for the medicine to start to "kick in" and Loren was well aware that I did not want anyone to know I was sick, including her, so she learned to "read" my every movement.

The Tigan usually helped, for the most part, but it really seemed that figuring out what to eat or drink made the primary difference. That day it was skim chocolate milk and a plain bagel. At this time I had not yet become Lactose intolerant as typically caused by the medicines.

The weather was chilly, but it was a clear pleasant day and the drive to Dr. Brooks' office was almost traffic-free. After the twenty-five minutes in the PUVA type radiation machine, I felt only slight disorientation and nausea. It was going to be a good treatment day after all.

"Do you still feel up to stopping at the store to get your fax machine fixed," Loren asked, aware that I was hiding the effects of the treatment.

"Yeah, I'll be okay," I said unconvincingly. "I really need to get that fax working though."

Loren drove to a nearby Staples store and we walked in. A strong odor of ammonia washed over me and my stomach and head immediately reacted. They were cleaning the floors. I began to feel light-headed. "Can you take this?" I asked, thrusting the fax machine at her. "I've got to get away from this smell."

While Loren took care of the fax, I sat on the curb outside, with my head between my legs, breathing heavily and working to regain my composure. I didn't want to worry my mother-in-law, so when I saw her coming out of the store, I stood up. Somewhat wobbly though, I did feel a little better.

"We'd better get you home. You don't look very good, your losing some color on me, Richard. Should we head back to the hospital? " She asked, unlocking the trunk for the fax machine. She quickly placed it there and unlocked the doors. I, of course, told her I was fine and just wanted to go home and rest. As I got into the back seat of her Lincoln Towncar, Loren realized that this was unusual and therefore I was not being completely honest with her.

She hurriedly got behind the wheel, started the engine and drove out of the parking lot. Another wave of nausea hit me, but after so many months of this, I was able to control it. As Loren entered the highway, a diesel truck pulled in front of us, spewing large amounts of black diesel exhaust fumes. Although the windows were up in the Towncar, the fumes made their way through the ventilating system, and with the acrid smell I felt another wave of mounting nausea.

"Richard, how bad is that smell affecting you?" Loren asked.

I was still managing to maintain my composure. I could see the worry on her face and didn't want to add to it. I could feel myself begin to get hot, and then cold; beads of sweat formed on my brow. I thought this might get worse, but as a reaction that I could still hide from her.

"I think I'll lay down back here. I'll be better soon," I responded.

As I stretched my legs out across the seat I began to shake uncontrollably, the convulsions were about to start. I knew I was in trouble, my stomach suddenly cramped and I pulled my knees up into the fetal position. I could see that my fingers and hands were turning blue. "Get me home now," I groaned, as I slammed my hand against the back seat.

Loren looked over her shoulder at me, the worry on her face had turned to panic, and in that instant she could see I was in a full muscular convulsion. I was in the fetal position, sweating profusely, my hands were cramping, with my muscles controlling my distorted movements. I could hear the roar of the engine as she floored the gas pedal.

"Richard, I really think I should go to the hospital, how are you doing back there?" Loren asked.

"Don't worry," I moaned, "I am used to this shit. Just get me home, I'll be okay."

I knew we were going fast, but in what seemed to be only minutes, she was pulling into my driveway.

By this time I was apparently doing better but was hardly able to stand, Loren helped me into the house and upstairs to the bedroom. She stayed with me for the next hour, until I told her, "I'm feeling better. You really don't need to stay around. I am just going to go to sleep."

In truth, I still felt awful. But the last thing I wanted to do was subject my mother-in-law to a bout of violent vomiting and diarrhea. I was holding it all in until she left. She stayed for another 30 minutes, checking on me three different times.

When at last I heard the car leave the driveway, I gave my body permission to react. It was like a volcanic explosion. The next two hours was spent in the bathroom with everything spilling out from every orifice. It was always the violent vomiting that took the hardest toll on my body. Often I would hit my head on the toilet or even the pedestal sink. The bathroom was usually too small for my body's violent and often uncontrollable reactions. The tub, toilet, and sink were all potentially dangerous objects to me, and also Cathi, should she get in the way of one of my unconsciously violent reactions.

I lay on the cold tiled bathroom floor completely drained and exhausted; I felt like shit. When I was finally able, I made my way back to the bed and collapsed.

Cathi got home at 5:30, and Max was not at the door to greet her. Something was wrong. She had learned to live with the fear of what she might find. Was I sick? Still in the hospital? Or, would she find me on the sofa, or upstairs dead? She checked the living room and did not find me there. She ran up the stairs to the bedroom and saw me lying on the bed. Quietly, she tiptoed to the bedside and reached out to check if I was still breathing.

"Hi," I said, sleepily. "I guess I don't look so good, huh."

"You look like hell," she admitted, as she quietly breathed a sigh of relief. "Bad day?"

I told her what I could remember about the fumes and the resulting convulsions. "Your Mom must have driven like a bat outta' hell. I swear she got me here in ten minutes," I grinned weakly.

She leaned over and kissed me on the forehead. "I'll go make some dinner and then come get you."

I vaguely recalled eating dinner with her and trying to watch some TV, but it was obvious that I was not going to be able to stay awake. "I think I'll go on up and go to bed," I told her. "I'm still awfully sleepy."

Just as I was getting up the phone rang. It was Cathi's brother Scott calling to see if everything was okay. I remembered speaking to him for about 15 minutes before giving the phone to Cathi and heading up to bed.

Just as I was lying down, the phone at the side of the bed rang again. It was Dad. "Dad, I'm pretty sleepy right now. Can you call back later?" I glanced at the bedside clock. It read 6:15. I hung up the phone and fell asleep.

The shrill ring of the phone awakened me again. I looked at the clock. It was 6:30. Damn, can't they leave me alone, I thought, I need to get some sleep.

"What!" I barked hoarsely.

"Rich, it's me, your Dad. How are you?" He asked cautiously.

"Damn it, Dad, can't you leave me alone. You just called a minute ago. I've been sick and I told you I need to get some sleep!"

There was silence on the other end of the line. I realized that I reacted too harshly and that Dad was worried, but I just wanted to get some sleep.

"Rich," Dad said slowly, "I haven't talked to you in a day. Do you know what day it is?"

I pulled myself up in bed. "What day is it?"

"It's Friday, Rich."

I had slept for 24 hours straight, but at least I was feeling much better.

This type of incident had begun happening about every 4 to 6 weeks. I did not want to complain to Professor Lambert for fear that he might reduce my treatments. That in turn could allow the cancer to grow.

Therefore, I confronted Dr. Martinez, my hematologist. Dr. Martinez theorized that from doing treatments four times per week my body was no longer processing out all the medicine. Hence, as each treatment came and went, my body progressively retained more and more of the pharmaceuticals until my body's tolerance level was reached. Then it would clean itself in these violent vomiting sprees.

This analogy made sense to me but I still did not want any adjustment made to my treatment schedule.

"I'll tough it out until we kill the cancer," I told the doctor.

"I admire your determination, boy—I don't think I ever had a patient with your attitude—but I don't think so, big guy". Dr. Martinez said. "I'll let Clark know you're having some bad reactions to the treatments and call Brooks' office. We can make adjustments in the medicines and your schedule to help subside this problem."

Unfortunately, now, Dr. Yang identified the second form of cancer, Lymphomatoid Papulosis or how it is usually referred to as "LyP". In it's beginning stages, LyP is clinically benign. However, some doctors believe it to be a precursor to malignant Mycosis Fungoides.

One important note that was often made to me was that Cutaneous T-Cell Lymphoma or MF was a non-Hodgkin's type lymphoma and there was no real evidence of it evolving into Hodgkin's disease. Conversely, some patients with LyP have developed Hodgkin's disease.

Of the three commonly accepted types of LyP, I had Type B, a malignant form, and it displayed itself externally as bumps, or nodules, that would grow, and even combine, and then ulcerate. It was common for the disease to disguise itself, as it had done with me, and therefore was not easily detected initially.

The accepted "start-up" treatment for the LyP was Methotrexate or a topical cream called *Carmustine* or *BCNU*, a nitrosourea alkyl-acting agent in wide use as a cancer chemotherapy. For us laypeople we just called it *Topical Nitrogen Mustard*.

Because I was currently on Methotrexate, Dr. Yang had me try the Nitrogen Mustard. The addition of this DNA altering cream was just one more medication that my body would have to assimilate.

Now some fun really began. Dr. Martinez contacted Dr's Lambert, Brooks, and Yang in order to be certain that all were updated about my occasional bad reactions to the aggressive treatment schedule. Dr. Yang contacted Drs. Lambert, Brooks and, simultaneously, Martinez to inform them of yet another cancer I was developing. This did not surprise Dr. Lambert.

Furthermore, due to differences in therapy regimes or treatments of each disease, and the now multiple possibilities of evolving into something more aggressive, Professor Lambert was now also having a bad day.

Dr. Lambert was now contemplating another disturbing aspect; my body was responding slower than he had anticipated.

I now had a total of 57 PUVA treatments, the majority of them 10 times the length of a regular patient. Their hope had been that 25 to 30 treatments would have brought the cancer under control.

Professors Lambert and Yang were not sure how long to continue this schedule. They were all in uncharted waters with an unusual patient that always was happy and willing to do more regardless of the side effects.

I met with Professor Lambert and realized my response was not what they anticipated, but I thought I could see a positive difference.

Lambert and I had a very casual "to-the-point" type honest relationship. Professor Lambert explained all the various diseases that could manifest in my body. Any one or any combination of these diseases could take my life quite rapidly. One added concern for the doctor was that I was now also showing signs of something called *Ki-1+* cells, pronounced "*Key One Positive Cells*" or large cell syndrome.

Professor Lambert gave a very detailed description of what was happening inside my body but my thoughts were still in their simplest form—"What do you want to do to kill it?"

Professor Lambert, like my entire medical team, did rely somewhat on my input and determination to continue. Lambert explained that, at this time, he preferred not to use the harsh cellular destructiveness of full body electron beam therapy (TSE), and suggested that I continue with the same treatment schedule for a while longer. If I thought I could handle it. I agreed. Lambert was pleased with my decision and explained that he didn't really believe the electron beam therapy would have solved the multiple problems.

For the next two weeks my treatments continued at:

One thousand mg. of Tigan two hours prior to PUVA.

PUVA four times per week, 27 to 32 minutes each, with 60 mg. Oxsoralen-Ultra.

Liquid Oxsoralen administered on all visible cancer sites prior to radiation.

BCNU cream every evening on all visible cancer sites.

Thirty-five mg. of Methotrexate injected on Friday night.

Five hundred mg. Amoxicyllin late every night.

The regime worked and the Cancer subsided to a more controllable form on my entire body and in my blood.

23
Spy Prostitutes Doctor

March 9, 1993—Still, during all these treatments, I was determined to stay in contact with John Reeves as to the progression, or lack thereof, of my Workman's Compensation Case and continue my medical self-education.

I familiarized myself with no less then 20 studies with titles like: "Human Cancer: epidemiology and environmental causes", "Exposures To Chemicals, Physical Agents & Biologic Agents in Mycosis Fungoides" and all of Dr. Turner's writings. By March 9th, I felt confident that Turner would support the conclusions of Lambert and Gochfeld.

Turner had been involved in a study in 1980 with Cohen. Based on test patients who worked as machinists, as I did, or as industrial electricians, their conclusions in this study substantiated that "the relative risk of encountering an industrial background among the cases was 4.3 times" greater for these individuals to develop CTCL.

When I read phrases like "a direct relationship between heavy usage of certain chemicals and the etiology of cancer," and saw references in these same studies to chemicals like Methylene Chloride, MEK, Fiberglass and liquid Styrene as being both *mutagenic* and carcinogenic,

I experienced little doubt of the Yale doctor's position in the ongoing debate about chemical exposure and my disease.

Dad took the day off to accompany me to Yale University Medical Center for the appointment with Dr. Turner. As we walked down the hall toward the elevator, Carolyn Fox and her husband stood by the elevator, talking with another woman. "Hi, Richard, Mr. Sabb. Right on time," Carolyn chirped. The other woman walked away. "Ready to go up?"

I had the distinct impression Carolyn was trying, once again, to ingratiate herself to us. As infuriated as I was, neither Dad nor I responded in a disrespectful manner.

We all stepped into the elevator together. Dad was upset with Carolyn, but realized he needed to stay calm. If I lost my temper, someone could end up severely hurt, and Dad was certain it wouldn't be me.

"So did you try to buy off the doc, yet?" I asked, my anger and sarcasm obvious and overtaking my congenial demeanor.

"Take it easy, Rich," Dad said in an effort to control a potentially volatile situation. "Let's just do what we have to do, and let the attorney handle the rest."

"Dr. Turner is ready to see you," Carolyn told us. "I spoke with him yesterday about what we are looking for." She was almost arrogant in her admission and made it clear that the good doctor had been bought.

Why was it, I thought to myself, that every time I'm around this woman, I fantasize about skinning her alive for intentionally destroying my life? I realized that I had to control my thoughts, as I glanced at Dad, I could tell by his red face he, too, reacted negatively to her comment.

"If this is supposed to be an independent examination, why was she visiting the doctor yesterday?" Dad murmured angrily so that only Richard could hear him.

We walked off the elevator and toward the office. An intern greeted us first as Dad and I entered the examination room. "Good morning. I have a brief questionnaire that we need to fill out first, if you could just have a seat."

I sat on the examination table and dutifully answered all the questions. They were all very standard: date of birth, education, and a very brief medical history. It took only a couple of minutes to complete.

Turner, a slender, distinguished-looking man, accompanied by his nurse, Carolyn Fox and another woman, entered the room just as the intern completed his portion of the form. I noticed that Carolyn's intent was to be in on the examination.

I objected to her being present, but she reasoned that she had been the one to set up the appointment and had the legal right to be part of the evaluation. The other woman that was talking to Carolyn when we had arrived was introduced as a witness. Carolyn's husband, not present, was seated outside the door.

"Please turn off the overhead light," Dr. Turner directed the nurse. "It might be too bright on his eyes."

My eyes were indeed sensitive to light; I appreciated the doctor's concern.

With the overhead light off, the only light left in the room was from some small, directional lights over the examination table. I felt like I was in the spotlight on stage. Dad took a seat close to the door.

Both women sat on the opposite side of the room, but in view of Dr. Turner.

I removed my shirt and loosened my pants as the doctor began to ask some preliminary medical questions. He asked about the treatments and about my work experience pertaining to various chemicals. I answered each of them in depth, specifically going over the accident. During this interrogation, the doctor was not even casually examining my body.

In talking with my doctors over the past five months, I had gained considerable knowledge about Mycosis Fungoides, but I always wanted to know more. Once Turner was finished with his questions, I began to ask more detailed, scientific questions referencing studies and researchers.

However, Turner's responses did not correlate with the information that the American Cancer Society and numerous other medical professionals supplied me. Plus, they were in direct conflict with the medical studies, including the papers Turner himself had written. I felt myself getting more and more angry.

From his vantage point, Dad could see everyone in the room. He noticed that after every question I asked, Turner would discreetly glance at Carolyn. It was almost imperceptible, but she would nod or use a hand signal. Turner's response would be adjusted to parallel her prompting.

"Have you had the opportunity to review the biopsies and test results that were submitted to you," Dad queried, aware of the mounting anger in me.

"No, I didn't have time," Turner, responded flippantly.

Now, Dad was angry. The numerous biopsies told an important story of evolution and Turner had not taken the time to even look at the extensive workup my medical team performed.

"Well, let's get to why we are here," Turner announced, cutting my questioning short. *"I find nothing to indicate that the cause of your cancer is in any way related to your work environment."*

Dad and I were both dumbfounded.

"There is no solid evidence to support the claim that industrial exposures cause Mycosis Fungoides," Turner continued, *"and especially the study in Scotland failed to show any causal relationship."*

The Scotland study was one that I was familiar with, and I knew that, of the 53 test patients in this study, only six had any exposure to carcinogenic chemicals as I had. Besides, this was in direct opposition to the conclusions reached in the 1980 Cohen, et. al., study I had read.

"According to studies you have been involved with…" I started, by now fuming with anger.

Carolyn quickly interrupted, cutting me short again. "So, what is your prognosis, Dr. Turner?"

"The prognosis looks very good for Richard," he stated. "The treatments seem to be working well, and as I stated before, there is nothing to indicate a connection between his work and his illness. I will have my report typed up and delivered to you. Is there any other information you need, Mrs. Fox?" he asked as he walked toward the door.

Carolyn thanked the doctor as she and the other woman followed him out.

The examination was obviously over. What had taken a group of eight scientists, doctors and interns hours, days and even months of intensive study to determine, this "expert" opinion had negated in less than twenty minutes.

"Why, you son of a bitch, I'll tear you apart you piece of shit!" I seethed, ready to ferociously harm the older man.

The doctor, witness and Carolyn practically ran out of the examination room while I scuffled to get my clothing back on.

Dad was furious but concentrated on calming me. "Rich, relax, John and Lambert can take care of this, and those assholes will not beat you. This is not a big deal. Don't let them get to you, you're better than that."

"Dad, then you tell me what the hell just happened!" I demanded, furious and frustrated.

"It was a setup, Rich." Dad could feel his blood pressure rising but stayed calm for me. "The entire appointment was orchestrated by Carolyn Fox. You couldn't see it; she was signaling as to what he could answer and what he could not."

We realized that not only did I have to fight the insurance companies, but also now a respected and world-renowned member of the medical community had joined the fray.

But what really defines the quote, "*respected world-renowned research scientist,*" I thought. Is it one that is paid to evaluate information supplied by the medical journals and make a decision consistent with the payee's thoughts or is such a person defined by their medical expertise and ability to evaluate medical information as it pertains to the patient's circumstances and condition, regardless of outcome or payment?

I called Dr. Lambert to apprise him of Turner's ridiculous pronouncement. "What an asshole, he actually was paid off, how can that happen at his level of expertise, and at Yale University no less!" I said disgustedly. "His evaluation was not based on what happened to me and was a complete contradiction of the studies he wrote!"

Lambert considered the news for a moment. "Well," he said slowly, "you never know how many hundred-dollar bills it takes to change someone's mind." He laughed. "Listen, Richard, don't let this bother you; when we get to court I'll take care of it. Let's concentrate on your health".

I knew that professionally Lambert could not say anything about Turner, but the disappointment in Lambert's voice was very apparent. This was all I needed to hear to calm me down.

That night, I related the events of the day to Cathi. I was still livid but having spoken to professor Lambert and hearing his confidence in his ability to explain my condition, we remained somewhat relaxed.

"They have so much money to fight us with, they are going to destroy us by paying everyone off," Cathi said, beginning to show her fear. "What are we going to do?" After five months with only her income we needed the help my parents were giving. The stress of my illness and the stress of the financial situation were starting to break her down.

"We still have all my doctors on our side. And, we have the truth on our side, too." I was not giving in so easily. "I'm meeting with John Reeves after my appointment tomorrow and we'll figure out how to handle this."

24
Oops, Wrong Lab

The appointment the next morning was one of the regular exams, which Dr. Lambert performed several times a month. As far as I was concerned, they were routine. And this morning was the same. I knew I would probably have to wait a while for Lambert and the others to show up, but I could at least be ready when they did get there.

The examination room was actually a private laboratory. There were dozens of them in the maze like hallways of the university, each assigned to different doctors and scientists. They all looked pretty much the same—tile floors, bright walls, and scientific equipment sitting around.

I entered the empty lab and began to clear a table to sit on. I found a towel to put on the table so that I would not have to sit directly on the cold surface. Then I stripped off all my clothing and climbed up on the table to wait for the doctor and his entourage of students.

After ten minutes, the door to the lab opened. Two young female interns walked in, followed closely by an older female doctor. They all hesitated near the door.

"Hey, how are you doing?" I asked pleasantly. "Nice to see you today. My name is Rich. Who are you?"

The women looked confused, but the two younger ones stepped forward and introduced themselves.

"Hi, I'm Karen," one said, extending her hand.

"I'm Sandra." The second intern also shook my hand.

I looked at the older woman, anticipating her introduction. When she said nothing, I explained. "Professor Lambert should be here anytime now."

"Well," the older woman began, "I don't think so. This is my lab and I am not Professor Lambert."

"Whoa," I exclaimed, jumping down from the table. "Are you telling me I'm in the wrong place?"

All three of the women were trying to resist the urge to laugh. "Rich," the professor said, maintaining her composure, "you're in the gynecology lab. I believe Dr. Lambert's lab is one hallway over."

At that everyone, including me, began to laugh.

"So, why are you still naked?" the intern Karen asked.

"I'm a lymphoma patient of Professor Lambert's, and I'm used to being naked for the examinations," I explained, obviously not contemplating what she asked. "I thought I would get a jump on things so I took off my clothes." I suddenly realized that I was standing naked in front of three strangers, answering questions.

The professor spoke up, still smiling. "Well, I guess you can put your clothes on now. I don't think we can do anything for you *gynecologically*."

"Naw," I teased, " I figured I would just walk down the hall this way. So many people have seen me this way, what's the point in getting dressed just to take my clothes off again?"

The professor was game for my jest. "Well," she responded, "we don't have any robes here, so I guess if you do want to walk down the hall, you should put your socks on to keep your feet warm."

"Oh, alright," I said, feigning resignation, "I guess I had better get dressed just in case somebody gets offended by my hairy butt."

Once I had dressed, the women all told me that it was nice to have met me. We all had a good laugh over my mistake. When I shared the incident with my other doctors, they too thought it was hysterical and couldn't wait to continue the fun by telling the gynecology personnel they had no clue who this person was.

Timelines Based on My DayTimer Calendars

1986	Jan.	
	Feb.	11th Overcome by Fumes
	Mar.	
	Apr.	
	May	
	Jun.	17th Spilt Resin on Foot / 18th Explosion
	Jul.	
	Aug.	Harold Dies
	Sep.	
	Oct.	
	Nov.	
	Dec.	
1987	Jan.	Henry Dies

1990	Feb.	24th Wedding
	Mar.	Purchased 3-Family
1991	Feb.	
	Mar.	
	Apr.	
	May	
	Jun.	Kenny Dies
	Jul.	
	Aug.	
	Sep.	Purchased Meeker House
	Oct.	
	Nov.	Rich in Colorado - Rash / Closed on Meeker House

1992	Jan. / Feb.	Max Joins Family
	Mar.	
	Apr.	
	May	Rich in Meeker - Rash
	Jun.	
	Jul.	
	Aug.	
	Sep.	Rich in Maine - Rash / 12th Rich to Dermatologist
	Oct.	2 nd The Diagnosis / 5 th Dr. Lambert - 1 st Visit / 6th Blood 3 vials & 2 biops. / 13th Dr. Martinez 1st visit / 13th & 15th Blood Work / 16th Blood work 10 vials & 5 biops. & 2 DNA Samples / 19th 2 biopsies / 21st Met with Eddie and Local 210
	Nov.	3rd Dr. Yang 1st time Suggests PUVA / 9th UMD Cat Scan, Chest Xray, Iodine Drink - Sick all afternoon / 13th Dr. Brooks / 16 th Began Treatments- 4times per week / Very bad headaches, forgetfulness, vomiting
	Dec.	4 PUVA treatments per wk. / 16th Carolyn Fox 2 hours / Very sick, disoriented, headaches, vomiting, now wearing special glasses

Timelines Based on My DayTimer Calendars

1993			1994		
	Jan.	15th Hired Dennis Murray 28 th Found out about John 4 PUVA treatments per week biopsy, vomiting, head noise, disoriented		Jan.	14 Treatments PUVA & Metha. 19 th WC Court -Gochfeld Testimony Rich on Stand
	Feb.	4 PUVA treatments per week 18th Fumes overcame me returning from Treatment biopsy, headache, head noise, disoriented		Feb.	8 Treatments PUVA & Metha. 2nd WC Court Canc.
	Mar.	4 PUVA treatments per week 8th Dr. Turner Apt. 31st WC Court -Rich on stand Lawyers away Biopsy & Blood test		Mar.	9 Treatments PUVA & Metha. 2 nd WC Court - Rich on Stand
	Apr.	4 PUVA Treatments per week 21 st WC Court - Cancelled 31st Rich on stand		Apr.	5 Treatments PUVA & Metha. Lambert & Rich on Stand
	May	12th WC Court Cancelled 25th Stopped PUVA Liver and blood tests		May.	6Treatments 3 PUVA & 3 Metha. 4th Prepared Lambert for court - Lambert on stand
	Jun.	23rd WC Court-Rich on stand 28th diagnosed - Inflamatoid papulosis NO TREATMENTS - Liver, blood tests		Jun.	8 Treatments -5 PUVA & 2 Metha. 8 th WC Court Cancelled Gochfeld on stand
	Jul.	13th -2 treatments per week 16th Called NIOSH Trip to Vermont Lambert discusses Surgery-Yang Says NO		Jul.	5 Treatments 2 PUVA & 3 Metha. 6th WC Court Cancelled 27th WC Court
	Aug.	2 PUVA treatments per week 4th WC Court- Rich on stand 25th Court Vacation		Aug.	3 Treatments Metha.
	Sep.	2 PUVA treatments per week 13th Talked to OSHA 14th Talked to NIOSH Lambert re. Removing Tumor		Sep.	3 Treatments Metha. 9th California Trip 7th WC Court Canc. 28th WC Court
	Oct.	6th WC Court-Rich on stand 12th -17th Chicago CTCL Symposium 12th Dr Kuzal NWU 26 th WC Court WebbTool, Bendix, Parkway Kew Released Rich on Stand 2 PUVA treatments per week		Oct.	1 Treatments Metha.
	Nov.	2 PUVA treatments per week		Nov.	3 Treatments Metha.
	Dec.	2 PUVA treatments per week 8 th WC Court- Rich on stand Cathi off 46 hours of work /yr		Dec.	3 Treatments Metha. 7th 2 vial of Blood 25th Vermont Xmas Trip with Family

Timelines Based on My DayTimer Calendars

1995			1995		
	Jan.	15 Office Visits - 5 Doctors 12th Lots of Bloodwork, Urine Sample, Xrays, EKG 18th Surgery - 7 sites 19th Home to Meeker 20 th Rich Passed out 23rd Removed Packing from Rt Hip 29th Train Show with Friends		Jul.	5 Office Visits - 3 Doctors 2nd On Vacation to Vermont 3rd Cancer is still growing all over 5th penis has new spots 20th Tony Deposition 18th Eddie Deposition 19th Brad Deposition 20th Jim Deposition 21st 3rd Party Court 25th Bumps all over and penis bad
	Feb.	13 Office Visits- 4 Doctors 2nd Removed Stitches 7th John Reeves Called WC Appeal 8th Bumps appearing, - Star Ledger Requests Interview, Art has cancelled 10th Dr. Martinez - Sezary 20 th New tumors growing 22nd Bethesda, MD turned down case 23rd new tumors growing 28 th 4 biopsies, 10 blood samples		Aug.	4 Office Visits -3 Doctors New Plaques coming out and old ones scaling 21st PUVA restarted Treatments - 3 PUVA & 5 Metha
	Mar.	8 Office Visits- 5 Doctors Lots of bumps all over body 7th took pictures of body and tumors 13th Called SS 18th Started Metha - 2 for month 23rd 0 T Helper Cells - Suppressor Cells 28th 6 blood Samples & 5 Biopsies		Sep.	3 Office Visits- 3 Doctors Treatments - 6 PUVA & 3 Metha 6th Calls to SS 7th New Plaques on Upper Rt Arm 8th Bought new Car 29th Rich Deposition - felt bad Breaking out all over
	Apr.	8 Office Visits - 5 Doctors 4 Metha Treatments 12th WC Court		Oct.	2 Office Visits- 2 Doctors Treatments - 6 PUVA & 4 Metha 13th Rich Deposition 20th Rich Deposition 24th-26th Rich Bad Cold 31st Very Sick - Plaques all over
	May	7 Office Visits - 2 Doctors 5 Metha Treatments 1st - Penus cracked 4th Cathy Home - Rich Sick 11th 3 biops. rt arm, 2 other biops., 10 blood samples		Nov.	3 Office Visits - 3 Doctors Treatments - 7 PUVA & 5 Metha 1st Papulas Very Noticeable 3rd Rich Deposition 10th Rich Deposition 10th Chest pain & Ankle Pain 11th Tried to go ice skating - Ankles & Knees hurt bad 19th Eddie brought Air Cast 29th Breaking out all month, Rec'd. injection to counteract, entire body hurt and Rash all over arms
	Jun.	5 Office Visits- 3 Doctors 4th Both to Art's to Review papers 4th Penis has white spots on shaft 9th Appellate Court Rendered WC Appeal Decision - We Won 13th Penis Worse 13th Art Rush Called - We are ready 14th Mike Deposition 20th Breaking out All Over Again 20th Cathi gave Rich Metha w/needle 30th Cancer definitely growing 30th Met with Eddie		Dec.	3 Office Visits - 2 Doctors Treatments - 6 PUVA & 3 Metha 4th Follicular Infection 6th took double medication, could not remember how much or what missed treatment would break out

Timelines Based on My DayTimer Calendars

1996			1996		
	Jan.	4 Office Vsts- 4 Drs 3 PUVA & 3 Meth. 5 th Deposition Cancelled. 8th Court Cancelled 17 th Scheduled Surgery 21 st Extreme Back Pain 26th Surgery 29th Art's Office & Lambert's Office 30 th Called SS re $18,000 31st Called John Reeves about SS		Jul.	3 Office Visits- 3 Doctors 2 PUVA & 3 Metha. 3 rd Art's Office Meeting Very Sick All Month 16th Dr. Roderick Deposition
	Feb.	2 Office Vsts- 2 Drs 4 PUVA & 3 Meth. 2nd Rich Deposition 6 th & 8th Review all other depositions 9th, 15th, 16th , 29th Depositions 14th Talked to John Reeves about SS 14th through 17 th Bad Cold 18 th Worked all day on SS		Aug.	1 Office Visits- 1 Doctors 2 PUVA & 2 Metha. 5 th Henry Dew's Office meeting. 5th worked on SS papers 6th SS Hearing 9th Henry Dew's Office meeting
	Mar.	3 Office Vsts- 3 Drs 4 PUVA & 4 Metha. 1 st Teeth, Gums, Side, Throat Hurt, head noise, cold 14 th Cancelled Dr. Appt. - Sick 22nd Mike 2nd Deposition		Sep.	0 Office Visits- 0 Doctors 3 PUVA & 2 Metha.
	Apr.	3 Office Vsts- 2 D 2 PUVA & 4 Metha. 2 nd - head noise, nrsot well - Dr. Appt. 12 th REM Ins. Called - Not Paying 12 th WC Court 15 th through 18th - Vomiting, Diarrhea, Chest , Teeth, Side Pain 25th Art's Office		Oct.	0 Office Visits- 0 Doctors 2 PUVA & 1 Metha. 25th Court
	May.	1 Office Visit- 1 Doctor 2 PUVA & 3 Metha. & Breaking out all over 9 th John Reeves called about SS 10 th 3-family fails inspection 13 th John calls re. SS - not good 14th Couldn't Sleep due to SS 15th Court 17th Drs. Appt.		Nov.	3 Office Visits- 3 Doctors 2 PUVA & 3 Metha. 2 nd 4 large papular on left forearm 10th Did a slot car show Donated proceeds to St. Jude's Hospital 18th Lambert took biopsy
	Jun.	5 Office Visits- 3 Doctors 2 PUVA & 2 Metha. 2nd Lambert & Art meeting 7th Lambert meeting 12 th Art's Office, Parent's Dep. 13th Play Softball with NY Giants 14th Mom & Cathi's Depositions 16th Gochfeld's Deposition 21 st Art's Office Meeting 28th Rich's Deposition		Dec.	0 Office Visits - 0 Doctors 2 PUVA & 0 Metha. 3rd John DayDeposition 5th Worked on Surprise 18th Dr. Birnkrant Deposition 20th Dad's Deposition cancelled 20th WC Court - Penalty for Paying Late 23rd Nightmare 24th Still Sick 25th Christmas together in Meeker

Timelines Based on My DayTimer Calendars

1997

Jan.

Feb.
24th-29th Anniv. Trip to Bahamas.

Mar.
1 Office Vst - 1 Dr   3 PUVA & 3 Metha
24th Dad's Deposition Cancelled
27th Scab still on Penis after 3 weeks
30th Large Scab off Penis, Not yet healed

Apr.
3 Office Vsts - 3 Drs 3 PUVA & 3 Meth
4th Blood work
8th Rich feels Art Selling Him Out
10th San Isabel Island to Visit Brian
14th Left Ankle gave out, Fell down stairs
15th Prepped for Friday's Court
17th Carolyn's Deposition, Dad's Depos.
17th Left Ankle Hurting Bad
18th Court w/ Art, Ankle bad, wear braces
22nd Rich with Art for Civil Trial
26th Kelliann's Christening
28th Called Bruce about SS, No call back

May.
2 Office Vsts - 2 Drs 2 PUVA & 2 Meth
9th Had to call 911 at 1:00 AM Rich
Muscle cramps, chest pain, turning
blue, very weak, blood pressure high
10th Still same with diarrhea now
11th better still had diarrhea 54 Imodiums
11th Lambert - Breaking out, diarrhea,
chest pains, left eye, penis
12th Headache & diarrhea
20th "Ricky" - Still having symptoms
21st Parents brought home van
22nd Art Worried about case
28 th Met Cheryl's fiance Mark
29th meeting Eric's office

Jun.
1 Office Vst - 1 Dr 2 PUVA & 2 Meth
Not feeling well all month worked on house
3rd Worked on SS paperwork
3rd Art called about $1.6million settlement
4th Spot on Penis
10 th Gochfeld Deposition
11th Worked on Paperwork for Art
12th Engineer Deposition, Rich Deposition
16th Rich & Gochfeld Deposition
18th Went to Hayward to look for Docs
23rd blood work
26th Blood good, Liver bad
26th Letter to Senator regarding SS

Jul.
Treatments - 2 PUVA & 2 Metha
1st Rich reads Depositions
3rd Worked on SS w/ Eric
16th Dr. Rocks Deposition
18th Dr. Platts Deposition
21st worked on Jama Report
23rd Interrog. w/Art & Lambert
24th Rich Deposition
25th Turner's Deposition

Aug.
1 Off. Vst - 1 PUVA & 1 Metha
Head hurts, throat, ankle, hips, eyes,
Papulos on Penis, also flaking
Had to buy Arch Supports
5th & 7th Depositions Cancelled
Bought new sneakers w/add'l supp.
21st - 23rd Paper work for SS
Still Breaking Out

Sep.
2 Off. Vsts, 2 Drs 2 PUVA & 2 Meth
2nd finished paper work for SS and
delivered to Judge Ryan's Office
8th Removed tumor - 6 Stitches
9th SS Court
11th Blood work
12th Jury Set for February
16th Dr. Shelley Deposition
18th Rich, Doctor, & Art Deposition
Sore on bottom lip, plaques over eye
on penis and all over body, new bumps

Oct.
Treatments - 2 PUVA & 2 Metha
2nd Fifth Anniversary of Diagnosis
24th Rich Sick, Cathi stayed home

Nov.
Treatments - 3 PUVA & 3 Metha
3rd & 4th Lambert & Art Met
11th Saw Lambert for review
12th Blood work
13th Dr. "Ricky"
18th Rich Deposition
26th Colorado Trip
New plaques in groin area and lips
Penis not healing - Very Drained

Dec.
Treatments - 4 PUVA & 3 Metha
5th & 11th Art for Review
19th Left for England
29th Rich burns - new bulbs in PUVA
no sleep - burns hurt, body swollen,
eyes hurt, penis & nipples hurt

Timelines Based on My DayTimer Calendars

1998			1999		
	Jan.	1 Office Visit - 1 Doctor Treatments - 4 PUVA & 2 Metha Rich Still Breaking Out All Over 8th Court Postponed, Not in Feb.		Jan.	
	Feb.	1 Office Visit - 1 Doctor Treatments - 2 PUVA & 2 Metha 17th Met with Art & Eddie Rich very drained, skin hurt, head noise		Feb.	
		Treatments - 3 PUVA & 3 Metha 2nd-3rd & 5th-6th Met with Art 9th Art & Lambert Review 10th Cathi & Art Review 11th Gochfeld & Art Review 12th Rich, Art, Dr. Shelley & Yang met for court 16th Trial Began 17th Jury Selection 18th Eddie on Stand All Day 19th Dr. Shelley on Stand, Case Settled 20th Went to In-Laws 25th Left for Vermont		Mar.	
	Mar.			Apr.	
				May	
				Jun.	
				Jul.	
	Apr.	Treatments - 2 PUVA & 2 Metha Tumors Still Growing			
	May	Treatments - 2 PUVA & 1 Metha		Aug.	11th through 13th - Cathi's Breakdown 24th Cathi Leaves
	Jun.	1 Office Visits - 1 Doctors Treatments - 4 PUVA & 4 Metha			
	Jul.	1 Office Visits - 1 Doctors 18th Richard left for Colorado 24th Cathi arrived Denver Airport		Sep.	
	Aug.	2 Office Visits - 1 Doctors Treatments - 3 PUVA & 3 Metha			
	Sep.	2 Office Visits - 2 Doctors Treatments - 2 PUVA & 2 Metha		Oct.	
	Oct.	Treatments - 1 PUVA & 1 Metha			
	Nov.	Treatments - 2 PUVA & 1 Metha		Nov.	
	Dec.	Treatments - 2 PUVA & 2 Metha		Dec.	

Toggle Injection Molding Machine

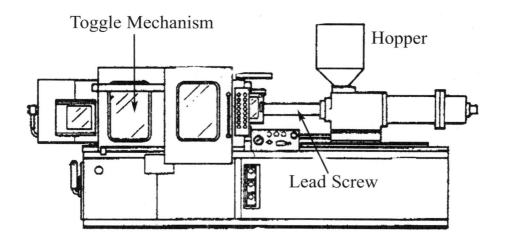

Toggle Mechanism

Hopper

Lead Screw

Toggle Mechanism

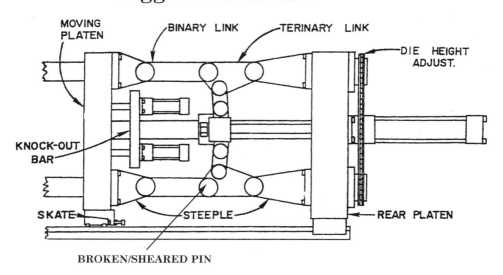

MOVING
PLATEN

BINARY LINK

TERINARY LINK

DIE HEIGHT
ADJUST.

KNOCK-OUT
BAR

SKATE

STEEPLE

REAR PLATEN

BROKEN/SHEARED PIN

Good Health - Summer 1986

Finished Test Ball
Rich's Skinned Knuckle
February 11, 1986

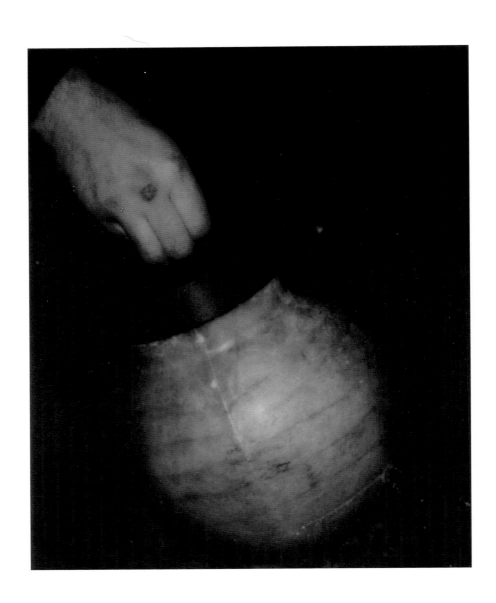

Basketball After Accident
June 18, 1986

Right Hip Plaque

Microscopic Cancer Cells
(black dots)

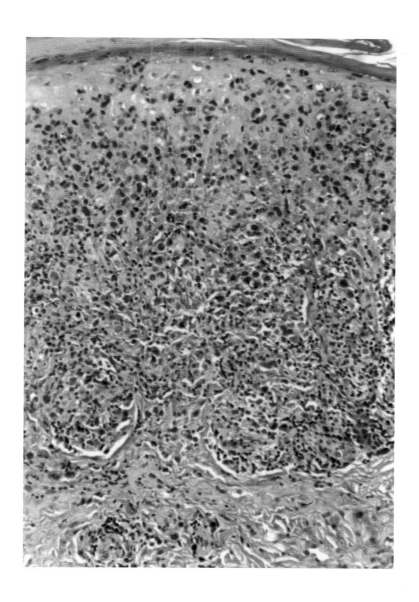

Some Surgery Sites

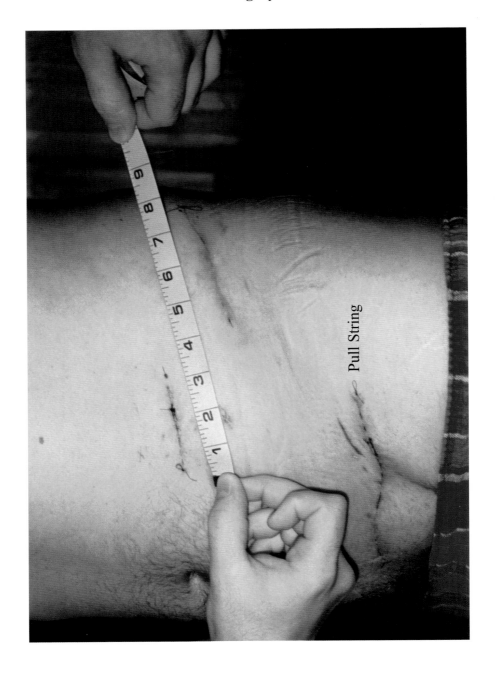

Pull String

Left Back Thigh
Skin Grafting Site

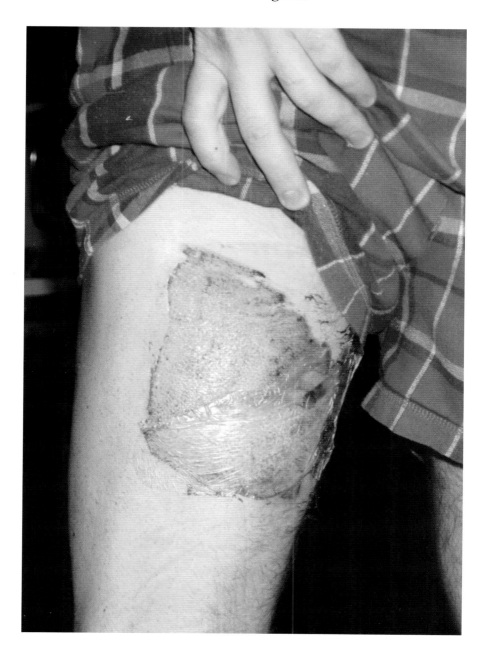

Right Ankle Plaque & Deteriorating Vein Wall

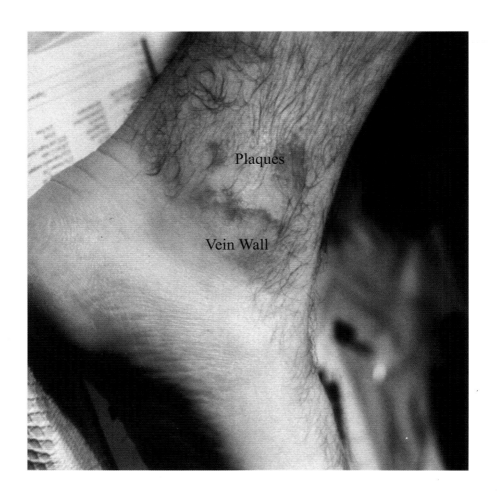

Plaques

Vein Wall

Arm & Shoulder
LyP Tumors

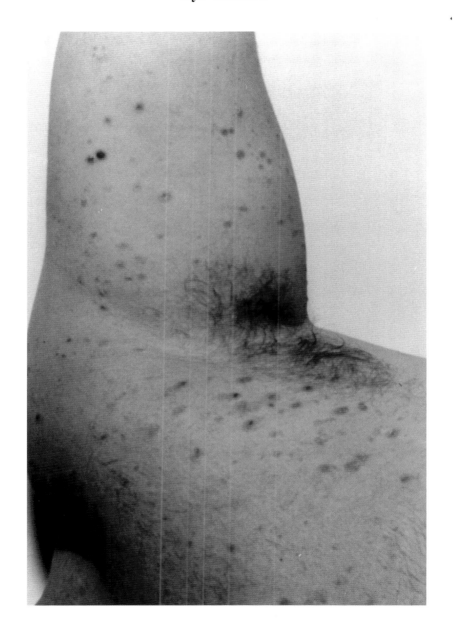

Arm & Shoulder
Plaques

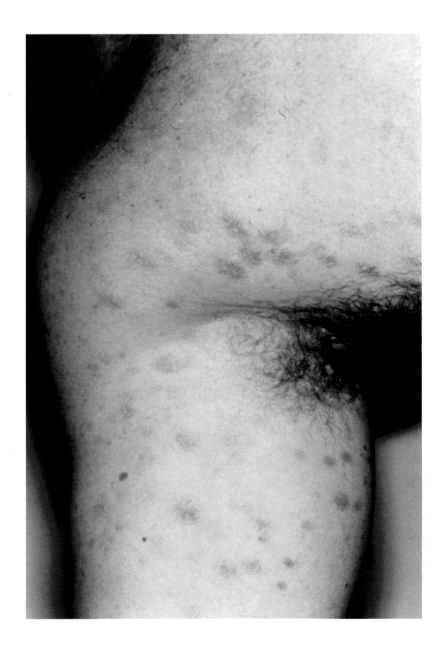

Train Auction Tumors
(after incision)

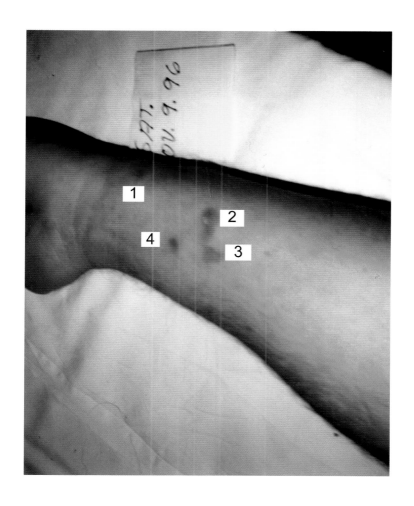

My Angel, My Protector, & Me
March, 1995

25
Preparation for WC Battle

March 10, 1993—Later that day, the tall, meticulously dressed John Reeves sat attentively, listening to me describe the Turner meeting from the day before. I respected the calm professionalism of this man and also appreciated the way he handled me. John would always ask how I felt, had I done a treatment, and when was the last time I had taken medication. But he was very careful never to ask if I remembered what our last conversation was. Rather, John would always recap, as though he was doing it for both of us. *John never lost view of the concept of dignity and treated me with respect.*

The attorney had recognized very early my desire to be part of the case. And, he admired my tenacity in my fight with cancer. Considering the number of treatments and the amounts of medicines I was taking, John was continually amazed at what I accomplished. My family and I never lost interest in the research necessary for the preparation of the trial.

"Richard, I don't want you to be too upset by this," John stated when I was finished telling him about Turner. "This kind of thing happens. In fact, the legal profession is just like any other; we all have 'whores' to contend with. Opinions and testimony can be bought. With

Lambert and Gochfeld's testimony, though, I don't anticipate any problems. Now, let's talk about trial preparation and that special project you're working on."

"John you're not going to believe it," I said. "I contacted the Centers For Disease Control & Prevention, (CDC), and gave them a brief description of the accident and my disease. They were quite helpful but told me there was at least a 1 1/2 year waiting list of requested safety investigations. And, the National Institutes for Occupational Safety & Health or NIOSH organized all investigations."

"As I continued and informed them of the tactics that Carolyn was using and that Dr's Gochfeld and Lambert were involved, they really became interested. They're putting a priority on my complaint and will have someone contact me in the next couple of weeks."

The two of us spent the next two hours reviewing questions, depositions and a list of all potential people to be deposed. John was quite methodical and tedious in organizing the presentation of the case.

"I doubt that we will have to call everyone to the stand," John told me, "but it is better to be prepared, just in case. We will be in Judge Rosati's court."

"What's he like?" I didn't want any more negative surprises.

"He's a good judge, very fair," John assured me. " He's going to be retiring soon, so he's not carrying a full case load. That may be helpful in speeding up this process."

The defense attorneys proved John wrong about the timing. At the first session on April 21, 1993, the attorneys representing Hayward Pool Company, Zurich American Insurance and Home Insurance opened with a motion to join my previous employers in the case. That meant that WebbTool Inc., Parkway-Kew Corp. and Allied Signal Aerospace (Bendix) would all have to be included in the proceedings.

John was thorough in his preliminary, or pre-trial, questioning and research of my past and, therefore, intentionally did not include my previous employers in the complaint. He knew it was a waste of time due to my lack of injury or chronic exposure to chemicals at any of my previous employers.

Judge Rosati, a soft-spoken man, recognized the tactic for what it was—*a stall*. He allowed the defense to present their reasoning but declined to grant the motion to "delay proceedings for more discovery time" and ordered that the hearing proceed as planned. The defense had to get organized in a timely manner.

26
Reconnaissance of Safety Practices

NIOSH 1993—Within days of the carefully choreographed Turner visit, (Tuesday, March 9, 1993) the Director of NIOSH Investigations, Dr. Edward Hoekstra contacted me. He explained to me that a formal but confidential complaint that included other employee signatures would have to be signed and then reviewed by NIOSH before any investigation could be considered.

Dr. Hoekstra was curious about what I had said to the initial interviewer at the CDC that enabled my verbal complaint to get his immediate attention. Again I explained the details of my condition, the doctors involved, the conduct of Mrs. Fox and the Turner visit at Yale University.

Dr. Hoekstra was appalled by the entire situation and agreed with the CDC that this case should be evaluated as soon as possible. He, too, was cautious with me, explaining that the likelihood of finding any remnants from an accident 6 years old was not likely to happen.

The investigation had to be based on the complaint of employees suffering the effects of exposures to chemicals and the effects they are having on employees at the present time. Furthermore, he explained, due to the rarity of my cancer, my young age, and the fact that the cancer had formed on the burn sites, he would definitely work with Dr. Gochfeld on the possibilities of my work exposure being the causative factor.

By June of 93 I had the signatures required for the NIOSH complaint and before the end of July NIOSH had approved an investigation with priority status.

In less than three months, on September 28 and 29, NIOSH investigators visited the Hayward facility in Elizabeth, New Jersey. Hayward was tipped off as to the inspection days and had a week to clean things up. No one ever expected to find a proverbial "smoking gun" associated to my accident. Instead, the investigation was intended to protect the workers from future chronic exposures.

The conclusions were filed in NIOSH record HETA 93-1013-2357, and made public in January, 1994. Hayward indeed received a clean bill of health—as far as the investigation was concerned.

What was not expected was that within the report an employee from the molding department stated that after the purging of heated PVC plastic or cleaning out the machine, the maintenance worker had to be hospitalized for a respiratory tract irritation immediately following the exposure.

Another benefit in the report was that the investigator had found an unlabeled, open, quart-sized can of methylene chloride. Hayward's representatives had been accusing me of being a distraught plaintiff who lied about exposures and the chemical labeling practices at the plant. The company now had some explaining to do.

The real surprise came during the cleanup or possibly during the NIOSH investigation. Realistically no one may ever know, but one thing Hayward's attorney was certain of was that I had made many friends at the plant and all knew that the company had accused me of making up various situations about the basketball project and the chemicals used.

Even Robert Zinn, one of the defense attorneys, conveyed to John that I had to be lying, there was no physical evidence showing a basketball was ever actually experimented on in the procedure I described, or that the machine existed, or that the woven fiberglass strands ever existed at Hayward, and liquid styrene in generically labeled one-pint cans was an illusion.

John took great pleasure in informing the defense attorneys that a Good Samaritan had dropped off a box at my front door while Cathi and I were at the hospital. It contained photographs, documents and actual products from the "basketball project." Mr. Zinn now realized his corporate client was falsifying information.

27
Workman's Comp Battles Begin

April 21, 1993—On the first Workman's Comp trial date of Wednesday, April 21, 1993, the first issue addressed was my disability. Hayward's insurance carrier's attorney knew that there was little reason to try to argue this point. Robert Zinn, attorney for Zurich Insurance stated into record:

"There's no dispute as to the diagnosis, your Honor. I think both parties agree that the diagnosis has been confirmed by the tests that were done. And neither party is questioning Professor Lambert's expertise in the field. The only real problem for you, your Honor, and for both parties, obviously, is whether this is causally connected to the work environment."

Cathi and I sat in the front of the courtroom listening to all the antics that some refer to as complicated legal discourse. Mom and Dad sat at the back of the room with my mother-in-law, Loren. Carolyn Fox was also in attendance, but refused to make eye contact with any of the family members.

I was prepared to testify that day, but with all the legal maneuverings of the defense, my participation was delayed until the next court date set for June. It was blatantly obvious that the defense was going to draw these proceedings out as long as possible. The unspoken gamble they were engaged in was that I would die before the end of the trial.

Over the next twenty months, in no less than a dozen court dates, all set one to two months apart, the defense attempted ploys to delay. However, the Judge was insistent on having the case heard and testimonies were heard as John planned. Month after month, to the exasperation of the defendants, I would be sitting in court, often suffering from the effects of my treatments, but never allowing them to see any sign of weakness or pain.

It was on Wednesday, June 23, 1993, that I finally was able to give testimony before the Honorable Judge Rosati. As I took the stand, the judge took a moment prior to the questioning to ask if I was feeling okay or if I needed a drink of water. I knew the judge's concern was genuine, and the questions were not just legal formality. I respected the judge for that and responded "I am fine your Honor, thank you".

With the excitement of having "my day in court" I wouldn't dream of saying, "Well Judge, I had tumors removed on my right forearm, right hip, and abdomen on Thursday and the sites and stitches are killing me from a rough treatment I had on Monday. I think the vomiting aggravated everything."

My testimony went perfectly. I described my various work place responsibilities and environment with candor and honesty. John couldn't have asked for more from a secretly distraught client.

Dr. Gochfeld took the stand on March 2, 1994, and was sworn in as an expert and Professor of Occupational Health Sciences & Environmental Biology. Dr. Gochfeld intrigued the court with his profound concern for the facts pertaining to my exposures and condition.

He openly admitted to the court that his expertise was not this form of cancer but rather determining the causative factors of a specific individual's condition. He used the supportive medical studies as an "additional" guideline to disprove my condition. In the process he and Dr. Lambert established causal relationship of the chemical burns to the cancer and the etiology or method of its formation.

On July 27, 1994, Dr. Lambert was sworn in as an expert and Board certified in Dermatology, Pathology, Dermato-Pathology, and Professor of Experimental Pathology. He stunned the court by describing the medical evidence that disproves any correlation of my cancer to chemicals as inconsequential because most of the studies were based on the disease being homogeneous or similar in structure instead of heterogeneous or dissimilar in structure. He described this to the court, in simplest form, as:

"In this regard, the category of disease known as Mycosis Fungoides appears to be many diseases that have many similarities with regard to the macular nature of lesions, thickening plaques, or tumors, but are nonetheless different diseases. As such the different diseases are caused by different things. Some are caused by dermatitis, some are caused by chemical exposures and some are caused by both."

The testimonies were so overpowering that the defense attorney only produced the written report from Yale University's, Dr. Turner. The attorney declared that the document was sufficient in this matter and the defense did not deem it necessary to take such a man away from his practice. John was quick to remind the court that the two professors that had testified surpassed Turner's expertise. Carolyn sat behind the defense team subdued and planning her next move.

Judge Rosati was not impressed by the defense team's evidence and on November 2, 1994, stated into The State of New Jersey Workman's Compensation record (# 92-066815):

"The court would not be remiss in this case, as in all other cases, if it did not comment on the testimony.

The court addressed questions at various stages of the proceeding to each of the witnesses. On each occasion the court would look directly at the witness and likewise on each occasion the witness would look the court in the eye without lowering his (witness') eye, giving the court the strongest feeling that the witness was being truthful, honest and forthright with the court.

The courtroom light bothered Richard Sabb, but he kept his spirits up, probably giving his wife, mother, father, and mother-in-law, who also attended all sessions as observers, courage and confidence. Not too often has the court heard or witnessed such forthright, honest and credible demeanor and testimony.

Richard Sabb admittedly is affected with a deadly disease whose prognosis is doubtful at best. He attended every court session and who knows what he was going through and what was going through his mind when his two medical experts almost gave him his death pronouncement.

He impressed the court with his honesty and credibility. He made an observation at one point when a minor discrepancy was brought to his attention and he said, "I am sorry. I am trying to testify from memory."

Dr. Gochfeld in his testimony admitted his area of limitation and he impressed the court with his honesty and sincerity.

As to Dr. Lambert, who impressed everyone in court, on Jul the 27th, 1994, he mightyly (mightily) impressed the court. On the particular occasion the court and attorneys were discussing an article on the pathogenesis of Mycosis Fungoides and Dr. Lambert said, 'This article, by the way, was cited by me. It was not provided by someone. I cited it in an attempt to be absolutely fair. I am paid for my time and I am nobody's advocate up here. I am just an expert.'

And the court does find Dr. Lambert is an expert witness who impressed the court with his total truthfulness and candor, and I view his testimony as entirely honest and forthright which reflected an honorable, believable, and believable and truthful person and witness."

On November 2, 1994, The Honorable Judge Rosati ruled in favor of me to receive Worker's Compensation benefits and declared me temporarily disabled.

The defense immediately appealed and the true battles began.

28
Fighting on Multiple Fronts

1993—During the time that I was subjected to the Worker's Comp trial, I was busy on other endeavors, finances being just one of my major concerns. By the time the trial had started, I had gone six months without a paycheck or any benefits.

The only steady income was Cathi's, but because she had to take off so much time to nurse me or attend depositions and trials, her income suffered, too. My parents were helping a lot.

Dad had spoken to the other three children. They were self-sufficient with spouses and families of their own, but Mom and Dad wanted to explain that they had to concentrate all of their financial strength on providing for themselves and subsidizing me while I fought to stay alive. "It will mean that we will not be able to give elaborate Christmas and birthday gifts," Dad had told them. "We've got to focus on Richard for now."

My siblings understood our parents' concern and tried to comprehend the struggle Cathi and I were facing.

It was an emotional roller coaster ride for Cathi and I; we lost our dreams of having a family, a normal life, and on a daily basis faced the possibility of death. We had sacrificed control of our finances, the real estate we had worked so hard to obtain, and a promising business.

It became necessary to dissolve my partnerships with Gary and John shortly after the diagnosis, both at a monetary loss to myself. With the specter of momentary death hanging over me, I could no longer function or contribute to the arrangements.

Cathi and I still owned the problematic three-family home that was built in 1921. It was where we had lived when we were first married. We managed to keep all three apartments rented most of the time, but the revenue only covered our mortgage on the building. There were many months that major repairs had to be made and my Dad was not only there to "foot" the bill, but also labored through the repairs.

Cathi and I surrendered our freedom, not just financially, but physically and emotionally. Together, we chose not to show the outside world the despair and anger we sometimes felt toward the life we had been handed.

I knew I had to do something to contribute. My only source of potential income was my childhood passion of early American electric trains. The model trains provided a dual solution. In order to maintain some normalcy in my life while taking treatments and attending to legal battles, I would work on my trains, refurbishing and fixing them. In essence it was my form of mental therapy; regardless of how traumatic a day was, an hour in the basement with the trains elevated me from that day's turmoil.

My grandfather started my hobby and each interlude of enjoyment with the trains enhanced my memories of him. Now I shared all the joys with my father, and it struck me that the natural order had been disrupted of father to son. As any hobbyist knows, with the advent of potential income comes the excuse of the addition to the collection. My dad fell prey to his lost childhood addiction and joined me in my passion. Cathi, she had been hooked on trains for years.

Still, the first order of business was the continual PUVA and chemotherapy. But once I had slept off the effects of the treatments, I would go to the train room and work there. I expanded into other collectible toys, such as Buddy–L Trucks and Aurora Slot Cars. Auctions and shows were held on weekends and posed as a form of solace for Cathi and I to interact with the "normal" world.

One April Saturday, I convinced my friend, Carmen, to join me for the day at a show being held at the Wayne Police Association Center. I wasn't going to set up a table, but I enjoyed the shows and would almost always stay for the entire 5 to 6 hour duration. It was my social outlet.

Within a month of starting treatments, the medications had begun to affect all of my joints, especially my ankles and knees. It had gotten to the point that any change in the weather would cause my ankle and knees to ache and swell.

The day of the train show was sunny and clear, but rain was being predicted for the next day. And, I could definitely confirm the forecast.

Carmen and I arrived at the show as it opened and slowly made our way from table to table, often stopping to talk with the vendors.

About midday, my ankles began to really bother me. They had swollen to the point that it was necessary for me to untie my high-topped sneakers, so as not restrict the blood flow. Rather than continue to hobble through the show, I found a strategic spot to sit and talk with friends.

There were always two main topics of discussion: trains, and my health. The folks at the train shows knew me and were genuinely concerned about my progress with my cancer. My determination and how I continually looked to the brighter side of things regardless of the moment at hand intrigued them, too.

Carmen worried about me and suggested in his colorful way that we might go home.

"Heck, no," I told him cheerfully. "I'm fine as long as I'm off my feet. Besides, I'm having fun. Relax, Carmen. Enjoy yourself."

Carmen respectfully stayed with me until the end of the show. When we arrived back at home, Carmen told Cathi, "Hey doll-face, your butt-ugly husband is fucking insane, absolutely nothing upstairs at all," laughing all the while and pointing to his head. "This dumb-ass of yours couldn't even walk, and insisted on staying until the very end."

Meanwhile, my friend from Hayward, Eddie, stopped by unexpectedly to see how I was feeling. It indeed turned out to be a Godsend. Eddie had a good laugh with Carmen's description of my hobbling around all day, but also brought good news. Eddie was now working for a new employer that made "air casts" for people with injuries to joints and specialized in ankle supports for athletes.

Eddie gave a brief description of how useful they could be and simply offered, "Guimo," (as Eddie referred to me), "Don't you worry about it. I can take care of this problem. When I tell my boss about you, he'll give you a pair for free. Try them for a week or so and if you like them keep 'em. If you don't give them back."

True to his word, Eddie was at my house the next day with the "air casts." The braces were made of a very light durable plastic that were filled with a "molding gel" that comfortably encased the ankle. From the first time Eddie put them on for me, I knew they worked. ("Still to the time of this writing and after eight years of use—they are still in use")

Through my sister, I was introduced to Tom Stange. Tom had met Cheryl through her job at Tek Investors.

Because of his involvement with the American Cancer Society, she told Tom about my ongoing battle with cancer. Tom was the chairman of a fund-raiser for the local chapter, and his firm, National Business Parks, was the event's primary sponsor.

Team members from the New York Giants football team played a softball game against local corporate teams.

I was an athlete and, at one time, had been a superb baseball player, so Cheryl was eager to introduce me to Tom.

Tom was thrilled to meet me and contacted me within two days. "It would be a tremendous help," he told me, "if you could participate in the softball game. It would be wonderful publicity for the Cancer Society and a great draw for the fans. The players could witness, first hand, how their involvement is having some positive results."

I did not hesitate. "Sure, Tom, I'd be happy to help. I think what you are doing is a great thing."

Tom was pleased at my willingness and called some of the pro football players to tell them about the cancer patient who would be joining them. He also put in a call to all the area newspapers.

I was able to play a portion of the game as shortstop, but when I was up to bat, and connected with the ball, everyone could tell that I was in pain. They graciously allowed me to take the base.

The game was a hit with fans and players. The New Jersey Star-Ledger interviewed me and ran a photograph of me and some of the teammates. *"I wanted to show that these events really do help,"* I told the reporter. *"The enormous cost of new cancer fighting technology is largely offset by organizations that depend on the public for support. And, much of that support comes from these local events where neighbors turn out to help their neighbors."*

After the game, Cathi and I were invited to join two of the pro players and their wives for dinner at a local restaurant. We were not football enthusiasts, which seemed to help the players and their wives feel more comfortable, giving them an opportunity to relax without the badgering of fans.

During dinner, they asked about my cancer and myself. The father of one of the players had recently been diagnosed with colon cancer. "I wish I knew more about that type of cancer," I apologized, "but if there is anything I can do to help? I will be happy to talk to my doctors and see if they could offer you any assistance."

We talked more about doctors and hospitals, comparing them, and how they treated their patients. The wives were particularly interested in how Cathi was caring for me. At the end of the evening, we all parted as friends, better for the experience.

Through the years, I participated in four other softball game fundraisers, but the first one always held a special place in my memory.

29
Entering the SS Battlefield

1993—I knew that I would be eligible for Social Security benefits. Shortly after the first Worker's Comp court date in April, I went to the local Social Security office to file my claim. Mrs. Cook was the name of the clerk who helped me. She was a kind woman, winning my confidence with her sincerity. She wore a gold guardian angel on her lapel and a gold cross hung around her neck. She seemed earnestly concerned about my health, and openly told me that she would ask her guardian angel to watch over me and that she would include me in her prayers.

While filling out the forms for me, she carefully covered the complex regulations of the agency. One of the policies stuck in my mind.

"Should you begin to receive any other benefits, Richard," the clerk explained, "you need to report it in a timely manner. Benefits from other sources will affect the amount you receive from Social Security."

"I have just started my Worker's Comp trial," I shared with her. "Provided I win the case, and let's hope I do, is that the kind of thing you are talking about."

"Exactly," Mrs. Cook answered. "When you receive those benefits, you need to report it in writing. Well, I think we have all the information from you that we will need." She had begun to organize the sheets of paper. "Richard, please call me anytime should you have a question or don't understand something. I will help you in any way that I can, and I will pray for your recovery."

"Thanks," I said, touched by her kindness. "I appreciate your help with all this and especially your prayers."

I assumed, as many do, that I would begin receiving the benefits within a month. It was not until five months later that the interminable red tape of the federal government at last netted me a check. It was retroactive to my filing date, but by the time I received the $6300, our debts surpassed that amount.

30
Mainstay of the Arsenal

1993—To add to my debt load, in July, 1993, my medical insurance ran out, and I had to go on Hayward's Local 210 Union COBRA plan. This meant that I was responsible for the monthly payments of $211. Additionally, I had to pay for all of my medicines out of pocket, then submit requests for reimbursement. As with most insurers, these reimbursements took months of fighting and often included threatening attorney letters. But considering the enormity of my medical bills, I felt that it was little to pay.

What the insurance would not cover were the vast amounts of vitamins and free form amino acids I was taking. The doctors had determined that one reason why my body had been able to withstand so many treatments and medications was the result of my healthy diet and the supplements I had taken while in training during the weight lifting competitions in my late teens and early twenties. My body contained high amounts of CD36 positive T-helper cells, which was believed to be what helped me withstand the onslaught of the harsh chemotherapy treatments. It was only logical that I would continue with this regimen now that I was on the treatments, but at the cost of $400 per month.

I was taking such massive quantities of vitamins and supplements, it was necessary for me to keep a written list, with amounts and when I was to take each of them. The list, which I tacked up on the wall, also helped me to remember to take them. The affects of the therapies were always a consideration. As I needed, I would update the master list.

One such partial list read:

NAME	AMOUNT	SCHEDULE
Vitamin A	10,000 i.u.	1 pill 1X day A.M.
B-Complex (1000 mg.)	5-7,000 mg.	2 pills 3X day Not on Treament Day
Vitamin C (1500 mg.)	30-40,000 mg. daily total	10+ pills 3X day
Vitamin E (1000 i.u.)	4-8,000 i.u.	2 pills 3X day
Calcium (1000 mg.)	4,000 mg.	1 pill 4X day
Lethicin (1000 mg.)	3,000 mg.	1 pill 3X day after meals
Ginseng (300 mg.)	3,600 mg.	4 pills 3X day
Free form amino acids (5000 mg.)	30,000 mg.	2 pills 3X day
Ultra Co/Q10 (100 mg.)	300 mg.	1 pill 3X day
Cat's Claw (500 mg.)	1,500 mg.	1 pill 3X day
Magnesium (300 mg.)	900 mg.	1 pill 3X day
Potassium	1,000 mg.	1 pill 3X day
Selenium (1000 mg.)	1,000 mg.	1 pill 1X day A.M.
Flaxseed Oil	2 teaspoons	1 teaspoon 2X day
Apple cider vinegar	2 teaspoons	1 teaspoon 2X day
Floressence Tea	1 cup	1 cup midmorning
Maitake Tea	8 -12 oz.	8 -12 oz. before bed

In the margin was scribbled, "shark cartilage 8-10,000 mg day." In 1992, when I first tried the shark cartilage treatment, it was still a somewhat new concept in cancer therapy. Dr. Charles B. Simone of the Simone Cancer Center in Lawrenceville, New Jersey spearheaded my initial nutrition schedule.

Dr. Simone conducted a thorough investigation of the functions of my body and my reactions to my treatments. By conducting intensive blood, urine, and liver testing he was able to determine a precise nutrition schedule that coincided with my treatments. Dr. Simone was one of this country's forerunners in this concept who has training in radiation therapy, chemotherapy, tumor immunology, cancer detection and prevention, and nutrition.

His extensive background enabled him to not only develop a comprehensive vitamin regime for me, but also an intensive and somewhat experimental "shark cartilage" therapy program that coincided with Dr. Lambert's planned chemotherapy treatment schedule.

Unfortunately, the "shark cartilage" program did nothing for my condition. Conversely, I learned the importance of a patient seeking all possibilities of therapy to cure or subside one's condition. I experienced firsthand the vast benefits of Dr. Simone's treatments.

All of his patients, including me, became considerably healthier, even if just for a short time, and for those whose course was predetermined by our creator, at least received some time to put life's responsibilities in order.

I often bought the large, economy-sized bottle of 1500 mg. Vitamin C tablets and emptied it within five days. I would occasionally try 50,000 mg., but that amount normally irritated my stomach.

I brewed my own Maitake Tea, which enhanced the immune system response. The tea was brewed from a black mushroom and the process was time consuming; a proper brew could take as long as eight hours. Not counting the liquids, I often took 65 to 75 pills each day.

The vitamins became a barometer for me. I could tell when I was healing internally by my reaction to Vitamin C, specifically. If I got diarrhea or stomach aches, I knew my body was healing and did not require as much, therefore I would cut back on the vitamin.

Marty, the pharmacist at the local Shop Rite food store could not believe the amounts of vitamins, minerals and prescription drugs I was ingesting.

"Richard," Marty said one day, "you're always so happy. You're the most positive cancer patient I've ever met, and I've met quite a few."

"Well, I just got through puking a few hours ago," I grinned, "and I feel great now."

Marty was not the only person who admired my enduring spirit. The doctors were impressed with my upbeat attitude. They also respected my awareness of my body. They encouraged me to continue with the vitamins and minerals, knowing that I was better able to gauge what my body needed than anyone.

Drs. Martinez and 'Ricky' introduced me to a simple technique to judge how my body would react to specific supplements and medicines.

"We call it the 'arm test,'" Dr. Martinez told me.

I was intrigued. "Well, how do you do it?"

"You simply hold the product or medicine in question in one hand and keep it at your side," Martinez demonstrated as he spoke, "and hold your other arm straight out, laterally extending it up directly from your side. If I am able to push your arm down with ease, it is not good for you. If you are able to resist the pressure, it is good for you."

"Come on, Doc," I scoffed, certain that the doctor was teasing me, "you're joking. That can't work!"

"No, it is not a joke," Martinez assured me. "Let's find Dr. 'Ricky,' he'll show you, he's amazing at this."

Certain that the doctors were playing a trick on me; I smiled expectantly, but followed Martinez into Dr. 'Ricky's' office.

"Doc.," Martinez said to Dr. 'Ricky' as he walked through the office door, "Richard does not believe what I told him about the arm test. You have to show him how it works."

"You two are pulling my leg," I grinned.

"Not this time, Richard," Dr. 'Ricky' told me. "Let me show you." Dr. 'Ricky' opened a desk drawer and took out a bottle of Vitamin C tablets. "Here Richard, hold some of these in your hand. Wait a minute. Let me make sure your body's electrical fields are stable."

The doctor placed his hand on my chest and rubbed in a circular motion where the thymus gland would be found. Then he took his index finger and gave me a stiff pop between the eyes at the center of the forehead. This, he said, was the center meridian for the brain and the impact shock was like hitting the reboot button on your computer.

Still skeptical and waiting for the punch line, I held out my hand. Dr. 'Ricky' poured a few of the tablets in my palm.

"Now," instructed Dr. 'Ricky,' "hold your arm straight out to your side and resist my pressure."

I complied as Dr. 'Ricky' pushed down on my outstretched arm, but was unable to budge it.

"God, I could do chin-ups on that arm," Dr. 'Ricky' teased. He stepped over to a shelf and picked up a bottle of Oxsoralen Ultra. "Okay, Richard, we all know that the chemotherapy that you are taking is, in essence, a poison to the body. Hold this in your hand and let's try it again."

I dutifully took the second bottle and stretched out my arm. As the doctor pushed down on my arm only slightly, I found that I was not able to resist.

"Damn," I said in disbelief. "Try that again."

This time, determined to resist the pressure, I steeled my arm. To make a point, Dr. 'Ricky' took only his index finger and pushed the arm down.

"I don't believe it," I exclaimed. "Does it work with everything?"

Over the next few minutes, we tried everything Dr. 'Ricky' had available in the office. I found that I didn't even have to hold the Oxsoralen Ultra; simply standing close to it achieved the same results.

Martinez spoke up. "You see, we were not joking." It is an easy way to tell what you should take and if it's done right, it works on almost everyone. "All the vitamins you are taking, I would imagine they would all prove to be very good for you. If not, change brands, *preferably to one that is hypoallergenic.*"

He was right, of course. Cathi and I tested everything that night. The chemotherapy medications all confirmed the validity of the test. They were poisons to my body, but poisons that were hopefully destroying the cancer.

I was always careful about what I ate and drank; well, almost always. I was not allowed to drink any type of alcoholic beverage during the first two years of therapy. But as my body adjusted to the medicines, and the treatments were decreased from four to two per week, I could not help but treat myself to an occasional beer or glass of wine.

This could have been dangerous, but I was careful. My last treatment for the week was on Thursday, and this allowed my body 48 hours to clean itself out. If I had a drink on Saturday, I also had 48 hours for the alcohol to be digested and eliminated. Everything in my life was based around my treatments and medicines. My body did not always comply with this theory.

My occasional splurging with alcohol was not the only product that caused great concern. The medicines often reacted with other food products and non-alcoholic drinks. If I had any type of warm or hot fluid, either when taking or while on one of my medicines, I would become violently ill.

The heated fluid causes the medicine to be digested at a much more rapid rate, causing it to shock the system and overload it too quickly. My body protected itself by causing me to become ill and regurgitate the substance.

Sometimes, even the vitamins could have an adverse affects. Vitamin B was one such culprit. Although this vitamin was typically part of my daily regime, the doctors advised me not to take it the day of treatments.

However, all the other vitamins and minerals were very important for me to take while doing therapy. All forms of chemotherapy do a great deal of damage to the body.

Chemotherapy is designed to destroy cancerous cells, or cells that have mutated. In the process of destroying those cells, non-cancerous, healthy cells are also destroyed.

Vitamins, healthy foods, and exercise were crucial in helping my body to rejuvenate itself, even if it is only to sustain more treatments.

31
Changing the Concept of Medicine

During one of my routine visits with Lambert, the doctor asked me into his office. "I want to go over some things with you, Rich," the doctor told me, "so that you can better understand how and why this cancer got started."

I was always eager to learn what I could from this brilliant man, and I settled into a chair, waiting to absorb what I could about my disease.

"First, let me tell you," Lambert began, "that your case is most likely going to be included in a book that I am working on with many other doctors from NATO's advanced scientific studies program. I am calling your case the 'Thymus By-Pass Model.' Before you showed up, it was only a theory that we had about the progression of the disease. But your medical and work history strengthened the theory. Until I had all the facts, I was not willing to say that the causal factor of the CTCL was the accident you were involved in at the plant. As you know from my testimony at your Workman's Comp trial, I attribute your June, 86 accident, the "basketball explosion," as being at least 70 percent the causative factor of your cancer. This I also believe is the accident that accelerated and intensified the effects of the chemical exposures you received at your job. Let me explain."

I leaned forward, intent on what the professor was about to say.

"Let me give you a brief definition of the Thymus By-Pass Model: I am proposing that some cases of CTCL are not due to the malignant clonal proliferation of thymus derived T-lymphocytes, or lymphocytes that should come from the thymus gland. Instead it's an error in the formation process where bone marrow derived precursors of T-cells "Bypass" the thymus and travel directly to the skin where an aberrant proliferation of cells occurs. This aberrant proliferation is a deviation from what is right in the process of the body producing Thymus cells. The deviation in the cellular process was most likely promoted by the body's attempt to produce self-antigens in the skin when you received the chemical burns. What this means is that the sudden shock from the chemical burns and fumes caused the body to malfunction at the skin and, the antigen-like cells or bone marrow cells evolved, over some years, into the malignant cancer you now have. Therefore it did not start as a T-cell lymphoma or thymus derived cells, it evolved into one."

"We will never know how quickly you would have developed cancer without the assistance of the main accident. We are fairly sure that you would have eventually, due to the chemicals you worked with on a daily basis and your first incident of February, 1986, when the fumes shocked your body. Many of the chemicals you worked with were carcinogenic and mutagenic. We know that carcinogens may or may not cause cancer. It depends upon the individual's body, exposures and time duration of exposure. It was the mutagens, which are cancer-causing agents, such as liquid styrene, methyl ethyl ketone, methylene chloride, and benzene, that would have caused your cells to mutate, quite possibly at the time of the primary accident in June, thus developing the foundation work, or evolution of your cancer."

"Dr. Gochfeld spent a considerable amount of time researching the possible causative factors of your cancer and we both agree that there were three primary conditions that hastened the progress of the cancer. The first condition was *inhalation*. You inhaled both carcinogenic and mutagenic fumes or gases, and in several different ways. As you were making the soaking mixture and the injection mixture, you were breathing in the fumes associated with the chemicals. This alone would have had a slow effect on your body. Next, you took those mixtures and added heat to them, making them even more potent. With the failure of the machine and the explosion, the gases were in their most volatile state. You were inhaling these toxic fumes and they were possibly affecting your bloodstream via the lung tissue and the process of oxygen being introduced into the blood."

"Second, was *absorption*. When you were cleaning the mixture of chemicals off your skin after the accident, you used Triclean (trichlorethylene). Triclean opens the pores of the skin, not only allowing the solvent to enter the body, but also the chemicals, which you were trying to remove. Additionally, the heat from the injection mixture opened the pores, allowing another avenue for chemical absorption and introduction to epidermal cells. The epidermis, being the outer layers of the skin."

"The third condition was *penetration*, by far the worst. Penetration meant that the chemicals got past the epidermis and into the dermal layer of your skin. The skin, specifically the epidermis, is the primary protector of the body. Penetration can occur through a cut or lesion in the skin. There was a picture of you holding up the basketball that showed a large cut on your knuckle. The mutagens penetrated through that cut. Also, the burns you sustained from the heated mixture provided additional penetration, multiplying the effects. This was clearly evident due to the precise location and distribution of the MF lesions on your body."

"Now, in most patients, we are looking for one of these conditions. With your case, we got all three."

"Kind of like three strikes, you're out," I interjected.

"That's right," Lambert nodded, and continued with his explanation. "The thymus also produces "T" helper cells that assist the body in warding off ailments. However, in your case, by instantaneously having your body shocked through inhalation, absorption and the penetration process, the cells actually mutated on the area of the body that was most affected. In your case, it was the burn sites. The bone marrow cells did not travel through the thymus; the malignant cells were formed on the skin due to the inflammatory conditions. Hence the name 'thymus by-pass.'"

"Studies have shown that there is a five to ten year evolution before these mutated cells manifest. Your cancer was right on target. The first of the rashes showed up in '91."

"After the T-cells become malignant and proliferate, they may circulate and then go back to the skin at different sites. And that is exactly what we have witnessed with your body. This is why every time we gain control of your cancer and then reduce your treatments, it comes right back. I also still believe that your primary burn site on your right hip is acting as a *"feeder"* site to your cancer. You know most of the other doctors are now agreeing with me, including Dr. Gochfeld."

"So what you're saying, Doc," I concluded, "is that because of my daily exposures to chemicals at Hayward and the minor accident in February, 1986, I might have, or probably would have, developed cancer through the normal evolutionally process of the body, but the June accident made it happen a lot faster and with a lot more severity through a non-typical process of the body."

"That's correct."

It was a lot to digest, but confirmation from someone such as Lambert made me more determined to find some justice for my condition.

32
New Strategist for the Civil Trial

1993—In 1993, when the defense had offered no arguments that would withstand the strength of our case, John Reeves explained to me about the New Jersey Worker's Comp laws. "Simply, the law states," John explained, "that, by filing the Worker's Comp claim, you cannot then sue your employer for punitive damages."

"Workman's Comp is devised to virtually guarantee the employee benefits and income for a work related injury. The injury just has to happen at the work place environment. If you wanted to sue Hayward for punitive damages you would have to prove that Hayward knew that the way you handled the chemicals and that accident would cause your cancer. There is no way they could have known that. In fact, I believe DuPont Chemicals is the only Company in New Jersey that has been sued for their direct knowledge of, and intentionally withholding information that caused cancer in an employee."

The deflated look on my face spoke volumes. "The bastards are going to get away with killing me slowly and painfully," I muttered.

In order to give me some hope, John hurriedly added, "You can, however, bring suit against the manufacturers and chemical companies whose products were involved in the accident." John detected a glimmer of hope on my face. "But Richard, my firm does not want to take that type of case. It's just not one we prefer to take on. Plus, I am too deeply involved in your Worker's Comp case. You will have to find other representation for your civil suit. I can make some recommendations for you."

I only nodded. It was a lot for me to digest. In my mind, I held Hayward responsible for my illness. But now, because of the way the law was written, I would have to change my thought processes to include the manufacturer of the injection-molding machine, Cincinnati Milacron, and chemical companies such as FibreGlass-Evercoat, Cadillac Plastics, Dow Chemical, and other smaller companies.

Plus, John, whom I had grown to respect, would not be handling the case. Could I possibly find another attorney I could trust? I was disappointed that John would not be able to represent me, but I was encouraged that there might still be a way to get some vindication. We would have to begin a new search for a firm to handle the civil suit.

"One last thing, Richard," John advised me, "I would suggest that you get started on the civil case right away."

My sister stepped in and put her efforts to assisting Cathi in the quest for a suitable attorney. A co-worker of my sister, familiar with my situation, recommended Art Rush from the firm of Bryan and Clark.

Cathi and I were busy interviewing many firms that were referenced by friends, family members, doctors and even previous attorneys. By now we had become methodical and astute in the questioning and evaluation process.

Cathi and I met with Art within a couple of weeks. He reminded us of Santa Claus, with his short, stocky, round body and big smile. We both liked him and during the interview he appeared very anxious to bring the case to trial.

He was compassionate and intelligent; there was one piece of information that helped us to make our decision. Art had settled a $1.2 million lawsuit against Cincinnati Milacron that year, and that meant that he was familiar with how Cincinnati Milacron worked. That kind of information could be invaluable in court.

Art also commented during the interview "that nothing in Richard's case appeared to be so insurmountable that it could not be tried before a jury, especially with the medical experts Richard had supporting him." Art was hired to represent us in the civil suit.

He began right away gathering names and information that would be needed to prepare the case. Together, we comprised a list of people that would be deposed. I, of course, was at the head of the list, followed by a machine design expert and my primary doctors.

Art wanted the names of other employees who were there the day of the accident, either present at the time of the accident or who might have been involved in the cleanup. This was a time consuming process and a lengthy list of basically all of my immediate management personnel and all the maintenance personnel in that day of the accident. Art justifiably included Cathi in the suit, since her life and well-being was also drastically affected by my illness.

I quickly recognized that this trial was going to take place on a much larger playing field. We were going to be up against some huge companies. But I also knew that my case was solid. My life had been destroyed due to the negligence of these companies and justice would prevail. On September 24, 1994, Art filed a products liability action, asserting 10 different counts, against 13 different companies and their subsidiaries.

33
Witness Tampering?

"Guimo, how are you doing?" It was Eddie on the phone.

"Doing good, Eddie. What's up?" I heard from Eddie often. In fact, Eddie was about the only person I now heard from who worked at Hayward.

"Some bad news, guy," Eddie began. "Dwight was involved in a motorcycle accident today and is in intensive care."

Dwight worked in the maintenance department at Hayward and had been the person who cleaned the lead screw of the injection-molding machine after the June 1986 accident. He was one of my key witnesses.

"What happened?" I asked, shocked by the news.

"He was coming back from lunch on his motorcycle and a garbage truck hit him when he was going through an intersection. He's in really bad shape. They're probably going to operate on him again today. He's got huge chunks of flesh taken out of his arms and legs."

I could picture Dwight in my mind. "It sounds really bad," I said. "Where did it happen?"

"It was really close to the plant, and they were both going pretty fast," Eddie said.

"Why would they be going fast? Those streets are all filled with kids," I asked. It all sounded very suspicious to me.

"Ya got me," Eddie replied. "But I thought you should know since he's one of your witnesses."

Dwight was going to be important to my case, but I still had Eddie. He had repaired the pneumatics and hydraulics on the machine. And, there was Billy, who had witnessed the accident. "How's Billy?" I asked.

"He's pretty freaked about it," Eddie responded. "I don't know if he's going to be willing to testify now. I think imaginations might be running wild now, but who knows."

"I'll talk to him," I said. "How are you doing?"

"Hell man," Eddie assured me, "I'm okay. It's gonna take more than that to scare me off."

I appreciated the loyalty Eddie displayed. "Thanks," I said. "But in the meantime, watch your back. This may get nasty!"

I knew that Eddie would stick by me. It was Billy I was worried about. Billy had been in the huge room during the accident and had suffered from the effects of the toxic fumes, also.

As good a witness as Billy might have been, I was more worried about the man's health. Billy worked with the same chemicals and plastics as I had, and often had bad allergic reactions to the substances. I had even noticed a rash on Billy's face and arms that looked very similar to the rashes I had suffered. I felt compelled to share this information about Billy with my doctors.

"Tell him to come see us," Lambert instructed. "He won't be billed. We'd just like to check him out; no forms or anything."

Billy despised the idea of seeing doctors. It took a lot of convincing on my part to get Billy to come with me, but I finally succeeded. Billy was obviously nervous. Before Lambert showed up, Billy got up to leave. "Listen, Rich," he said, his eyes full of fear, "if I'm going to die, I just want to go. I don't want to do what you're doing." And, he turned around and walked out.

After Dwight's accident, I tried to call Billy, but all of my attempts were refused. I finally had to admit to myself that Billy was not going to testify, and there was no way that I could force him. It was a civil case, not a criminal case; therefore, even if he were subpoenaed he would not have to testify due to his fifth constitutional right. I would have to be satisfied with the people who were willing to help me.

34
Evolving Strategies

April 1994—In April, the doctors reduced my PUVA treatments to twice a week, but added the topical nitrogen cream. A month later, we reduced it to once a week. This was an attempt to scientifically determine if we were gaining control over the disease.

None of us were satisfied with the results we were getting. By early June, we stopped the PUVA treatments all together, but continued with the topical nitrogen and the monitoring of the cellular processes in my tissue and blood.

This halting now served two important purposes: first it gave the medical team the opportunity to thoroughly evaluate my progress without the intervening effects of chemotherapy; and second, it gave me the chance to exercise more vigorously to regain strength for future therapies. Drs. Martinez, Levy, Weiss and Zuel all confirmed that my body needed this time to rejuvenate. My liver function had dropped off substantially and my heart's mitral valve was now fluttering, causing me chest pains.

Later that month, I began to develop bumps and tumors over my entire body. Dr. Yang added Tetracycline, an antibiotic, to the medications. After only a month off of the chemotherapy treatments, the doctors started me back on them twice a week.

We were trying everything we could, but I continued to develop plaques and tumors in different areas of my body. The medications would help temporarily, clearing the problem, but then something else would show up.

The Tetracycline caused me to itch severely. I continued to suffer from the affects of the chemotherapy, with sensitivity in my eyes, headaches and ringing, or Tinnitus, in my ears and the occasional adverse reactions to the treatments. Nausea and disorientation continued to be commonplace in my life.

The continuous urgency of my medical well being, added to the pressures of our financial situation and, compounded by the stresses of two legal suits, did nothing to help the relationship between Cathi and I. The constant pain I suffered made me irritable and antagonistic, a side of me that was, again, not usually being displayed to the outside world.

Cathi was most often the recipient of these mood swings and absorbed them with the instilled strength of understanding that I was suffering the effects of my treatments. My family members often, inadvertently, would interfere, always taking my side and causing Cathi to feel like an outsider in her own home.

I was the patient, and no one wanted to do what I did on a daily basis. But too often it was forgotten the strength and endurance that Cathi needed to maintain a job at Makita and the emotionally destructive job of caring for me. Despite frequent arguments, Cathi was still standing strong.

35
A New Weapon in Medicine's Arsenal

July 1994—In July 1994, Dr. Lambert presented Cathi and I with a frightening, yet extraordinary offer. "For some time now, I have been suggesting that we try to remove the primary source of your cancer. It seems that no matter what form of therapy we try, we cannot control it. As you know, I believe this is due to certain places on your body that serve as "feeders" to the cancer, primarily the area on your right hip".

"We have developed in conjunction with a Japanese industrialist who we also believe to have CTCL, a prototype of a machine which has the ability to scan and pinpoint cancerous cells in the human body."

"We only began to seriously think of this device when we started working on your case. There are so many new technological procedures that held possibilities, all possibilities that we needed to address. We have never witnessed such a hyper-proliferation of cancer without the person dying a relatively quick death. You present us with the opportunity to gain a better understanding of the disease, an opportunity that has never been available before. The information we could gain from this procedure could be priceless in cancer research. It could assist in breakthrough technologies that many scientists have spent years researching."

Well, the doctor certainly had my attention now. Was there a hope of controlling this life-threatening condition? I leaned forward to listen more attentively.

Dr. Lambert explained about the machine. "I call it a *'scanning multi-focal cellular image analyzer.'* I suppose we'll have to devise a better name for it. The basics of how it works; is that cancer cell information is programmed into the computer. While each individual has a unique genetic structure, cancer has familiar and even predictable traits, regardless of whom it affects. We have gathered and will include information from leading cancer facilities all over the world."

"Once the information is installed, cell information from a specific patient, derived from blood and tissue samples, will be entered to give us the parameters necessary to identify the offending areas."

"What I am suggesting," Lambert's voice had taken on a soft, caring tone, "is an experimental operation. With the help of the prototype, we would locate the most adversely affected areas in your body and remove them. This will allow us to eliminate the 'feeder' areas, subsequently enabling us to control or destroy your disease with fewer treatments."

"Please understand that this procedure is highly experimental. It has not been done before on anyone in your condition. There is no way we can guarantee the outcome. We could gain invaluable information, but because it would be such a radical invasion of your already ravaged body, it could kill you."

"This is not going to be an easy decision. And, it is not one that I expect you to make right away. It is going to take some immense soul-searching. I will educate you on the technology we have used in creating the prototype, and on all the drawbacks to the procedure. After you fully understand what I am proposing, then I encourage you to contact other doctors and scientists to get their opinions."

I realized that I had been holding my breath. As I took a deep breath, a flood of emotions inundated my thoughts. Even with the little amount of information I had, my mind was already at war with itself. It was going to be a classic struggle between the good for mankind and self-preservation.

But, was it really? I had defied the odds so far; having stayed alive fifteen months longer than expected, I still lived with the knowledge that any day the cancer could explode, causing my death.

"Tell me everything you can, Doc. I would really like to have a better understanding."

For the next few hours, professor Lambert took the time to show me the machine and even some cells that he had been studying. (Many were mine.)

Together we talked things through and I asked a multitude of questions. Lambert explained his concern with anesthesia. The belief in the medical community is that when a person suffering from a full body cancer, such as CTCL, is placed under anesthesia the body falls into a deep sleep, or regressed state, causing the internal functions to slow down dramatically.

Additionally, this deeply regressed state allows the brain functions to "relax" preventing it from signaling the proper cellular functions that ward off diseases. Therefore, when an incision is made, the body can be shocked to the point that the cancer can grow rapidly, or metastasize, at an even faster uncontrollable rate. Because the immune system is slowed substantially, and oxygen is introduced, the cancer is quicker to respond, again, giving the cancer more opportunity to spread.

He went into more detail about the machine, trying to explain it in a format that I would retain. The professor wanted me to be able to take the information to Cathi and my parents and tell it in a way that they, too, could understand.

I asked about the significance of the knowledge to be gained from the surgery. Lambert emphasized that there was no way to know how far-reaching the research might be, but it would be unprecedented.

As I often did when I had an important task to perform, I set about methodically calling doctors and scientists throughout the world, individuals recognized to be the leading authorities in the field of oncology and lymphomas. I quickly developed a pattern to my approach. I would explain who I was and then describe the proposed operation and ask for their opinion.

Responses were consistent. Everyone I spoke with was pessimistic about the outcome of such a radical procedure and some added that I would be better off by proceeding with Total Skin Electron Beam Therapy (TSE).

Only after receiving their initial response would I tell them that the procedure was Lambert's idea, and would be organized and directed by him.

Once again the responses were consistent. With the mention of Lambert, every expert reversed their previous position and expressed their approval. Had anyone else proposed this surgery, they would have lost credibility almost instantly. Dr. Lambert's solid reputation and expertise swayed their judgment and erased any doubts. In addition, almost every doctor I spoke with told me that the operation would produce significant information about my body's reaction and likely promote research to find a cure.

I spoke with Dr. Lee, who had been one of Dr. Lambert's students. She was now working out of Stanford, and was becoming a respected scientist in her own right. She told me she was honored that I would call her, and emphasized that her background was nothing comparable to that of Dr. Lambert's. Nonetheless, she offered a wealth of information. She reiterated the possibility of the failure of the operation, and reminded me that an incredible amount of information was certainly being derived from me while I was alive.

Dr. Foon of the University of Kentucky had already been using my cell lines and tissue samples in an attempt to create anti-viruses and other forms of laboratory-generated retroviruses, which could stimulate the body to defeat diseases like leukemia. "The knowledge that could be obtained from the operation could also accelerate these outcomes. But again, we can do this without you dying from an operation."

I would end such conversations with each of the scientists with one final question. "If you were me, would you trust Dr. Lambert with this procedure?"

Without exception the response was the same. "Yes, only Lambert."

I was all too aware of the possible impact this operation would make in cancer research, but at what cost to me? Was I heroic enough to sacrifice myself? I knew that the burden of the decision once more rested squarely on my shoulders. I talked with Cathi and my parents, and as much as I valued their input, I would decide the final answer. Was it the prospect of a speedier death that I feared? The disease that was daily overtaking my body was working to that end anyway. Did I refuse the operation and continue as before, never knowing the direction or ferocity the cancer might take? Or, did I opt for the risk of death versus an opportunity to gain more control, and longer life expectancy, contingent on my body's response?

At the time of Lamberts proposal, the unknown outcome of the Worker's Comp. and civil trial also prejudiced my decision. I wanted to wait to at least get a decision from the Workman's Comp. trial before committing to such a surgery. Many scientists had openly admitted that they did not understand why CTCL acted in such a disparate manner among some of its victims, and typically could not determine the cause.

By far, the greatest causative factor in my development of this cancer was environmental influences, despite the failure of America's legal system and big business to recognize this fact. My personal ambition was to at least live long enough to see Hayward lose.

I truly believed that pharmaceutical companies do not fund programs that seek a cure. They fund programs that seek the discovery of a treatment that includes pharmaceuticals or medicines that allows a patient to live with a disease. Full disclosure of the causative factors and potential cures is unfavorable and detrimental to their financial interests especially when doctors promote nutrition.

I wanted my case to be recorded as another instance where doctors attribute the development of cancer to the human body's exposure to chemicals.

Every response, every thought added to my dilemma. And, as only those who have experienced the responsibility of a life altering decision, my mind began adapting and working with heightened clarity. I began to see beyond the doldrums of daily life and to search for a deeper meaning.

I became more intuitive and my sense of purpose was becoming more defined. Small things influenced my thoughts: a movie, a comment. I began to feel compelled to go through with the operation, knowing that my sacrifice could answer the question of my purpose in this life.

Even before the answer had crystallized in my consciousness, I was preparing for the outcome. I began with the process of forgiving and renewing relationships. I attempted to better understand the other person's point of view. I made it a point to inconspicuously spend time with each individual in my family and circle of friends. I felt the desire to correct any ill feelings I might have intentionally caused and strengthen the bond with those important in my life.

A life-long dream of mine had been to experience glacial ice climbing. Together with my older brother, we planned a trip into the icy wilderness of the Northwest. But he was becoming uncomfortable with the potential dangers of the pilgrimage. "I don't want to be the one to have to carry you out in a body bag," he explained to me. "Maybe we should rethink this."

Cathi, too, shared his concern. She understood my need to experience this dream, but worried about my well-being. After some discussion, the trip itinerary was changed to a grand tour of California's Mammoth Mountain and Yosemite National Park.

This relieved some of Cathi's apprehensions, and because she understood my reasons for this adventure, she mentally shelved her concerns and helped with the planning. The question of what supplies and medicines I should take with me was a big one. Should I take back-ups? Were there medical facilities available in case of emergency? Was I physically up to the rigors of hiking and camping?

The trip proved to be one of the greatest experiences in my young life. The awesome grandeur of nature quieted my thoughts and nurtured my spirit. We brothers hiked and fished and camped in the shadow of God's handiwork. Our adventures took us through rain, snow, and a small earthquake.

My thoughts were continually on Cathi as we trekked through the beauty of the wilderness. I could feel her by my side, just as she had been throughout my entire ordeal. I knew I was extremely fortunate to have her trust and loyalty.

The peace that comes with acceptance blanketed me. I knew what I must do.

When I arrived home, I called Dr. Lambert. "Go ahead and schedule the operation, doc. Let's see how this machine of yours performs."

"Are you sure, Richard? You understand all the possibilities?" The doctor was torn between the thrill of exploration and the care for this patient who had become like a son to him.

"I'm sure, doc. Let's 'boldly go where no man has gone before.'"

I could tell that the professor smiled at the reference, and agreed quietly, "Okay, let's. I'll get everything set up and let you know when I have a date. There will be a lot of preparation and you are going to have to meet up with a surgeon that I have picked out specifically for this. Also, I want you in here a few times a week so that my interns can monitor your body more closely. And Richard, you know you can change your mind at any time up until we put you under. There is no pressure and I want you to understand that I would be just as comfortable as if it were my son. I'm going to take care of you."

The highly experimental operation was set for January 18, 1995, a little more than two months away. We had just received the ruling on the Worker's Comp. case, and I was hopeful that I would soon begin to receive the benefits. However, the appeal quashed any hopes for a quick remedy to some of our financial problems.

I instructed Art Rush to put the work on the civil trial on hold. "If I make it through this, Art," I told him honestly, "and, there is a big 'if' about it, I will have to recuperate from the surgery. Someone will let you know the outcome. Hopefully, it will be me."

As every medical and legal professional that had come before him in this saga, Art had grown to respect the attitude and spirit I possessed. "I'll be waiting for your call," he said, blessing the future with his positive response.

In spite of the certainty I felt in my resolution to proceed with the operation, doubts would still creep into my thoughts. All of the world-renowned experts had initially told me that the plan was foolhardy. Their faith and belief in Dr. Lambert's abilities was the only thing that had swayed them. But what if they were all wrong? I didn't want to die. In my bouts with fear and anger, I would try to reason my way out of my decision. Why should I try to "save the world?" Fifty percent of the people out there were assholes, anyway.

During these periods of negativity, I would have to force myself to stop. I trusted Dr. Lambert, and I knew I was doing the right thing, both for myself and possibly others. If I only knew, either way, what was going to happen, I thought, I could prepare for it.

36
Soul Bonds Reach New Realms

November & December 1994—In the two months prior to the surgery, the bond between Cathi and I intensified to the point that our dreams began to parallel one another.

What Cathi didn't realize was that I was practicing "Lucid Dreaming." Before going to sleep I would concentrate on her, focusing on understanding what question she was thinking, how she was feeling emotionally about losing a husband (and knowing when it was to happen) and intentionally using my rational thoughts to recognize when I was dreaming, I would have control over the events and their outcome. I also realized that this must be used only for positive thoughts and outcome.

One night, I purposely willed myself into a dream Cathi was having. She was sitting in a green reed grass field, overlooking the ocean. I walked up to her and began talking to her. She asked what I was doing there. I replied, "I wanted to visit you in your dream."

The next morning as we lay in each other's arms, I asked, "So, how were your dreams last night?"

"I dreamed about you," she told me. "I was in a field close to the ocean talking to you."

I smiled. "And, I told you that I wanted to visit you in your dream."

Cathi was amazed at this remarkable connection we had made. She was not aware that this type of dreaming was possible.

Christmas had always been a special time to Cathi and I, but the holiday season of 1994 took on a different meaning. There was a strong likelihood that this could be my last holiday season.

Sometimes doubtful, I was most often at peace with my decision, knowing that should I not make it through the surgery, I had made a long-lasting contribution to humanity or at least the scientific community. My life would have been meaningful.

Although difficult, Cathi understood and supported me in my decision. Her prayer was that I would survive, but she prepared as best she could for the worst. And, she had made up her mind that she would sacrifice everything to make what could possibly be my last days enjoyable and full of love.

She began by decorating the entire house. The large fireplace was bedecked with poinsettias, holly and trains. It created a Currier & Ives effect, with the fire blazing and the park scene through the huge picture window covered with snow. The tree, stunning with lights and decorations, was encircled at the base by her favorite Lionel train. The home emanated the warmth of holiday cheer.

My sister had rented a home in Vermont for the holiday and invited the family to spend it the mountains. Cheryl typically used the holiday for travel but this season included the approach that "this may be Richard's last and he likes to ski; what better way for us to all be together." This, although sounding, and definitely intended, to be pleasant for all, broke Cathi's heart. I never turned down a chance to ski and Cheryl knew that.

Cathi wanted to spend her last holiday with me, just some "quality time alone." Cathi (and I), planned on sharing gifts around the well-decorated tree and having friends over for relaxing drinks in the hot tub.

But with my excitement to go ski, she did not want to deny me what might be my last time. Cathi considered these actions for what they were, selfish. Her feelings of what this holiday was to her were intentionally or innocently (?) overlooked. Gracefully, she declined and waited until the 28th for my return.

Upon my arrival home Cathi greeted me with her innate strength that only love could provide. She was pleased that the family ski trip now contained memories of pleasure that spanned generations from the grandparents to the nieces and nephews. She focused on the upcoming days and the New Year's Eve Party that were spent at home with our friends and me.

One week before the surgery, I was roused from a deep sleep. Something had made the bed shake and awakened me. I looked at the clock. It read 3 A.M. Cathy was sleeping soundly next to me.

At the foot of the bed, I watched as the vision of my long-deceased grandfather, Oscar, appeared before me. This old man, with whom I had been so close as a child, stood looking over me. Although no words were spoken, I heard the message strong and true, "Everything will be alright."

To assure myself that I wasn't dreaming, I did a reality check. I looked around the room, I touched the bed, and I touched Cathi. The image remained. I was convinced that I was fully awake and conscious.

Thanks Gramp, I thought, and the vision smiled again and began to fade. I knew with certainty that what I had just experienced was not a dream.

The next morning, I had already been up for an hour, working in the basement repairing some trains, when I heard Cathi above me in the kitchen preparing breakfast. I was eager to tell her what had happened during the night. As I walked into the kitchen, Cathi was at the counter, her back to me. She was pouring a cup of coffee and had a bagel in the toaster.

"Hey, how did you sleep last night?" I asked, frightening her and causing her to jump.

"Jeez, Rich, do you have to do that to me," she snapped, but quickly regained her composure. "Good. How did you sleep?"

"Well, it was an interesting night for me," I began. "I woke up about 3 A.M. and saw Gramp at the foot of the bed. I really think I was awake. It wasn't a dream. He didn't speak to me, but it felt like mental telepathy. He was telling me that everything was going to be fine. I guess the surgery will be okay. What do you think? Am I nuts?"

"Well, you're not nuts," Cathi answered, beaming. "I dreamt that he was here, watching over us, too. You were with him, talking, in my dreams. See, you're going to be okay. You'll live through this. There is nothing to worry about."

We continued to talk with fascination about the night we had experienced. More importantly, we began to share a common bond of faith and trust in the professor. We believed in our hearts that my grandfather was watching over us. The early morning visitation had changed us, for we now shared a heightened awareness, which brought serenity into our lives, a serenity that is often lost in the lives of others.

37
Removing the Underground Feeder Routes

Monday, January 18, 1995—It was 4:30 A.M. and the alarm woke me up from a peace-filled, spiritual-like sleep. It was the best night's sleep in my life. As I turned off the alarm I realized Cathi had been up and quietly observing me as if this is to be our last day together. I could only imagine what she was thinking as she mentally prepared herself for my experimental surgery that was scheduled to begin in only two hours.

As she got out of bed I realized that Cathi was functioning in what appeared to be a mechanical mode. The night before, she had laid her clothes out on her grandmother's cedar chest and preset the coffee pot to 4 A.M. Cathi was dressed in a minute and "bee lined" down the steps of the two story colonial home, got her coffee, and was is in the bathroom styling her mid shoulder length blonde hair before I even stepped out of bed. The realities of what the day's events "might be" were now affecting us. I rolled over and couldn't prevent my mind from reflecting on all the years I had enjoyed with my childhood sweetheart.

I calmly got out of bed and strolled into the bathroom to shower, but instead started to comb my hair. As I looked into the mirror my mind worked at lightning speed flashing my life experiences before me in amazing detail. My mind focused on all the highlights in my life, which were many, from my grandfather to my first camping trip to Lake George with my brother and sisters, to my many moments with Cathi, and family and friends. I looked down at my side and loosened my pants to take a look at the tumor on my right hip, and then I looked in the mirror as I lifted my shirt—only to see more tumors. I said to my reflection, "this shit has gotta come off."

Cathi, now standing at the bottom of the steps, called cheerfully to me, "Don't do that honey, everything will be fine. So get showered and dressed, your parents will be here soon. Remember, the professor wants you clean for this."

My mind was still reminiscing the past and future as I stepped into the steaming shower. I was prepared, mentally, emotionally and spiritually. I was at peace with myself and I knew I could not show any signs of fear or weakness in front of Cathi or my parents. I was compelled to make the day's events somewhat easier on them.

"Your parents are here," Cathi called, coming up the stairs. "They come early on the day everyone thinks you are going to die," she continued laughingly.

I grinned, "Maybe they're in a rush to get rid of me, or maybe they want to see me a little longer for one last time."

This statement brought a realization to Cathi that they too were sharing the emotional turmoil of potentially losing a loved one. Cathi realized that neither parent nor wife could understand the other's emotionally traumatic point of view.

I dressed in oversized sweat pants and a loose flannel shirt. I knew my clothes were not going to be on me much longer and the professor instructed me that extra room would be required for bandages when they were through. I dressed quickly while Cathi waited and we went downstairs together to greet my parents at the back door.

As I walked down the steps, every square inch of the house became alive with instant detailed flash backs of the times Cathi and I spent together with family and friends rebuilding and enjoying our truly beautiful home. As we entered the kitchen it was obvious that the task of hiding our emotions could become difficult.

Cathi greeted my parents with a big smile. "Come on in, you didn't think we were going to leave without you, did you. Come on in the kitchen. I have coffee ready and we have some time."

My parents stood in the kitchen with dazed looks upon their faces, but wanted to appear calm.

"Well, you all set for this? You listened to your doctors and haven't eaten or drank anything, right?" My dad was stumbling for words and "the right thing to say" without upsetting anyone.

Cathi jumped in laughingly, "Yea Dad, I cooked him a big steak last night and we got drunk."

Dad was startled, not sure if "maybe" we did, for one last time.

Cathi could see the concern on his face and immediately went over to hug him and replied, "Come on Dad, lighten up, you know I take good care of him. He didn't have anything."

Cathi then went to my side and put her arm around me. "You know, Billy stopped by yesterday," she said to my parents.

Billy had been a friend of mine for years, but when the diagnosis was made, he couldn't face me. The thought or reality of losing a close friend was too difficult for him to handle, and to compound matters his brother had been just diagnosed with a brain tumor. I understood his difficulty and often spoke to his parents about how Billy was doing.

Cancer often has a more profound emotional effect on the surrounding loved ones than on it's victim.

Billy's parents were very helpful in getting Billy to come to terms with his emotions and bringing the two of us together. Billy stopped by and maintained his strength of character.

"Hey, buddy, I hear you're going in for some wild surgery tomorrow. Well, I have a little gift for you; it's a guardian angel. I had it blessed for you. You know I am sorry I have not been around for you."

I understood the enormity of the emotional hurdle Billy had to overcome and was proud that my friend had conquered it.

"Shit, don't sweat it buddy—you're here now and that is what matters," I said smiling. I just wanted to make sure my friend knew that I understood the difficulties that everyone tried to endure.

As Cathi and I finished telling the previous days events, my mom looked at her watch and said, "It's getting late, it's almost five, we better get going, just in case of traffic; or the doctors might want to see you early."

Cathi handed me my overcoat and began to put hers on.

"Let's get this show on the road," I said, opening the door and ushering everyone out before me.

Max came to sit by the door. I squatted down next to him, "I will try and come back but if things do not work today, I need you to watch after your Mommy," I said softly.

Max looked at me with big sad eyes and I knew that he understood that this was serious. I gave the dog a kiss on the head and walked out the door into the early morning sunrise.

The New Jersey Parkway was free of traffic, and the trip to the University Hospital was quick. Mom pulled up to the entrance of the huge medical complex and let Cathi and I out. Dad had followed in his own vehicle just in case he was required to work that day. We were able to park in the official spaces near to the entrance and within minutes the four of us were together again. We walked quickly down the hall, accepting the well wishes of many staff members. Through my dad and Cancer, we had become well known at the University, and at least for this day, Cathi and I were in thousands of prayers. I held Cathi's hand tightly.

Dr. Lambert met us at the door of the outer area to the operating room. Beyond the door, I could see the surgical team hard at work, preparing for the intricate surgery. The computer or Scanning Multi-

Focal Cellular Image Analyzer stood close to the operating table. I could feel the nervousness well up inside me.

"Good morning," Dr. Lambert greeted us. "Bob, you and your wife can go on to the waiting room. Richard and Cathi need to come with me. And, Bob," Lambert put his hand on Dad's shoulder, "I'll take good care of your son. I won't let anything go wrong."

We all appreciated the reassurance from the doctor. "Good luck," Dad said, turning to me, "and we expect to talk to you later."

Mom kissed me on the cheek, tears glistening in her eyes. "We love you," she managed.

I watched my parents reluctantly walk down the hallway. "Mom, Dad," I called with more bravado than I felt, "don't worry about this, simple stuff happening here. I'll catch you guys later."

"Richard," Lambert spoke as I turned back to him, "I've come to think of you as a son, and would never have recommended this operation unless I felt confident that it would work." He sensed that I, too, might need a verbal confirmation that my decision had been right. "I would have proposed the same thing to one of my own children."

I saw the genuine concern on Lambert's face. "Somehow, I knew that, Doc," I replied, putting my arm around Dr. Lambert's wide shoulders. "If I die, don't let it bother you. I know you care and you're just trying to save my life, or at least buy me some quality time. Besides, I've already beaten the six-month death sentence I was given when this all started. So, let's just do it!"

Professor Lambert was not a surgeon and therefore turned over that aspect of the procedure to Dr. Patel, an acclaimed micro-surgeon. Dr. Lambert would be by his side directing the entire procedure. I could see Dr. Patel through a set of doors, conferring with interns and nurses.

Mike, Lambert's top intern, was finishing the checklist. When he saw Cathi and I enter, he turned and smiled. "I prayed for you last night, and I am making sure everything is set up perfectly." Mike spoke softly to me, and smiled again.

Others on the team greeted me and assured me that everything was ready. Everyone took their own individual moment to privately wish me well and assure me that they are ready. I knew I was among caring, thoughtful friends.

"Well, Mike, do you think a double check of the equipment is needed?" I playfully asked. I knew how exacting and thorough the intern was. During the preliminary tests two days before, Mike had confessed to me that this operation would probably be the highlight of his entire career, and he promised that he would not let me down.

Mike knew that my comment was meant as a joke, but he still turned to the others and said, "Let's go through everything one more time." He sent the team into another diagnostic frenzy.

Cathi helped me remove my clothes, carefully placing them on a stainless steel cart by the door. While the doctors and interns began the process of photographing my entire body, she held the thin, white hospital gown. I was used to being naked around this group and posed comfortably for them. I even tried to be relaxed and joked, "So, do I look like Schwarzenegger?" Cathi and the team laughed and added to my antics, thankful that I was not letting fear get the best of me.

When the photography was completed, Mike added, "Arnold has nothing on you today."

Cathi helped me don the skimpy gown. I got up on the cold table, and lay down. I looked at Cathi; she gave me a kiss and said, "I love you." As the nurse rolled me through the swinging doors into the operating room, I looked back saying, "I'll see you later okay." Cathi smiled, holding back tears as her lips quivered. She inconspicuously waved goodbye.

Dr. Patel turned to greet me. "Good morning, Richard," he said in his proper Indian accent. "I am afraid we have more photographs to take. This time it's for the computer charting. Then let's see if we can get you set up on this "bean bag" like apparatus. This is what we are going to use to help us move you around during the surgery. Pretty neat toys we have, don't you think?" Dr. Patel also helped in keeping the atmosphere light.

"No problem Doc. This toilet paper gown isn't really doing anything any way. Wait a minute, you plan on flipping me around, Doc?" I asked with curiosity.

"Well, yes—if that's what it's going to take."

Again, every inch of my body was photographed. It was cold in the operating room and I was feeling chilly. Once the photographs were completed, I got back up on the cold metal table and lay down. Now I was starting to shiver.

One of the nurses noticed me shivering and within seconds, someone handed her a stack of warm towels. "Here, you look like you could use these," she said, as began to cover me.

"Thanks," I said appreciatively, and began to relax a little.

Just as I started to relax the nurse opened up the arm extensions to strap me to the table. I looked into her face and became frightened. I questioned if this was what I should be doing. As she continued strapping me to the table she said, "Don't worry, everything will be fine." I looked over my right shoulder and saw Cathi. She had snuck back in to see me. The nurse instructed her to leave.

"Is there any way that she can stay?" I asked Dr. Patel.

"I am sorry, not this time, but she can stay until you are asleep," the surgeon responded kindly

I was thankful, but said nothing. I kept my eyes on my beautiful young wife as the injection of sodium penathol was administered. The last thing I saw and heard was Cathi, as she leaned over, quietly, and tearfully said, "I love you." Then I slid into unconsciousness.

During the surgery I experienced a sensation of being on a journey. I felt warm, tranquil and secure. As I was able to see, I discovered that I was floating, moving forward through white clouds with light gray linings. I continued traveling for what seemed to be miles and the clouds gradually became brighter and thicker. I could feel warmth and peace surrounding me, and I began to travel faster. Everywhere it was getting brighter until I had the impression that a perfect white sphere encircled me.

Then the sensation of movement began to subside. I noticed a figure in the distance. As I neared, silhouettes of others appeared behind the central figure. I couldn't make out their faces. I realized, as I got closer to the small crowd, that I was no longer floating, but was walking. A gentle wave of recognition washed over me and I recognized the person standing in front was my grandfather with my grandmother to the right.

"Hello, Richard," my grandfather greeted me.

"Hey, Gramp," I replied. I could not see the faces of the others standing behind, but had the sense that I might know them or at least they belonged.

"Richard, you can't stay here, it is not your time. Cathi is waiting for you."

"But Gramp, I don't want to go back. This is wonderful!" I felt sheltered in an envelope of serenity.

"Richard," my grandfather instructed, "you have to go back for Cathi. She is waiting."

My grandmother stood smiling at me. "It is not time yet, Richie," she said. "You have to go now."

Resigned that I must return, I slowly turned to leave. As I did, I saw my old friend from work, Kenny, standing alone, off to the distant side. "Don't give up," I heard Kenny say.

I tried to speak, but was unable to mouth the words. I felt as though something was guiding me away. I kept my eyes on Kenny as long as I could, until the image faded away.

In an instant I was back and exhaustedly was opening my eyes. Slowly, as my vision cleared, I could see Cathi at the foot of the hospital bed rubbing my feet. Momentarily I was filled with rage for having to leave such a tranquil place, but rage disappeared in Cathi's smile and turned to love. I knew that she was the meaning of my life. She was why I had to live.

Cathi stood at the foot of my bed, rubbing my toes. "How do you feel?" she asked with a gentle smile.

I managed a faint smile and whispered, "I'm fine."

"You really gave them a workout in there," Cathi said softly, the relief evident in her face, "but you are going to be okay. I love you." She came to my bedside, gently rubbed my forehead and bent to give me a light kiss, as I drifted off to sleep.

The operation was scheduled for 2 to 3 hours but lasted a little over six. During that time, the surgeon masterfully made a fourteen and one half inch incision on my right side to remove the primary tumor. It weighed in at seven pounds, four ounces and took slightly over 500 sutures to close. The medical team rightfully named this tumor "Little Richard." (It was a boy.)

Also a six-by eight-inch layer of skin was removed from the back of my left leg and grafted to the primary surgical site of the right hip. This was needed to close the massive depth and width that the tumor had temporarily called home.

Toward the left region of the lower abdomen, closer toward my groin, a 10-inch incision was made to remove more tumor-ridden tissue. Moving up my abdomen about at the belly button line a four inch incision was made to remove still more tumors.

Then Dr. Patel worked his way to the left, making a nine-inch incision and removing that tumor. Remember that beanbag that the doc. joked about? Well, it came in handy for removing a tumor from the top center of my little butt.

But yet another concern was one of the smallest, it was approximately one-quarter inch from the spine and about six inches above my waistline. The concern was that this tumor might have attached itself to the spine, which could have meant death, or paralysis. Fortunately, it had not attached.

Relatively speaking, this was my lucky day, I was still alive to piss off defense attorneys and I had about 600 sutures and seven surgical sites to show for it.

The medical team was ecstatic and Professor Lambert was proud. The operation was a definite success and the Scanning Multi-Focal Cellular Image Analyzer had done its job.

Outside the operating room, Cathi and my parents had tearfully spent those grueling six hours waiting for news of the worst, praying for the best, their emotions on a terrifying roller coaster ride. Every sign of movement from the area of the operating room would cause their stomachs to tighten, prematurely preparing for words of disaster.

When at last the exhausted Professor Lambert came through the doors, my parents jumped to their feet, Cathi stood behind them anxiously waiting. Professor Lambert gently pulled Cathi near to him so he could speak to her individually, face to face. The smile on his face relieved her deepest fears.

"Richard will be fine but he is in a tremendous amount of pain!" Professor Lambert instructed.

Cathi's emotions ran wild inside her, she was excited, relieved, and frightened by how much damage I might have sustained and how much care I would need. She stood strong as the Professor spoke and never lost composure. She wanted to hug the Professor but feared she may hurt his recently broken arm. "Thank you, doctor." She sighed in relief.

"You should be very proud of Richard," Lambert said with a sign of relief. "They just brought him into the trauma ward and he is resting. We are trying to keep him as comfortable as possible, but again he is in a lot of pain. We had to operate on seven parts of his body; to say the least his recovery will be very slow."

The doctor's excitement was now starting to show. "I really feel good about what we accomplished here today. It looks like we removed the entire 'feeder' tumor; this operation is a success. I strongly believed that main tumor was going to kill him.

"We are planning to send samples of the tumor to many different universities. Doctors and scientists around the world will be studying his tissue and conducting research with hope to learn much more about the disease." Dr. Lambert paused for a moment. "Would you like to see 'Little Richard' before the lab technicians dissect it?"

Cathi looked somewhat apprehensive. "Yes, I would like to see what you found."

The doctor held out his right arm, motioning the family members to enter the lab next to the operating room. A small table on wheels stood in the corner of the lab. On it was a large metal pan covered with a cloth. They made their way through the maze of high-tech computers and analytical equipment.

Dr. Lambert slowly lifted the covering for Cathi, proud of his handiwork, yet concerned that the family may not be prepared for what they were about to see. What had been 5 to 6 inches wide, 14 inches long and two inches thick was now spread out in the pan, soaking in blood; seven and a quarter pounds of shapeless grotesque tumorous mass, larger than some newborns.

Dad stepped between Cathi and Lambert to sneak a quick peek. As he looked upon the tumor his emotional turmoil peaked: "Oh my God, Oh my God, Oh my God," he moaned.

Cathi gasped, repulsed by the sight, but more shaken up by her father-in-law, she stood conscious that this had been inside me slowly killing me. Bombarded with the reality, she turned and ran from the room, sobs of hysteria escaping from her lips. She ran down the hallway until she found a chair and collapsed into it, still sobbing uncontrollably. She felt the warmth of some arms around her and realized it was my mother consoling her.

"Is he really going to be alright?" she managed between sobs. "Did he really make it? I wasn't dreaming, was I?"

"He's going to be fine," Mom reassured her, and continued talking to her, confirming all that the doctor reported.

Cathi again showed her amazing strength and was able to compose herself within a few minutes. She returned to the lab room to apologize to Dr. Lambert for her outburst. "I'm sorry," she said sincerely. "It was just too much for me to handle all at once, I guess. I really do appreciate you showing me what was growing inside him, though."

The doctor was sympathetic. "It is alright, Cathi. Would you like to see Richard now?"

"Yes please." She was still subdued.

The Professor led the three down the main hospital hallway and stopped outside the room. He allowed Cathi and my Mom in for a moment. I lay motionless sleeping on the bed. My Dad took a peek into the room to see if I was okay and the nurse asked that Mom leave. They only wanted Cathi in the room when I awakened. Mom gently kissed me on the forehead and quietly walked out the room.

Cathi went over and began to rub my feet. I stirred and opened my eyes slightly.

"How do you feel?" she asked.

It was a moment before I could speak, but managed a weak "I'm fine." I heard Cathi tell me that she loved me, and then I slipped back into sleep.

Cathi stood at the side of the bed gently caressing my forehead; my eyes were swollen from tearing and she gently wiped my face and cheeks. With the touch of her hand I again slowly opened my eyes.

"How do you feel honey?" She softly spoke. I just looked at her. "Try not to move, if you need anything just tell me."

"I'm thirsty," I replied.

Cathi asked one of the nurses for some water and when she would be able to take me to a private room. The nurse said I would have to 'pee' first before they could move me and she returned with a can of 7-Up stating it may be better to help make me 'go.'

Cathi was a little confused and asked the nurse, "What if he doesn't 'pee.'"

The nurse smiled and held up a 12-inch catheter tube saying, "Well, then we'll have to make him go by putting this 'up' him."

Cathi smiled as she looked over to me. I had horror written on my face. "They're going to stick that up your 'weenie' if you don't go." Cathi said.

My eyes opened wide. "Oh shit, please make me 'pee,' I'm in enough pain as it is."

Cathi held cold cans of soda against my feet and massaged them for about an hour—finally I went.

During that time I was in excruciating pain all over my body. I knew something was terribly wrong but was not sure how to ask Cathi or if I really wanted to know. Finally, as I motioned to lift the bed sheet to look down upon my body, Cathi spoke abruptly.

"Rich, I don't think you want to do that, you really gave them a workout in there."

I was frightened. "Cath, I can't move anything but my head and arms. My whole body is killing me. Why are my back, legs and groin hurting so badly? I thought they were operating on my hip? And shit, I feel like I'm missing something—did I lose the jewels?"

Cathi knew she had to tell me the truth but didn't think I needed to see the actual damage yet. I was strong but this was not what anyone expected or usually dealt with in life, unless maybe you were victim of an explosion of a hand grenade.

"Listen Rich," Cathi said somberly, her face flush. She pushed my hand away from the bed sheet.

"The operation went perfect—the machine worked perfect, but the Cancer was much worse than Dr. Lambert expected. They operated on seven areas of your body and most of your side was removed. It took Dr. Patel over six hours; not the two we all expected. We can do this; you're going to be okay. And I'll be here to take care of you and Art will get them. We are not going to let them get away with this. Now you need to get better so just relax and go to sleep. Dr. Lambert and I will take care of everything."

Then Cathi smiled saying, "And yes, you still have the jewels."

I was terrified. I knew I was in trouble but I didn't like seeing Cathi scared. She had been through hell with me and I realized she was going to have to be even stronger through this. But still, just how much of me was missing was driving my curiosity. I was tired and left my trust and life in Cathi and Lambert's hands. The pain medicines helped me slip back into a deep sleep.

By the next morning, Cathi was exhausted and fully aware that a teaching hospital was not the place for specialized individual care.

Unlike the attention I had received in the surgical unit, the trauma ward was severely lacking.

Cathi had spent the night changing my bed sheets, checking my bandages and performing nursing duties that the staff should have been responsible for.

I was losing enough body fluids and blood to warrant continual monitoring by hospital personnel, but the nursing staff made the assumption that Cathi would handle it. She quickly learned that when I began to moan, it was time to change the dressings or the blood soaked sheets.

The first few times she tried to get help from a nurse, but instead she received sarcasm that she was being annoying. Immediately, Cathi helped herself to the supply cabinet and laundry storage closet. Throughout the night Cathi meticulously tended to my needs and only slept momentarily in a recliner chair that Dad had brought in earlier that day.

It was 6 A.M., and Cathi had run out of clean towels. Worn from lack of sleep and angry from lack of care for me, she went to the nursing station to get more towels.

"We cannot allow you to take any more towels," the nurse told her nonchalantly. "You used up all the ones you're allowed."

"I have used all of them," Cathi raising her voice and becoming very agitated. "And I need some more."

"I'm sorry, but our policy is that we cannot give you any more towels."

Cathi was tired and 'pissed-off.' "Do have any idea who I am, or who is in that room? My father-in-law is going to have your ass; you're not getting away with this."

Just then, Dr. Lambert walked up to the nursing station. "What is going on here?" he asked, aware of the exhaustion on Cathi's face.

"This nurse," Cathi told him, sarcastically emphasizing the word 'nurse,' "will not let me have any more towels. I need them to clean up Richard and the bed, he's been bleeding all over."

Cathi had never seen the large man angry, but the flush on his face told her that she was going to get some satisfaction from this nurse.

"You get this woman anything she wants, and you personally make sure that she continues to have anything she wants. I will speak to you later about this."

The nurse, mortified by this doctor's command, scurried off to get more towels.

Turning back to Cathi, he calmly asked, "How is he doing?"

"He's awake and alert, but still in a lot of pain. He seems to be doing fine as long as I keep the bed dry and the bandages fresh," she reported. "Dr. Lambert," she continued, her face showing the wear from the long night, "I had no help from the nursing staff all night and the drainage pump that is connected to his side kept falling out and usually I pumped it by hand. I have been changing his bandages and keeping the sheets clean. I can do the same at home, and I know that he would be much happier there. You know how much he hates hospitals."

The doctor paused to consider the proposal. I was scheduled to spend the next ten days in the hospital recovering from my surgical trauma. Lambert knew that Cathi was certainly capable of performing any nursing duties that were needed. She had demonstrated that even before the previous night. But could he risk the possibility of some complication? Not dismissing the idea, he told her, "Let me talk it over with Dr. Patel and the others. Now, let's see to this patient."

"So Richard, how we doing today?" Professor Lambert said with a big smile as he entered the room.

"Great Doc. I hear you did a really good job. Can I go home now? I really don't like being in here."

"Richard, are you in any pain?" The doctor looked at me with more concern.

"Come on Professor, you know I can't say yes to that. I want to go home. Cathi took care of me all night—she can do it at home. Besides I know I really gave you a run for your money in the O.R. yesterday. Let me go home, and then I'll start on the pain pills again."

"Let me see what I can do and I'm not promising anything. You're really in bad shape and you shouldn't move. If we work something out, you must do what she says; she's the boss, understand."

Shortly before noon, Dr. Lambert returned. "The discharge papers are being prepared now," he announced to Cathi. "You must agree, that at the sign of any problem, you will call me immediately at the hospital or at home. And don't hesitate to use my beeper number."

"Thank you, Dr. Lambert," Cathi gushed, " I promise that I will call." The broad smile on her weary face was infectious, and the doctor found himself smiling with her. Even I was able to manage a faint smile through the pain.

Shortly after this announcement one of the surgeons came in to check on me. We talked casually and I demonstrated my usual showmanship of over-simplifying my condition and demanded that I was going home. The doctor gave me a routine bandage check but accidentally opened the drainage valve as he left.

Cathi noticed I was losing color fast and noticed a small pool of blood forming on the floor. She started checking my bandages to locate where all the blood was coming from. In seconds she identified the problem and stopped the bleeding.

Just as she finished a large male nurse came in to move me into the wheel chair. The nurse's name was Rich and though of massive size, he was able to ever so gently pick me up off of the bed and place me in the wheel chair, never breaking a stitch or causing any further bleeding.

Preparations were quickly made to convert the living room at our home into a hospital room and the sofa bed into a bed adequate enough to accommodate me. Dad secured padding and thick foam from the hospital to construct a bed thick enough and soft enough to afford some comfort. By the time he was done the makeshift bed was at least a foot thick.

Tables and furniture were moved to make space for medicines and bandages. The large recliner was pulled close so that Cathi would have a place to sleep for the first few nights. She was running on nervous energy, but was grateful to be able to bring me home.

Despite the smooth ride of Dad's new Cadillac, the hour-long ride home was very painful for me. I could feel every pebble in the road. Drained from the ride and unsteady from the medications, I was glad to be home. I quickly fell asleep on the converted sofa bed, and the family was elated to have me home.

Cathi got very little sleep over the next few days, acting as my private Florence Nightingale. She would often awaken in the middle of the night to change bandages or to give me pain medication. As tired she was, her protective instincts overrode the exhaustion.

She was contented, at least mentally, to be in control of my care. She was an expert nurse/maid, cleaning and dressing my wounds, making meals, cleaning up after visitors and tending to all my needs.

I know what the casualties of war felt when they opened their eyes to the vision of a lovely lady tending their wounds and seeing the compassion and caring in her eyes. I would awake to see all the tremendous love, compassion and caring framed in Cathi's brilliant blue eyes, and the halo of golden hair confirmed for me that I had a wonderful guardian angel in this harsh world.

I, too, preferred the security of our home to the sterile atmosphere of the hospital. However, I was still in excruciating pain. Due to the major incision on my right side, I soon learned that it was best to do things with my left hand, since even the smallest task, like lifting a glass of water, would cause me intense pain. In spite of the pain, I was thankful to be under Cathi's care and to be where my spirit was most comfortable.

The first two days were somewhat easy on Cathi, this was only due to my being out cold on pain medicines, but on the third day I wanted to try to stand. Cathi was reluctant. Dr. Lambert wanted me completely immobile for five to seven days. Cathi had seen the tumor and had daily dressed the 14-inch gash in my side, in addition to cleaning the other sites on my body. She did not believe that I would be able to do it without suffering.

But, I was insistent. "I just want to try," I told her.

Unable to resist my pleas, and always supporting me in my efforts to strengthen myself, she at last agreed. "But we are going to take it very slowly, and you let me know if you want to stop. The last thing we want is for you to end up back in the hospital."

A plan had to be devised on how to move me to the side of the bed. Then, we had to determine how to get me to a standing position without breaking any stitches. Because all the medical apparatus was on the right side of the bed, we figured the left side was the way to go. Cathi helped me gradually move my body toward the side of the bed, an inch at a time. By the time I had reached the edge, we both needed a rest.

Cathi made sure that Max was outside. She didn't want the over-zealous puppy to jump up on me and knock me off balance.

With Cathi standing by my side, we were ready to go. Very gently, she moved my left leg off the side of the bed, then the right, being ever so careful not to disturb the main incision. With my legs off the bed, I tried to pull myself up. Instantly, I realized that the incision in my right side was too large and too painful to use any lower body muscles. It seemed as if every muscle in my lower body was connected to my right hip and was causing me intense pain. Amazing, I thought to myself, I have six other incisions that are 4 to 9 inches long, and I'm not even aware of them.

"Come on, Cath. Let's make this work," I said, noticing that my hip was bleeding slightly. Cathi knew how badly I wanted to do this. She gently put my arm on her shoulder and slowly lifted. Working together, I was able to stand. It was an arduous task, but I did it. Standing triumphantly, but feeling dizzy, I smiled at Cathi. "I guess I still had quite a bit of pain medicine in me when they moved me from the hospital."

"How about I go stand by the fireplace," I suggested, once I had caught my breath.

"Well, how about we do it together," Cathi said, "and if you can lean there, I'll clean the blood from the bed and floor and make things a little more comfortable for you."

Slowly, we made the long five-foot walk to the fireplace. I was able to hold myself up by leaning against the brick. Certain I was secure, Cathi hurried to change the sheets. As she worked, she noticed I was trying to lift my right foot off the floor.

"Hey what do you think your doing?" she reprimanded me.

"Well, the doc said exercise will do me good, when I can," I said, slowly lifting my foot three inches off the floor.

"I think that's enough for one day," Cathi instructed, "and you're bleeding even more, so stop! And I know you're in pain. I can see you clenching your teeth."

Over the next few days, I stood as often as I could, requiring less and less help from Cathi. I began to venture a few steps from the sofa bed. I was feeling more confident and Cathi's spirits lifted as she witnessed my progress. She marveled, as she watched me push myself to take one more step, when only a few days before she did not know if she would return home with me. Now, despite my haggard appearance, she felt a burst of energizing hope.

I decided that it was time to try the trek to the bathroom on my own. Although it was only 25 feet away, it was going to be a major accomplishment if I was able to make it to and from my goal. I did not tell Cathi my plan, knowing that she would object. It was only as I shuffled through the kitchen area where Cathi was preparing some food, that she became aware of my little jaunt.

"What the hell are you doing? Are you out of your mind?" she scolded.

"I'm going to the bathroom," I stated nonchalantly, as I slowly crossed the kitchen floor.

Before I entered, Cathi rushed into the bathroom and placed bath towels over the mirror. She always realized that having been a once solid-bodied weightlifter, I might not be ready for the sights of my surgery. As I entered I realized what Cathi's intentions were. "Hey, Cath, I guess I look pretty bad?" I questioned.

Cathi stood by the door in case something went wrong and said, "When you're ready, we'll take a look."

I stood in front of the mirror wondering, "How bad is it?" I asked as I pulled the towel down. Stunned by the size of the bloodied bandages that covered most of my mid-body, tears trickled from my eyes. The gruesome reality of my cancer hit hard. As quickly as I could, I placed the towel back on the mirror.

I was worn out by the time I had finished the first leg of my trip, but I basked in the glow of accomplishment, and being able to pee on my own. I considered myself lucky, regardless of the tale the mirror told. I was ready to stand strong.

Taking a deep breath and steeling myself for the trip back to the living room, I stepped out of the bathroom. Only a few steps into the kitchen, I began to experience tunnel vision. Cathi was watching me closely and could tell that something was wrong.

She quickly grabbed a chair and put it under me. I slumped down onto the chair, and as if in suspended animation, completely numb to the pain, I sat there momentarily in a state of semi-consciousness. Then I continued to slide to the floor. I landed face down on the tile, the force of the impact causing all my incisions to begin to bleed.

Cathi didn't panic. She grabbed the cordless phone and quickly dialed 911. In less than two minutes, the Old Bridge police and EMTs, familiar with the calls from Cathi, appeared. She had tried to make me as comfortable as possible, lying there on the kitchen floor, bleeding.

The paramedics stepped in and expertly rolled me over onto my back. I could see and hear them talking to me but I could do nothing; my body was completely shut down. They lifted me onto a gurney and rolled me into the living room, monitoring my vital signs as they worked. I muttered incoherently, "I don't want to go."

Slowly, I began to regain consciousness and started to moan from the intense pain. One of the EMTs asked me questions to make sure that I was becoming cognizant of what was happening while another EMT was quite busy tending to my bleeding. I had ripped open some stitches as I fell to the floor, causing blood to flow more freely around the packing gauze.

A young police officer gasped when the EMT removed the bloodied bandage from my right hip and saw the size of my wound. "God, look at the size of that! It's amazing that your wife is able to take care of you! Cathi are you sure you don't want us to take him to the hospital this time?" the officer questioned.

"No, I have everything I need here to take care of this, and I have four doctors willing to rush here if I need them. I just couldn't move him on my own without causing more damage."

The emergency team tended to my wounds and gently moved me from the gurney to the bed. The officer and the EMTs stayed about an hour to make sure that I was all right. When they left, I was sleeping peacefully on my makeshift hospital bed. Cathi, exhausted from the emotional and physical trauma, dropped into the recliner and fell asleep at my side.

Every day was a new experience for us. Tasks that would have petrified Cathi two weeks earlier were now considered routine. She had begun to routinely cover the mirrors in the downstairs area, protecting me from the sight of my ravaged body. It had taken only one glimpse in the mirror for me to be shocked by the affects of the surgery. Cathi now expertly cleaned and dressed the huge gash in my side. It continuously oozed blood and body fluids, and had to be constantly cared for.

I was accustomed to a more active lifestyle and I complained about my lack of mobility. I hated feeling so helpless. I was either in pain or doped up with pain medication. I felt worse when I complained or snapped at Cathi, knowing that without her aid and assistance, I likely would not have survived. When I was able to think clearly, I was in awe of her commitment to me.

On February 2, slightly more than two weeks after the surgery, it was time for Cathi to take me back to Dr. Patel for the stitch removal.

At his office in the university hospital the doctor gave me some *Lidocaine* injections to help relieve some of the pain.

The doctor attempted to be diligent as he removed the stitches from all the so-called smaller surgery sites, but my ravaged body was still very tender. It was apparent that more pain relief would be needed for the primary site.

Cathi used all her strength and her entire body to hold me down as the doctor pulled out more and more of the stitches. I sweated profusely as I held a tight "death" grip to the table. Finally, after about a half hour, when the doctor completed all of the smaller sites, he admitted that they all needed to take a break.

My well-deserved break only lasted about fifteen minutes. Dr. Patel realized opening the main packing in the "hole" in my side was going to be traumatic for Cathi and I. The doctor brought in two nurses to help, one male one female. He knew Cathi had been caring for all the other surgical sites and even the primary site, but the main packing was still in place.

"Well, are we ready for this?" He gestured to Cathi and I, but focused on Cathi.

"Sure, Doc. Let's get this over with," I said and Cathi agreed.

The male nurse held my chest down firmly to the table while the female nurse held my legs together and flat on the table. Cathi stood next to the doctor as he removed the "hold down" sutures that stabilized the main packing that held my insides in place.

The doctor looked at Cathi as he raised the bandages from left to right, as if he were opening a door to my insides. The skin grafting was still transparent and Cathi could see all the fibrous muscle and inner tissue of my body. Instantly she passed out.

From my vantage point, I could see the flushed panic look on her face, and then she disappeared. "Now you see her—now you don't." The doctor took care of me as the two nurses tended to Cathi, "You okay, any pain?"

"Not at all Doc. I think you better help her, though."

The nurse positioned Cathi on her back while she was still lying on the floor. He gave sudden claps in front of her face and then gently slapped her. She "woke up" with the gentle slap, and immediately looked up, stating, "I want to do this, Doc.; show me how to take care of that."

The doctor and nurse helped Cathi to her feet while the other nurse handed her some water. Again they stood at my side; Cathi took hold of the bandages and lifted. I could see the terror written on her face as Cathi said, "Oh God," sighing, gasping for air and losing color in her face.

"Well, show me what to do Doc."

Doctor Patel was impressed by her strength and demonstrated how to sterilize, clean and tend to the massive wound. He did it in a light-hearted teaching format, describing the various muscle and fiber tissue that she would be touching. This enabled Cathi to relax and maybe even accept the situation a little easier. Dr. Patel then had Cathi clean, repack and bandage the wound. She completed it impeccably.

Once all this was completed, the nurses assisted me off the table. Dr. Patel then showed me a problem stitch that was still attached internally toward my groin area. He instructed me to use warm compresses two to three times a day and "work" the last stitch out by gently pulling on the piece that was still sticking out. I was still quite sore down there and did not allow the Doctor to demonstrate.

That evening Cathi was helping me clean my body and decided it was time to give the stitch a pull. I agreed, but wanted to do it myself. As I pulled, my 'weenie' popped up.

"Holy shit, did you see that." I burst out in laughter.

Cathi laughed, saying, "Boy that must be one long stitch if you're pulling at your side and 'it' pops up."

Although I was still in substantial pain, the diversion of trying to get that last stitch out added some fun to the dilemma. Two or three times a day Cathi would remind me that it was time to "warm up the puppet—and pull it's string."

After about three days of tugging to no avail, I was frustrated and sore. I decided it was coming out now. I warmed the entire nine-inch upper groin surgical site for about an hour and had the skin good and soft. Cathi was prepared; she had ice, bandages, gauze, tape, and the phone, which was preset to call 911.

I tightly pinched the area above the "jewels" and just yanked the thick thread. To our amazement it was over seven inches long and attached to the end was a small piece of inner body type tissue. It took about 10 minutes for Cathi to stop the bleeding and once again I was on the floor in severe pain. Finally, and somewhat psychologically relieved, that last stitch was out.

38
Return to the Civil Trial Fray

1995—I called Art after the surgery. "Richard," Art cried, as he picked up the phone, "I can't tell you how glad I am to hear your voice. The surgery was a success?"

"Well, I'm still here, but I'm moving very slowly. And," I added, "I'm ready to start back up on the case."

"Great," Art replied, a smile evident in his voice, "we'll pick up where we left off. I really believe we have a heck of a case here, Richard. If hot coffee at McDonald's can bring in millions, we should be looking at tens of millions."

In reality, there were 24 counts in the suit. We were going to ask for $10 million per count. This was going to be the largest dollar amount for any case that was not a class action.

Cathi and I maintained a realistic outlook and hoped for even a fraction. Plus, now we were more familiar with the workings of the justice system: slow, tedious, and full of delays. But in the long run, I had outlasted the ploys of the insurance companies. And, I vowed I would do it again.

Benefits would eventually run out. My medical condition would be a factor as long as I lived, plus I wanted to make sure that Cathi did not have to struggle when I did die. Some financial security was the least she deserved after being forced to give up on her dreams of children and a normal life.

39
Dead Man Walking

February 1995—While incapacitated, my life consisted of sleep, medications, television, and reading medical or legal reports. I always believed there was something more I could do to help my doctors and attorneys during my healing process. Occasionally, Cathi would set me up with some trains to repair, but this too could cause some unforeseen dangers with the sharp edges or oils. Reading and watching TV were her preference for me. *Jurassic Park* had become my favorite movie, and I watched it over and over.

For the most part, she overlooked my outbursts, knowing that the pain was causing my occasional vile disposition. Cathi was rarely blessed with a full night's sleep, having to get up to change bandages or administer medications. And, as always, she worried about me the few times she was away.

The last few days of February were tough on Cathi. I caught a mild cold that could have caused problems with my healing schedule and Cathi was still tending to my surgery wounds. She had done some food shopping and on the way home decided to stop to rent a video. She could not bear to watch the dinosaur movie one more time. She was looking forward to the weekend, knowing that she would be able to nap

nap and recoup some of the sleep she missed during the week.

The two of us had just settled down, after dinner, to watch the movie. Ten minutes into it, the phone rang. Irritated by the interruption, I answered the phone, "Hello."

"Richard, this is Pedro Martinez. I have some test results I need to go over with you."

At the sound of the doctor's voice, every muscle in my body had tightened. " It's nine o'clock at night. Can't this wait until tomorrow? Then I can see you?" I asked, hoping that it was something that could wait, and not wanting to interrupt our planned relaxation.

"I really think we should talk about this now," the doctor responded, the gravity in his voice evident over the phone.

Already preparing for possible bad news, I turned off the TV. "Well, okay. So, how did yesterday's test results come out?"

"I finished your blood test late today, and I thought I better call you."

"Yeah? So, what do they say?" I questioned.

"This is pretty strange," the doctor told me, "but you're dead. Your blood Sezary count is 34 percent. How are you feeling lately?"

"Thirty-four percent!" I shouted. "That's wrong! You know that! I think you need to give your intern a failing grade this week. Besides, I feel great today. I even have a beer and some potato chips."

"I ran the test myself, Richard, twice. That's why I am still here, and I'm the boss," he said jokingly. "And what do you mean you're having a beer and potato chips? You shouldn't be having that while you are on medication."

I was undeterred. I maintained my lighthearted attitude. "Listen, Doc, I only have junk food once in a while. Besides, if I'm dead, or going to die, I'm gonna have some fun. And, listen," I added, "I'm not coming in tomorrow. I know the rules. You're going to put me back in the hospital and put me on photopheresis."

I never had to do photopheresis. And I didn't want to. The process of removing the patient's blood, separating the white and red cells, radiating the cancer cells that have bonded with the interjected drug methoxsalen (normally found in the white cells), occasionally adding other medicines to assist in the process, then remixing and sending the blood back into the body, was not something I wanted to even try. "I'm just not up to it this soon after the operation."

With most people, eight percent would mean that a person was critical. I knew that with that amount of tumor cells in my blood I should not be feeling well. "Doc, I feel fine. So, what do you want to do?"

"Come in tomorrow anyway. We will change some of the medications, take some new blood samples and rerun the tests. Maybe your body is cleaning itself or going through some changes due to all the tumor removal and trauma. This is not an unusual phenomenon, but I have to make sure. And, I promise, I won't put you in the hospital unless Lambert tells me to. Deal?"

"Okay," I sighed, "we'll see you in the morning."

Cathi sat waiting, expecting an explanation of what she had overheard. She had been through this kind of situation too many times, but could never really get used to it.

I hung up the phone and looked at her. "Well, honey, I'm dead," I laughed as I turned the TV back on.

Cathi was frustrated with what she overheard, and with my comment, but on the surface, she laughed. "So, I guess we better go to the hospital tomorrow."

I hated being the bearer of bad news again, but knew I had to tell her. "Yeah, my Sezary count hit 34 percent, so they want to monitor me more closely for the week or so. No big deal though, I'll be fine." We had both hoped that the surgery would alleviate this kind of daily stress.

Later that evening my parents stopped by to see how I was healing. I was still casually digesting Dr. Martinez's information and decided to share it with my parents. They looked at me with concern and jokingly said, "You're dead but you're still drinking BEER and eating potato chips."

I assured them that I was going to the hospital for more tests and that everything would be fine. When they were about to leave, they were still slightly angry about my lax attitude. My dad turned to Cathi, declaring, "When are you going back to work to bring in your fair share?" I just looked at Cathi. Neither one of us knew what to say.

I was thinking, "She takes care of me day in and day out, saved my life twice, and now she find's out I have 34 percent blood Sezary syndrome. What the hell are you thinking?" I sat there awed by my father's comment. It was apparent that the responsibilities and complex psychological effects of my nearly three-year-old medical battle with death were now breaking down my *supporters*.

Cathi replied, "Soon."

What caused the proliferation of the tumor cells in my blood, the doctor did not know, or at least he never conveyed it to me. But as Lambert predicted, almost as quickly as they appeared, in a few short days, they disappeared. The illusion of well-being had, yet again, been shattered for both Cathi and I. As before, we continued to live with the immediate threat of my death.

40
Friends Protective Circle

Spring was in full bloom and I was feeling much stronger. I was able to go on brief walks outside, but stayed close to the house. After my one episode in the kitchen, I was more careful not to push myself. But as my strength returned, I wanted to venture out more. I had read in the newspaper about a local train show and began to formulate an idea I hoped Cathi would agree to. After making some phone calls to other friends, I presented my idea to my wife.

"There is a train show this weekend. Carmen, Pete and Gary have all agreed to go with us." All three of these men were also model train enthusiasts. I hurried on, not wanting Cathi to stop me until I was through explaining. "They know that I have to be very careful and not overdo it, and they promised to stay with me and protect me from anyone getting too close or bumping me. If I get tired or start to bleed, we can come home. I also called, and the show will have some wheelchairs available if I need one. It would give us both a chance to get out of the house and do something."

Cathi thought for a moment. The doctors were very encouraged by my progress, and it didn't take a genius to realize how antsy I was just staying around the house. She, too, would welcome a little diversion.

"Well," she began slowly, "if you are sure that you will take it easy. You know that just one bump from someone and you'll probably end up in the hospital. If the guys will protect you from the crowds, I guess we can try it." She could not refuse the eagerness in my voice.

"Sure," I agreed, breathing a sigh of relief that it had taken less to convince her than I had thought it would. "They want to help out." I didn't have to be reminded of the kind of pain I was in, and I knew I was taking a big risk, but with the three men running interference, I should be all right. Besides, I felt very secure with Carmen around; he was big and protected me like he was my brother.

The show was being held at the Wayne Police Association Center, and was very popular. When we arrived, 30 minutes before the opening, lines were already forming. I was moving very slowly, but my escorts were patient. The police were aware that I was coming to the show and they knew that I was recovering from a severe surgery.

As we made our way toward the entrance, one of the policemen serving as security spied us and came over to ask if we would like for him to go with us to make sure no one bumped into me.

"You think I can just see where you had the surgery real quick," the police officer asked, overcome by his curiosity.

"Which one do you want to see?" I joked. "You wanna see the big one?"

"Yeah," the officer responded excitedly.

"It's pretty gruesome," I warned. "And, you're lucky, 'cause it's not all bandaged up right now."

Cathi would often let the wound 'breathe', helping the healing process. Because I could still only wear very loose clothing, all I had to do was raise the T-shirt and slightly lower the waistband of the sweatpants I wore.

Although healed tremendously, the site of the surgery still displayed angry ulcerations and red muscles and tendons beneath the thin layer of grafted skin. It took only a quick glance and the police officer's color left his face.

"My god," he said, sucking in his breath, "What happened to you?"

"Well, it was an awfully big tumor," I responded, watching the awe in the officer's face. "We call it 'Little Richard,' and it was 7 1/4 pounds."

"If you need anything, anything at all, you just call," the officer directed us, still struck from the sight of the huge gash. "I'm surprised you can walk. Come on, we'll get you in before the doors open for the crowd."

As we slowly made our way to the entrance, one of the patrons waiting in line called to the officer, "Hey, why can't we get in ahead of time?"

"If you're wounded like him," the policeman quipped, "I'll let you in early, too!"

The huge center held about two hundred and fifty different vendors. I probably knew three-quarters of them, and they were all eager to talk to me. It was the first time they had seen me in months. Cathi, Pete, Carmen and Gary surrounded me making sure that no one got too close. Everyone respected the distance, but wanted to hear about the surgery. Over and over I shared the information with small groups of well-wishers. We made our way through the aisles, stopping often to talk.

At one table, Gary spied a rare colored No. 402 engine, something he had been seeking for a long time. Excitedly, he turned to me. "Rich, I want you to take a look at this for me!" As he spoke, he slightly tapped me on the right side, forgetting about the wound.

I crumpled to the floor immediately, in torturous pain. Carmen, a big muscular guy, turned to see me fall. He had been busy making sure no one got near me.

I lay on the floor, looking up at the huge man.

"What the hell are you doing down there?" Carmen asked, shocked. "What happened?"

Gary, aghast at what he had just done to me, was wailing. "Oh, my God, I just touched him in his hole! I just touched him! Richard, I'm sorry. Are you okay? I'm sorry!"

It took a few minutes for me to recover from the agonizing pain centered on my right hip. When I could speak again, I told my friend, "Gary, it was an accident. I'll be okay, but I do think we had better go."

A police officer rushed up with a wheelchair. "Are you alright? Do we need to call the EMTs?"

"No, no," I told him. "I'm fine. Just a little pain." Cathi helped me to my feet. Everyone stood back, afraid to touch me, Gary's face still twisted with guilt and concern. I told him again, "I'm okay, Gary. It was just a mistake."

I took advantage of the wheelchair, still weak, and valiantly gestured to the people standing around. "Good to see everyone again." Cathi wheeled me away; the three men followed, still surrounding me.

41
LyP Takes Battle to Multiple Fronts

It had been over five months since the operation and I did not have any PUVA treatments during the entire time. I stopped chemotherapy and medicines just prior to the surgery. There had not been any other scares since the elevated Sezary count.

But toward the end of May, a unique phenomenon began to happen. Small spots began to appear all over my body, spots that looked like small pimples. They were Lymphomatoid Papulosis tumors, but unlike their progression prior to the surgery, they did not join to form larger tumors. They remained individual.

My doctors were concerned. I had well over 700 of the small tumors with many being located in lymphoid regions. Professor Lambert still felt that the main tumors were removed and that this represented a more controllable aspect of my disease. The surgical sites healed well enough for me to resume chemo and PUVA therapies, but at a much lower dosage. Lambert's theory was now being tested.

After only three minor treatments, the small tumors began to disappear. The doctors were thrilled. The rapid results assured them, once again, that the concept behind Professor Lambert's operation had been successful. They could now control the growth of the cancer with treatments, but it also meant that I would have to continue therapy for the rest of my life. The cancer was far from cured, but it was definitely more manageable.

The other concern was still the quality of the air in the city. Dr. Gochfeld felt certain that the high amounts of Benzene in the air affected the growth of my cancer. He conferred with Dr. Hönigsman of Vienna, who concurred.

They knew that the cancer did not grow as quickly when I was away from the city and they discussed the advantages of moving to other areas where the air quality was much better. The doctor even referenced the possibility that the air pollutants may have played a part in my massive LyP manifestation. But I knew that until the Worker's Comp. and the Civil suit were completed, we could not even consider moving.

42
Workman's Comp Appeal

June 9, 1995—Finally, on June 9, 1995, almost eight months after Judge Rosati's ruling, the attorneys for the insurance companies had exhausted all their efforts for the appeal.

In a brief prepared by John Reeves for the State Appellate Court, John cited:

Judge Rosati was extremely forthright in his judgment by stating: *"...the cancer from which (the) petitioner now suffers was caused by, exacerbated by and/or accelerated by his employment activities and workplace exposure while employed by (the) respondent (Hayward Pool Products)."*

Judge Rosati later included: *"To come by any other conclusion would be to say that the petitioner's diagnosed in 29 or 31 areas of his body where he sustained either thermal burns or chemical spills is strictly coincidental and this the court cannot permit, because the court would in effect be burying its head in the sand and not affording the testimony the merit it so richly deserves."*

John explained how *"Dr. Gochfeld based his opinion upon the following factors. First, Mr. Sabb is considerably younger than (sic) the average age of the individuals who normally come down with Mycosis Fungoides. The average age of individuals with a first incidence of the disease is fifty-two years. The unusual circumstance of a short latency period in a young man exposed to chemical carcinogens strongly influenced Dr. Gochfeld's views of causal relationship in this regard."*

The brief went on to say, *"Second, Mr. Sabb had lesions appearing in the exact areas that were damaged by thermal chemical burns from chemicals that were known carcinogens. Dr. Gochfeld opined that it was highly improbable that the disease would have occurred by coincidence at the exact same site of injury from chemical burns."*

In reference to Dr. Turner's report to Carolyn Fox and Zurich Insurance Company, and his determination of my condition based on the Scottish study, Reeves' brief countered the Yale doctor by stating: *"Notwithstanding some conflicting case studies, Dr. Gochfeld opined that as a clinician he is forced to look at the individual patient; scientific/medical literature cannot dictate the entire conclusion in all situations."*

Furthermore Judge Rosati included; *"Respondent presented no lay nor medical witness on its behalf. It did not contest the factual evidence submitted by and on behalf of Petitioner. It caused this matter to be prolonged solely for the purpose of determining the extent of the responsibility of each of its compensation insurers carriers, and not necessarily to contest its obligation to Petitioner."*

John named 16 different chemicals, chemical solvents and resins that I had been exposed to on a daily basis while working at Hayward. All were, at the very least, irritants; many were carcinogens, some were mutagens.

The three judge appellate panel ruled in my favor. They were in total agreement with Rosati's judgments. I was awarded $409 per week, retroactive to October, 1992. They were to continue paying that amount until I was able to return to work, or for a total of 400 weeks, the maximum allowed by the law.

Since the doctors had already determined that I would never be able to return to work, I was to receive these payments for the next seven years and nine months, if I lived that long. Court costs and attorney's fees were reimbursed to the amount allowed by law. The insurance company even had to repay me for the COBRA payments I was making.

Home Insurance was responsible for 85 percent of the judgment, and Zurich-American for the remaining 15 percent. The judgment was in total favor of my case.

43
A Hollow Victory

July 19, 1995—The insurance companies had not sent the payment after four weeks from the judgment date. The defense attorneys filed their last and final appeal with the State Superior Court of New Jersey. John Reeves and I had waited long enough and John had no reason to believe the defense could win their final appeal.

Again, it was just another "stall" tactic by Home and Zurich insurance companies to delay paying the money. On July 12, John filed a motion to enforce payment. At last, on July 19, 1995, some 2 1/2 years later, I finally received a check in the amount of $49, 328.05 for allowable wages lost. The appeal continued.

But even with the winning of the case, my victory was hollow at best. The laws allowed that the respondent, in this case the insurance companies, were obligated to pay only 80 percent of the attorneys fees. Also, the expert witnesses, Dr. Lambert and Dr. Gochfeld, had each submitted a bill for $8,550 and $1,400 respectively. The law allowed only $250 per expert witness. I was to be held liable for the remainder.

Dr. Lambert was furious about this. He told me that he would not take any money from me, but would only take what the insurance companies would pay.

When Lambert received a ludicrous $16.75 check from Home Insurance Company, it became a source of great humor between my doctors and myself. Often during our visits, Dr. Lambert and I would joke about using the money to go to lunch together, but Lambert would laugh and say, "it won't even cover a fast food place like Mc Donald's."

In one of his more serious moments, while referencing the trial expense, medical research and experimentations, Dr. Lambert told me, *"I didn't do it for the fee. I did it for you."*

By the time I paid my portion of the legal fees, witness fees and medical fees, Cathi and I netted less than $20,000. Yet there were still accumulated living expenses and credit card bills to be paid.

The other concern was Cathi's car. It was on its "last leg" and giving her a lot of trouble. She was going to have to have more reliable transportation. The money we had left over from the Worker's Comp settlement would have to go to buy a car for Cathi.

With Cathi's paycheck the only consistent source of outside income, we needed a car she could depend on. Even with the addition of the monthly checks from the insurance companies, every extra cent went to general living expenses, vitamin therapies and other medicines that the medical insurance would not cover.

Discouraged by the length of the process and our negligible net gain, I could only hope that the civil case would be more beneficial. I was counting on what Art had told me a couple of months before the surgery.

44
Notification of SS of WC Judgment

September 6, 1995—On Wednesday, September 6, 1995, I called and faxed information to the local Social Security office to report the Appellate court's decision on the Worker's Comp suit and its pending appeal to the State Superior Court level. My primary reason for contacting them was to check to see if I could spend the remaining monies or if I could be held liable to pay back monies to the Social Security (SS) department as well as the insurers, should I lose the appeal. I included a copy of the judgment, along with a picture of my surgery site, and my treatment schedule as proof. Also included were copies of living expenses. I did all this pursuant the advice of John and a Social Security (SS) worker that I had spoken to in *August.*

I called John on Monday Sept. 4, to review my conversation with the SS worker and to ask him if he felt it was okay for us to purchase a car with the remaining monies. John agreed with the SS employee and didn't believe there could be a problem. But, John was cautious and advised me to make another call to the SS Department and speak directly to my original case handler, just in case a problem could arise.

I called Mrs. Cook at the Social Security office to let her know that a letter was on its way.

"This is Mrs. Cook. May I help you?"

I remembered the woman and how helpful she had been in initially filling out all the paperwork two years earlier. During our first meeting, she had worn a necklace with a cross on it and had the figure of a guardian angel pinned on her right lapel. I recalled her concern for my well being, and her parting comment that she would pray for me.

"Mrs. Cook, this is Richard Sabb."

"Yes, Richard, how are you doing?"

Surprisingly, she remembered me immediately. I was pleased. "I'm doing pretty well, the surgery was a success and I am still healing. I called to let you know that I just faxed a letter pertaining to the Appellate judgment in my Worker's Comp case. It was in my favor, but it, too, was appealed. And, I have some other questions."

Per Mrs. Cook's request and curiosity, I went on to explain my surgery, my treatments, and the adverse affects I suffered from them. Then, I asked if a penalty could apply if I won the appeal or if a penalty could apply due to my accepting money from the court decision. Could the Social Security Department have inadvertently over paid me from the July 9, 1995 decision, *less than 2 months earlier?*

Mrs. Cook specifically responded: *"If there is actually an overpayment, don't worry about it,"* she assured me. *"You did what you were required to do and will not be held responsible for any overpaid monies."*

I breathed a sigh of relief, and continued. "My wife still drives a long distance to and from work, and her car is old and worn out. I've been concerned about her safety and I would like to use what's left from the settlement to put toward a new car for her?" I just wanted to make sure that I was not using the money improperly. In essence, I was asking this representative of the Federal Government's branch of the Social Security Department for permission to use the money. I also made clear that I was asking if the money was indeed rightfully mine to spend.

Again Mrs. Cook confirmed, *"Yes, you can go ahead and do that. And, again, don't worry about an overpayment, you are not at fault for anything; the money is yours."*

Encouraged by Mrs. Cook's comments and her understanding of my situation, my spirits perked up.

On September 6, one day after my thirty-third birthday, I faxed the information to Mrs. Cook at the Social Security Office, just to be sure I had everything confirmed. Then Cathi and I purchased a car that evening. Maybe it wasn't going to be so bad, I thought, and maybe I wouldn't take too much of a "hit" or reduction in the benefits I received. For about the next four months, I continued to receive the same amount in my Social Security check. It was logical to assume that my benefits would not be at jeopardy and my settlement money was mine.

45
SS Overpayment Letter

December 1995—Shortly after Christmas of 95 Cathi and I were greeted with a form letter from the Social Security Department. It began, "We are writing to give you new information about the disability benefits which you received." The letter went on to state that my monthly benefits were being reduced by more than 50 percent to $556 per month, due to the Worker's Compensation decision. It also stated that I had been overpaid $18,217.40, dating back to my first benefits received in 1993.

This can't be right, I thought, stunned by the amount the agency expected me to repay. I didn't receive any Worker's Comp money until June 12, 1995. How could I have been overpaid in '93 and '94? How could I have been overpaid at all when I reported everything to them?

Before I broke the news to Cathi, I wanted to talk to John Reeves.

"John," I said to the lawyer once he was on the phone, "I don't understand what they are saying in this letter. How could I have been overpaid that much? I reported the court decision on Worker's Comp last August ('95) and called again as they directed me to in September. Mrs. Cook, the lady I talked to, said that everything was okay and to wait for the appeal decision, which has not been made yet."

"Richard, don't panic," John told me. "Fax me all your Social Security paperwork and a copy of that faxed letter. I'll check into this. It may take me a little while, and I may have to turn it over to another attorney. I am not well versed in Social Security laws. But in the meantime, try not to worry about it. It's probably the government bureaucracy bungling things up, again."

I was somewhat relieved, and knew the letter was going to upset Cathi. When I showed it to her that evening she became emotionally distraught. "How can they say that we were overpaid when we can't even pay our own bills now? It's no wonder so many people just give up and die, especially when you have to deal with this kind of crap from a government agency that is supposed to be helping you." Cathi was in tears and pacing back and forth from the kitchen to the living room.

"Cathi," I said, trying to calm her, "John said not to worry. We'll get this taken care of. Besides, I did everything they expected of me. It's just a misunderstanding and many of their dates are wrong. We'll get this worked out." My confidence helped her to relax a little.

"It's just that it's been so hard," she said, her eyes filled with tears. "When are they going to stop screwing with us?"

Although she settled down emotionally for the evening, another battle was taking shape.

By early February (1996) John had turned over my SS case to Henry Dew, one of the firm's young new members that specialized in SS law. Henry immediately contacted me and instructed me to request forms for a "waiver of over payment." The forms were really quite simple and straightforward. It was particularly interesting filling out pages six and seven that itemized "Household & basic living expenses, and then income."

Cathi and I filled them out honestly by using actual receipts (supplied to the SS) and were in shock. Monthly expenses totaled $4,857.49 and income totaled $3,341.68. Now for those readers who are not blessed by the incompetence of the SS department's "mathematics" and reasoning, the difference is a *negative $1,515.88.*

We were receiving money and having bills paid by my parents. But until that day, we did not realize how far in the hole we really were. Mom and Dad were usually very casual about the bills and did not want to add any pressure to our lives. The bills were paid and nothing was said.

Dad repaired and purchased trains with (or for) me, and Mom spent time with Cathi redecorating and adding treatments to our home. Cathi and I were their main priority and they sacrificed their lifestyle and assets for us. My parents felt privileged that they had the ability to help us keep our home and some feeble definition of quality of life.

That summer my parents realized the growing emotional turmoil that Cathi and I were contending with. They basically stood helplessly on the outside watching their children struggle with an ongoing appeal to Workman's Comp., a mounting Social Security battle—with the threat of losing half or all benefits—weekly depositions for a Civil Trial, recovery from massive surgery, ongoing treatments and their reactions, and the likely probability of another operation for me.

My parents sold their retirement property in Williamsburg, Virginia that year and decided to have some well needed repairs done to our home. Cathi was ecstatic. Our home received new paint, windows, curtains, gutters, front step railings, repairs to the steps, and new entrance light fixtures. And that six-foot by eight-foot wooden parquet and glass window that Cathi loved, Dad spent nearly a week scraping, sanding, caulking, and re-varnishing it until it was new.

On June 22, 1996, house remodeling under way; I received a letter from W. Burnell Hurt, Director, SS Administration located in Baltimore, Maryland. I was excited; how could anyone side against me when I did exactly what Mrs. Cook told me to do and she personally said I was not at fault. Besides, I told Cathi and my parents, "were $1,500 bucks in the hole every month and you guys aren't legally responsible for me" I said, gesturing to my parents.

The letter started: *"This concerns your request for waiver of recovery* *of the over payment of $18,217.40. We cannot approve your request for waiver of recovery of your overpayment."*

Other inserts from the presumed cognitive intellectual decision making included: *"Our records show that you received the settlement November 28, 1994.* (Not true—received June 12, 95) *You failed to report the settlement before September 1995.* (Not true—Aug. '95 I contacted them and within the 90-day time frame of actual settlement) *You could not have avoided being overpaid for April 1993 through November 1994.* (Ah—does he think?) *However, had you promptly reported the award, the overpayment for December 1994 through December 1995 could have been avoided."*

"Based on the above evidence we find you are without fault for accepting the incorrect payments for April 1993 through November 1994, totaling $14,640. However, your financial statement shows no hard ship would be caused by repayment. (Yes, W. Burnell Hurt believes that a negative cash flow of $1,500 per month was not enough debt or financial hardship.)

Mr. Hurt made reference to Section 204 of the SS Act that states: *no recovery of an overpayment shall be sought when the person liable for repayment is without fault and the recovery would deprive the person of income for ordinary and necessary living expenses or would be unfair for some other reason. Both conditions must be met.* (Incorrect, this actually identifies three conditions and it is the start of undefined terminology and phrases that the SS intentionally uses to control situations to their benefit.)

The paragraph continued: *Although the individual from whom we are attempting to recover the overpayment may need substantially all current monthly income to meet current and necessary living expenses, recovery of the overpayment is required unless the person is also without fault in causing the overpayment.*

This statement should not be interpreted as redundant or a repeat of "no recovery of an overpayment shall be sought when the person liable for repayment is without fault" as stated in the start of Section 204 of the SS Act. This difference in terminology allows the SS

Department to determine fault. In so doing they apply "three distinct tests" that have a total of nine criteria that you must meet.

The letter continued: "*The first is weather (whether) you made an incorrect statement or a statement which you knew or should have known was incorrect. The second is weather (whether) you failed to furnish information timely which you knew or should have known to be material. The third is weather (whether) you accepted payments which you either knew or could have been expected to know were incorrect.*

It is this type of terminology that allows the SS department complete immunity to fault of any wrongdoing. Hence, this terminology allows the SS department full discretionary power to instill complete fault on the recipient regardless as to whether or not the recipient was actually at fault. Therefore, a government devised for "we the people" has now been manipulated by lawmakers to "you're screwed and it's your fault!"

As I read the letter to Cathi and my parents, they all became livid with boisterous sarcasm toward Mr. Hurt and the government as a whole. Surprisingly, I stayed calm, telling them the letter was just the start, and I planned on fighting it. The letter clearly stated that I had the right to a personal conference with a SS administration employee where I could present testimony, witnesses and even bring an attorney. I assured Cathi and my parents I would contact Henry Dew and have him schedule the conference as soon as possible. This temporarily brought focus back to the home renovations.

46
Cancer Takes Battle to Genitals

Summer of 1996—Throughout my ordeal with cancer, I had experienced about 100 minor biopsies to remove small Mycosis Fungoides tumors. Most of the time, the interns did the cutting right in the laboratory, with more than one site excised. The incisions would usually require from 0 - 2 or 3 stitches. If Dr. Brooks or Dr. Patel did the cutting, again, it was often in their offices. Cathi even assisted on a few occasions.

During the summer of 1996, I noticed a tumor in an area that caused me a great deal of alarm. A growth appeared on my penis. In spite of the familiarity that the medical team had of my entire body, it was difficult for me to tell the doctors about this new development. When I thought of the possibility of a surgery, even a minor one, I broke into a cold sweat.

I don't want them to cut me down there, I thought. What if they slip?

When I did muster enough courage to tell Dr. Lambert about the developing tumor, I was surprised by the response.

"I've been anticipating something like this," Lambert told me. "You see, Richard, there are certain areas of the body which are extremely susceptible to your form of cancer—the linings of your nostrils, eyelids, lips, the nipples, and the groin. These are all areas that are more susceptible. So, I am not surprised by this development."

It would have been nice to be forewarned, I thought. But I knew, as open as the doctors were with me, they couldn't predict everything.

"So, Doc, are we going to have to cut it?" I asked, hoping the answer would be no.

"Let's take a look at it, before I make that determination," Lambert said.

I stripped off my clothing while Lambert called for Drs. 'Ricky' and Martinez and several interns. I sat on a table while they all gathered around me.

Lambert's face broadcasted the verdict. "I don't like this," he announced. "It's got to come out."

Dr. Martinez inspected the site and agreed. Dr. 'Ricky' made it unanimous.

"I gotta say, Docs," I said nervously, "I'm not real crazy about the idea of someone with a knife down there. Is there anything else that can be done?"

"Unfortunately, no Richard," Lambert said sympathetically, "let's not play any games with this one. Let's just take it off. We need to get one of the interns in here and have them take care of this now."

"Okay," I said cautiously, "let's do it now. But, who's going to do it. All you guys are scientists, not cutters."

Dr. 'Ricky' spoke up. "We need to get a surgical intern in here."

"Well, make sure he's a damned good one, I'd like to keep what I have," I commanded.

It wasn't that easy to find someone willing to perform my delicate surgery. The first few interns called in were male and really did not feel comfortable practicing on such a delicate area.

I quickly let them off the hook.

Two more interns, females this time, were brought in. They were more receptive but also commented, "That's not a good location for a tumor."

So many interns had examined the jewels that the situation became somewhat humorous. I was certain they were just trying to make me more comfortable. But this intern was relaxed, intent in thought as to the procedure, and more delicate with her touch.

She looked at me and spoke directly to me. "I can take care of this for you, if you want me to?"

Finally I was able to calm down. "You know, I feel more comfortable with you. I'd like you to take care of it. Please be careful."

Relieved that I finally found someone, I sighed. But in the same instant, my body tensed, fearing what was to come.

A plastic chair was pulled up for me to sit in. The intern prepared for the procedure.

"Here," Dr. 'Ricky' said, handing a book to me, "a little light reading for you. This way, you have the option of watching or reading."

I took the book. It was about Mycosis Fungoides. "Thanks, Doc," I said facetiously.

The intern wanted to make sure that the area was completely numb. The first needle filled with Lidocaine felt like fire to me. "Damn," I swore, "that sucker hurts." I gripped the chair tight enough to leave permanent imprints, but never twitched on her.

The following shots did not hurt as much, but the sweat was pouring out of my body. Two interns left the room, commenting that they couldn't watch. "I would never let anyone cut me there," one male intern said as he walked toward the door.

"Yeah, thanks," I called to him, "you're really making me feel better."

The female intern worked quickly and expertly. Within minutes the tumor was removed. It was one of the larger tumors that had been removed in-house. It was approximately 3/4 inch in length and 1/4 inch wide. The intern closed the cut with a few stitches and was done. I sat in a pool of sweat, grateful for her steady hands and thankful that the procedure was over.

47
What Does Truth or Law
Have to Do With It?

August 6, 1996–May 28, 1998—Henry Dew, my Social Security (SS) attorney, was quick to respond to the administrative notice and was able to successfully pressure Jacqueline Stern, office manager of the Iselin, NJ, office, to schedule a personal conference on August 6, 1996 with SS representative Mr. Newton.

By Tuesday, August 6, 1996 Henry was fully prepared and laid out chronologically all my actions and all the errors of the SS administration. He even organized statements of fact that pertained to the various sections of SS law. He and I organized full documentation of my ongoing medical condition and living expenses. Henry also invited my father to give testimony regarding their payment of bills that Cathi and I could not afford on a monthly basis.

The three of us met outside the SS office at 9:30 A.M. Henry wanted to be a half-hour early in order to answer any last minute questions or settle any last minute preparations.

As I stood in the elevator with my Dad and Henry we joked about how we were going to destroy this evaluator. We clearly had everything in order and could conclusively prove no fault on my behalf. Henry cautiously agreed and warned: "we have to take this one step at a time,

Social Security Law is obscure and subject to interpretation. Let's just hit him with everything we have and then see what happens."

It became apparent to me that things still could go wrong. Although I maintained a smile, intense anger was building up inside me. My Dad and I suddenly questioned our confidence to ourselves.

Upon meeting Mr. Newton, we realized we were in for trouble. He sat behind a simple desk with his head down and did not even stand to shake our hands during Henry's stylish introductions. When I asked for his first name, he responded, "You can call me Mr. Newton."

I couldn't help myself and I slipped out a semi-private laugh. Henry looked at me and smiled, my Dad poked me in the back of the leg, and I gave "Mr. Newton" an extra little squeeze as I shook his hand. When he attempted to withdraw his hand from mine, I held on, forcing him to look up at me. I intensely peered directly into the center of his eyes and he realized he was dealing with one "pissed off" cancer patient that would proudly make his children fatherless.

The success of my attempt at intimidation was quite evident in his facial expression, yet before letting go his hand, I sarcastically added, "by the way, do you need me to introduce you to Mrs. Cook, she is sitting across from you."

Henry took control of the situation and started to format the proceedings. He thoroughly reviewed all the events and the dates of their occurrence. He presented all my bills and expenses, and released copies of receipts as proof thereof. He diligently reviewed the SS laws and provided explanations and evidence as to why I should not be held liable. He included the SS administration letter that identified their fault and the lack of mine. And finally, he concluded with testimony from my father qualifying that they pay substantial amounts of money to help maintain a stable lifestyle for Cathi and I.

Henry realized he was dealing with an intellectually indigent person and explained that my parents are not legally liable for me or my expenses and that they in fact could individually gift Cathi and I a total of $10,000 per year each, for a yearly total of $40,000, if they were able to afford it and chose to do so. The SS could not count this as income nor could it be included as guaranteed yearly gifts. Mom and Dad simply can't afford to do this and were indeed tapping into their retirement funds to pay the $1,500 per month.

During Henry's meticulously executed dissertation, Mr. Newton showed some sign of life by occasionally taking a note, accepting evidence to add to his file, and looking up at Henry and stating, "Da, ah, could you repeat that?"

I was well informed by Henry as to how he planned to execute the meeting. With Mr. Newton's mundane responses and complete lack of interest in what Henry was saying, Henry cut his dissertation short.

In less than a half hour, I was back in the elevator leaving the building. Henry was quick to evaluate the situation and respected my intelligence by being honest. "Richard, I don't think we stand a chance with this guy. I think we should just forget about what happened today and plan on going before a judge."

Henry was good about keeping me calm. I had had about all the shit in life that anyone could dish out and still stood with a smile. He realized my emotional turmoil. Part of me wanted to rip Mr. Newton apart, and part of me felt sorry for him. After all, he was the mindless puppet on a government string.

For the next eight months the SS administration dragged it's feet in settling my complaint. Instead, they asked for me to resubmit all my bills and expenses once again. Henry continually corresponded with Mr. Newton and, as expected, got nothing accomplished.

Finally on April 11, 1997 I received notice from the SS that according to Mr. Newton I have a surplus of income over expenses and that a total refund of the over payment of $18,217.40 should be made within 30 days.

It is important to note here that the SS administration, through Mr. Newton's letter, had now blatantly falsified information and was planning to "illegally" collect funds. Mr. Newton wrote in his April 7, 1997 letter that: "*Mr. Sabb claimed during the personal conference that at the time he received a favorable decision regarding his Worker's Compensation case, he was too concerned with his medical condition to be worried about his reporting responsibilities to Social Security.*" This is not true.

Although my medical condition is indeed my primary concern, my attorneys and I all knew that the decision was immediately appealed. I acted upon the guidance of the Judge, my attorney and an SS representative. Mr. Newton failed to acknowledge my attorney when he pointed this out. Therefore, he is simply manipulating words and blatantly making things up in order to find me at fault. This is how the government works when they are at fault.

Further into the three page letter he falsely states: "*A number of financial statements were obtained but the Sabb family income was consistently understated since he failed to use the correct weekly multiplier to convert weekly income into monthly income. His monthly income appears to be understated by approximately 25 percent.*"

Mr. Newton continued by stating that my expenses were inflated and that Cathi's 401k retirement plan and her car should be liquidated in order to pay back the monies.

Mr. Newton concluded: "*It is therefore determined that relief from repayment of this overpayment of $18,217.40 cannot be granted. Refund of the total overpayment of $18,217 should be made within 30 days.*"

What fascinated Henry and I was that Mr. Newton's report made no sense even when applying his own statements. Prior to his determination statement, Mr. Newton wrote: "*In summery (summary), a revised financial statement indicates a surplus of income over expenses and there are other assets available for repayment of this debt.*"

"*Recovery over a 3 year period from current Social Security benefit payments would not deprive Mr. Sabb of income necessary to meet current living expenses.*"

We could not figure out this form of government math. Henry attempted to manipulate my numbers and receipts to conform to Newton, but still concluded with me being over $1,000 per month in debt. Even a local accountant that helps cancer patients now and then could not figure out the SS administration's math. Henry was frustrated and informed me he would start the paper work to bring this before an "Administrative Law Judge."

About six weeks later Cathi and I received a real shock. Cathi's employer, Makita Power Tools, informed her that SS was attempting to remove and/or put a Lien on her 401k plan. Makita did not allow it and demanded authoritative proof from SS.

This delay allowed my newly appointed attorney, Eric Green, to stop the SS administration dead in their tracks. Mr. Newton and Mrs. Stern had forgotten that even within my own letter, case law reference was made to: *"Posnack vs Secretary of Health & Human Services",* (and others), where the SS administration does not have the right to seize or place lien upon a spouse's retirement monies or any tangible item or asset that is required for everyday living.

The morning after learning about the lien, I was scheduled for a treatment. My truck wasn't running well, so I had made arrangements with Cathi to use her car. I took the Oxsoralen Ultra pills, staring out the kitchen window, still angered by the events of the previous day.

In the car, the traffic was bad on the Parkway, but I had allowed enough time. I tried to think of other things, but my mind gravitated back to the conversation with Stern, and my anger renewed. Torture would be too good for her, I thought to myself.

I had been crawling through the traffic for forty-five minutes, and I began to feel bad. The medication had started to act. I exited the Parkway and got onto Route 280, hoping that this would speed up the trip. I was still functioning by the time I reached the stretch of the highway which became Summit Road.

The local police officers, and even some of the state officers, knew me. More than once, I pulled over onto the shoulder to drive during bad traffic. They would stop me, and I would explain that it was a medical emergency, and give them details of the chemotherapy. With an understanding of the situation, they would then escort me to the hospital.

For some reason, this day I did not pull over, but remained in traffic instead. It was the wrong decision. A few miles from St. Barnabas Hospital, I began going into violent convulsions. I was just able to pull over to the side of the road and park the car. I grabbed the cell phone and dialed 9-1-1. By now, my entire body was beginning to cramp.

A state patrol officer answered the 911 call. It was difficult to speak, but I forced myself to tell the officer what was happening. The cramping from the convulsion was so severe that my legs had begun to pull up. My hands were cramped so tightly that I could not let go of the steering wheel in one hand and the phone in the other. My vision was blurred and my breathing had become labored. I was doubling over, my nose and forehead pressing hard against the steering wheel.

"Sir," the voice of the patrolman came over the phone, "you have to try to tell me where you are."

" I don't know. I can't get up to see. I think I'm still on Summit Road, but I'm not sure where," I managed.

The officer was concerned. That highway ran through three different towns. "Okay," he told me patiently, "try to look out the window and tell me what you see."

I struggled to pull myself up enough to peek over the dashboard. I saw, and then remembered, that I was near a university. I forced myself to speak again, "I see a university."

As I looked out the window, a car had slowed and the driver was straining to see what was wrong.

I formed the words "help me," hoping the woman would be able to read my lips. Instead, she looked at me in panic and sped off.

"That damned woman just left me!" I cried, gritting my teeth as another cramp seized me. "I can't move. I need help now."

At the mention of Summit Road, the officer had dispatched police and ambulances from all three towns. The officer continued to talk to me, asking me questions, making sure that I stayed conscious.

It took several minutes, but a young police officer was the first to arrive. The young man opened the door and was reaching to retrieve the cell phone from my hand.

"Do not approach the victim," came loudly over the police officer's shoulder radio. "He is in muscular convulsions."

Basic training taught all officers to exercise extreme precautions with anyone experiencing muscular convulsions. They could often have the strength of ten men.

The blood drained from the officer's face, and he immediately released his grip on my hand and backed away. "Sir, please don't touch me!" he shouted, and turned to warn the other emergency personnel who had begun to arrive. He quickly went to the back seat to gain a better position to grab my arms. His objective was to pin my arms down so that I would not harm myself.

When I was somewhat upright, I could see three ambulances and nine or ten police cars surrounding me. The entire road was blocked off.

With the young officer holding me securely, another police officer opened the driver's door and helped hold me. At the same time, a female paramedic entered through the passenger side and stabbed me, through my clothing, with a full injection of Lidocaine.

"This should help," the paramedic told me.

"Oh, yeah," I breathed, already beginning to feel the effects.

Another police officer grabbed me around the shoulders. "I'm giving you some oxygen," he warned, as he planted an oxygen mask over my face. I felt another needle as the EMT gave me another shot of Lidocaine. With three policemen holding me down, two doses of Lidocaine and oxygen, I was feeling better.

It was visually evident, too, that I was getting better. The color was returning to my face and hands, my muscles were relaxing.

"We're going to start to let you go," a police officer told me.

"Are you okay?" It was the paramedic. "Are you clenching?"

"No, no," I assured them both, "I'm feeling pretty good."

Very gradually, the police officers released their hold on me, warily watching every move I made.

When they had fully released me, two other EMTs stepped in. They took my vital signs and listened to my heart rate.

"Are you having any chest pains?" the EMT with the stethoscope asked.

"Yes," I explained, "but I have a fluttering mitral valve as a result of all the medications I take."

Aware that their patient knew what he was talking about, the other EMT asked, "So, you don't think you are having a heart attack on us?"

"No, it's just my mitral valve."

They moved me onto the gurney and strapped me down, continuing to test my muscles to make sure that they were not still tensed. They put me into the ambulance and raced for the hospital.

According to my instructions, the police had notified my in-laws. They were over two hours away, but they drove back from the Jersey shore to pick up Cathi and rush to the hospital. Cathi's car was towed and parked at the police station.

Dr. Brooks was already on alert at the hospital and waiting as the ambulance drove up. "We're going to have to get that medication out of you," Dr. Brooks warned me. "This is going to clean you out."

A staff member gave me a shot.

Within minutes, I could feel the effects of the third shot. "I'm going to lose it," I informed a nurse standing close by.

"We want you to lose it," she told me and helped me to the toilet.

For the next twenty minutes, I was throwing up and wrestling with diarrhea. I had no doubt that my system was cleaned out.

Cathi and her family showed up and waited until the effects of the medicine had worn off. Cathi and her mother helped me, while her father and brother went off to retrieve the car.

"You just like driving fast in an ambulance," Cathi teased me. She knew I was going to be all right. "We ought to call you the 'Energizer Bunny!'"

I grinned, "Yeah, I just keep going and going."

When we arrived home, I went up to our bedroom, feeling the affects of my ordeal. I lay down on the bed and slept soundly for the next eighteen hours.

By now I was going through my days with a ferocious anger toward Newton and Stern. I often drove home from the hospital wanting to take a detour off the NJ Parkway to dismember the government's henchmen.

My treatments often fueled my anger toward my many legal and administrative adversaries and my hostility was becoming apparent.

The pressure was mounting; I respected my attorneys, but none of them wanted me to go public with my situation. I was still doing treatments two times a week, and meeting with Art for all the intricacies of Civil trial preparation.

And if that was not enough, I also started my Civil trial depositions with as many as 14 defense attorneys. But with all the villains in my life, one defense attorney managed to surpass them all. Mr. Eaten was hands down the winner of *"The Perpetual Prick Award."*

Eric Green was now my new SS attorney and by July of 1997 he had successfully inundated Jacqueline Stern with more case law than her paper shredder could handle.

Finally the SS Office Manager was giving in (or was she?). She contacted Eric with a proposal that if I agree to a monthly withholding of $100 per month, she would reinstate my benefits until we were able to go before a case law judge.

She also stated that it would take at least 18 months to 2 years to get a trial with a judge. If I did not agree to her offer I would lose all my benefits and be held liable for the full $18,217 in 30 days.

She even stated that I would have to start this filing process from the beginning. I had no choice but to agree and for those readers who do not know, this situation is recognized by law as being forced to settle or comply under duress.

What Jacqueline did not know was that in early June, 1997, I had written a letter to New Jersey Senator Frank R. Loutenberg outlining my medical condition and the antics of the Social Security department. I also included numerous documents as proof.

The Senator was well known in New Jersey for standing up to government bureaucracy and helping to solve problems versus just talking about them and finding someone to blame. In other words, he actually did something. So, I thought he would be a good person to ask for help.

Within two days of their office receiving my letter, one of his aides contacted me. Mrs. Mada, the aide, was shocked by what I had sent and was more beside herself after talking to me. But she warned that the Senator was very busy and that she needed proof before they could get involved. Basically, she wanted to hear from my attorney.

On July 7, 1997 Eric sent a letter to the Senator's attention outlining all of the events and even made reference to the 18-month wait for the up coming administrative hearing. At that time we were asking the Senator if it would be possible to have the hearing pushed up to a more reasonable time and if the Social Security Administration was conducting themselves properly.

The Senator was quick to have his aide respond. They successfully contacted Mr. Hurt at the main office in Baltimore and enabled me to receive a hearing only two months later on September 9, 1997. Mrs. Mada also made reference that it is possible to file suit against the government but certainly not an easy task.

Eric and I were quite surprised at the Senator's ability to help with scheduling a hearing in a timely manner. There really was no preparation needed on my behalf, due to most of it being "my every day life." But Eric was new to the firm and wanted to make a good impression by winning his "FIRST" case.

He called me on my birthday, September 5, and wanted to review his procedures. I think I really floored him when I responded; *well I would really like to do this with you but I did just get home from a treatment and I had a small tumor removed.*

Eric knew it was my birthday and he never had the opportunity to see me showing any distress or even see me lose my composure. Momentarily the phone was silent. Cautiously he asked, "Well do you think Monday will be okay?"

Monday morning I called Eric to start the review. This time he floored me. He had worked on my case over the weekend, reviewing every document, phone call, receipt, and anything he could get his hands on about me. He knew more about me with SS than I actually did. I could not ask for more.

On Tuesday, September 9, 1997 my parents, Cathi and I all met Eric in front of the Newark, NJ, Federal building. Once in the hall Eric outlined his procedures and asked that my parents wait outside the courtroom. He was so organized that he did not even want me to give testimony unless the judge asked for it. After we entered the courtroom the Honorable Judge Gerald J. Ryan entered. As he took the stand he commented, *"So you're the fellow who had the Senator change my schedule."*

It was obvious the judge was not happy, and Eric looked to me and said, *"Shit, don't worry, I can handle this guy."* And handle him he did. From memory alone, Eric meticulously identified every situation, explained it, and chronologically identified all the errors made by the SS administration. He often referenced documents, but still maintained 90 percent of the case at the tip of his tongue.

When Judge Ryan did ask questions, Eric immediately responded with accuracy and professionalism. It would have been easy for him to make a mockery of the SS department, but he never did.

Judge Ryan concluded the case with, *"If you do not have anything else, I will get back to you with my decision."*

Eric, Cathi and I realized the judge was quite annoyed that we were able to get Senator Loutenberg to change his schedule. But Eric really presented a perfect case. We realized we still could lose, because after all we were asking a government employee to side against the government. And the SS administration did not even send a representative. The judge was theirs.

Our past proved the government lies, changes documents and statements to conform to their needs. This was nothing new to us. Without knowing if we won or lost, the next day Cathi and I sent a letter of praise and recommendation on Eric's behalf to John Reeves and the partners of Winslow and Abby. Eric's professionalism and dedication warranted the action regardless of the outcome.

It would take another eight months for Judge Ryan to make his determination and when it arrived it startled all of us. The judge stated in his findings that:

"1. The claimant was overpaid benefits in the amount of $18,217.40.

2. The claimant was without fault in causing or accepting the overpayment not only for the period of April 1993 through November 1994, but for the period of December 1994 through December 1995 as well.

3. Further recovery of the over payment would not defeat the purpose of Title II of the Social Security Act, especially with respect to his current payments of $100 per month.

4. Recovery of the overpayment is not waived."

Signed, May 28, 1998, Gerald J. Ryan, New Jersey Administrative Law Judge.

What happened here was, Judge Ryan recognized Eric's identification of all the facts and realized the SS administration was at fault. But, by Jacqueline Stern forcing the $100 per month payment upon me back on July 16, 1997, the judge felt, in essence, that if my parents could afford to pay the $1,500 per month to help their son and daughter-in-law, what was another $100 per month. The judge failed in his appointed duties to society and me by not finding in my favor.

The judge knows that nowhere in the laws does it state that my parents are liable for me and their gifts to me cannot be counted as assets. Furthermore, the Judge failed to recognize that Jacqueline, while representing the SS administration broke the law herself by forcing the ultimatum of $100 per month payment or full immediate recovery of $18,217.40. This defines the statement of "an action under duress."

Eric politely contacted me some days later to find out if I decided to continue with an appeal. I told him that after speaking to Cathi and my parents we decided not to move forward. After three years of the Social Security Administration's bullshit, none of us thought it was possible to get a fair trial from the U.S. government.

I also told him my doctors were quite certain that the stress from all the simultaneous litigation was affecting my health. We felt it would be better if I focused on the Civil Action and my medical well-being.

Eric knew I had experienced more than most, but when I told him that I have now completed or was still involved in; five different litigations, nine operations, and some 400 treatments, he understood my desire to end the battle and accept the incompetent judge's decision.

48
Strategic Planning for Romantic R&R

December 1996-February 1997—One day in mid-December, I was working in my train room on some prized turn of the century Lionel 2 7/8 gauge trains. I had been sick most of the month and never stopped treatments or attending depositions for the "civil action." My ongoing battle with Social Security took up some of my time, but my attorneys handled the bulk of the work. It was the emotional strain that caused most of the damage to my personal life.

Cathi worked all day at Makita and came home to care for me, usually at all hours of the night. When I was sick, which was quite often that month due to a persistent cold that severely affected my treatments and recovery. I was usually in bed before 2:30 in the afternoon and only got up to eat dinner with Cathi. Then I would graciously keep her up all night with some sort of ailment or medical emergency.

I was feeling guilty about this and having a difficult time enjoying my recently acquired treasures. For this was going to be a special year. Christmas, Cathi's favorite time of year, was only a week away. I had not yet purchased her a gift, and February would also be our seventh wedding anniversary. I wanted to do something extraordinary for my loving, caring wife.

My mind kept wandering to her. Five of our seven years of marriage were hell for her, continually living day to day not knowing if I would regain some median of health and valiantly standing strong at my side caring for me without hesitation. Cathi could not even be sure if one day we may be granted retribution from the obviously liable manufacturer or this country's failing justice system. She had willingly sacrificed everything for me, meaning with all her heart the marriage vow: *"til death do us part."*

I stopped what I was doing and simply stared out the window contemplating my life. It was cold and rainy. Heavy clouds blocked any chance of sun and it had been this way all week. Cathi loved the beaches in the Bahamas; we have not been on any vacation that did not include some family or the family paying for it. I was broke and our only spending money came from my parents. The Workman's Comp trial was over and that money was spent to pay off credit cards and a car.

"Screw this," I thought, "We need a break from everything and everyone."

My disease did not allow for me to do anything without a plan. I needed to know where hospitals were located, if doctors could handle me in an emergency, if "Flight For Life helicopters" were available and, of course, permission from my doctors. This trip was going to be a complete surprise to Cathi and therefore a full-blown "Covert Operation"—at least from the family.

I immediately called my friend Gary, whose wife was a travel agent. "Gary, I am taking Cathi to the Bahamas for our seventh anniversary. Have Judy book me first class airfares and a room over looking the water from Monday February 24 to Friday the 29th. Have her use my credit card, she has it on file."

"What? How are you going to pay for that? Oh my god, are you going to die again?" Gary was quite concerned and confused.

"Relax, I'm okay. And I'm not going to worry about paying for the trip until I get back. Maybe I can get lucky and make a train deal or two. But you are not going to believe what I am up to."

My plan was elaborate; I checked with my doctors and received their approval. I decided that for total surprise and secrecy I would buy Cathi all new clothing and luggage. This would prevent her from noticing anything missing from the house. I asked my sister-in-law, Chris, to help or actually make the clothing purchases. I would rent a limo for airport transfers. Then, I would make secret arrangements with her boss at Makita so Cathi could have the week off. And, most importantly, I did not tell any family member until the last possible minute.

It was good that I acted on my instincts and contacted Gary and Judy to help me with my plans. Only three days later on December 23, while driving to the hospital for a treatment, I had a bad reaction to the medicine and ended up, once again, in the emergency room. Christmas was difficult, but I recovered quickly, and on December 26 treatments resumed.

Shortly after New Year's, I called Cathi's friend and immediate supervisor, Karen. "Karen," I said when she answered the phone, "this is Rich. I need to talk to you about a plan I have. You have a few minutes?"

Karen was surprised to hear from me and curious as to what I wanted. "Sure. What can I do for you?" There was a touch of apprehension as she remembered our conversation three years earlier.

"I am planning a surprise for Cathi. It's our seventh wedding anniversary in February, but I need your help with it."

Her anxiety dissipated and was replaced with my infectious enthusiasm. "What can I do to help?"

I outlined my plan for the trip to the Bahamas. "Can we arrange for Cathi to have a week off, but not let her know about it?"

"Don't worry, I'll take care of it for you," she said excitedly. "Will you take me with you?"

I laughed, knowing that my plan was going to work.

49
Romantic R&R for Soul Alliance

February 24-29, 1997—By January 1997 Karen, Cathi's boss, was starting to move Cathi's workload to other employees. She was worried that they might want to fire her due to all the lost time from work. Many days she came home practically in tears, wondering why they would consider letting her go, when she was at work, she worked hard and was conscious of her responsibilities.

I was well aware of the daily turmoil she was enduring. Cathi was part of the civil action and my bad reaction to medicines over Christmas was still fresh in her mind. And the ongoing problems with the SS Administration were not making her life any easier. I knew if I told her about the trip it would relax her somewhat and give her something to anticipate. However, holding out and not telling her would certainly make the trip a truly magnificent surprise. I opted for the latter.

One day in early February she came home with swollen eyes. It was apparent she had been crying on the drive from work. Cathi didn't want to upset me after the day's treatment, but couldn't refrain from asking if I heard anything from the lawyer about Social Security. I tried to console her but the "no" answer was not what she wanted to hear.

Then she stated that Karen was splitting up her clients to other employees. To my surprise, when I told her that it was likely due to the market slowing and that Karen was just keeping everyone busy, she believed me without hesitation and the dilemma was over.

My doctors were as excited about my plans for Cathi as I was and they adjusted my treatments according to the plan. With only a few weeks before leaving I decided it was time to let my sister-in-law, Chris, in on the plan. After all, I planned on purchasing Cathi all new clothes and luggage for the trip. Chris's input was definitely needed.

"Chris, I need you to go shopping with me."

"Shopping?" Chris questioned. "What would you need me for?" Suddenly, Chris realized that our anniversary was coming up. "Are we going shopping for Cathi's anniversary present?" She was excited, knowing my history of saving for nice gifts for Cathi.

"Listen, Chris," I explained. "You can't let anyone know about this, I really have a big surprise for Cathi this year. I suspect everyone in the family is going to be real pissed off when they find out what I am up to. You know, I haven't been able to do anything nice for her since the diagnosis and on our first two anniversaries, we were broke from all the home repairs on the 3-family."

"Don't worry, I won't tell anyone anything, but are you okay? You didn't get any bad news from the doctors again, did you." Chris was worried. Was this another medical problem that I didn't want the family to know about? Or did I just want to enjoy my anniversary with Cathi, regardless of the consequences?

"No, Chris, I'm fine," I said quickly, relieving Chris' anxiety. "Listen, I bought first class plane tickets to the Bahamas for our anniversary. I even got us a beachside room. I am having Rick, the limo driver, pick us up at 7 A.M. next Friday. I already spoke to Karen at Makita, and arranged for Cathi to take vacation time. No one in the family, and especially Cathi, is to know anything about this."

Chris was giddy with excitement, but contained herself in case someone was nearby and able to hear the conversation. "Richie, this is unbelievable! She's going to go nuts over this! I can't believe you did all that! You guys really deserve some time away from all this trial bullshit, and your treatments. Wait, you can't go to the Bahamas. What are your doctors going to say?"

"Don't worry, Chris, I took care of that, too. The docs have been changing my treatments and my medicines so I can go. All I need is my blood results and then, this is a go. Besides, you know me; I really don't care what my blood tests read. I'm going."

"So, how can I help?" Chris asked.

"Well, I want to meet you at Woodbridge Center tomorrow and go clothes shopping for Cathi. We're buying everything: socks, sandals, underwear, bathing suit, the works. Oh, and I need to buy luggage, too. I'm getting everything new, so that there is no way she could suspect anything."

"My god, Richie, this is unbelievable. I am glad it's only a week away. I'm not sure I could keep this a secret. Of course, I'll meet you there. But listen, I know this is none of my business, but how are you paying for all this?" Chris knew we were struggling financially and receiving money from my parents.

I was almost glad that Chris asked this personal question. I didn't want her to worry that I was voluntarily putting Cathi in a bad financial position should I die anytime soon. "Listen, Chris, I don't mind you asking. I know you worry about what will happen to Cathi when I'm gone. But my attorney tells me that our case is precedent setting, and is worth multi-millions. My cancer won't quit and could kill me whenever it wants. So, I figure, charge it on the credit cards. If I die, Cathi gets the insurance money and pays for it. Or, we win, and this is no big deal anyway. The only problem is if I live and lose the case. Then, we spend the next couple years paying for it."

"Richie, I really admire you," Chris said approvingly. "You do so much regardless of the shit everyone gives you, and I am including the families too, you know. How about I meet you at the mall around 2:30 tomorrow. We'll need time to get this done in a day."

"Works for me, I'll see you tomorrow."

As my cover story to Cathi, I told her I was going to my friend Don's house to fix trains for the day. Cathi was somewhat relieved to have a free day to take a relaxing walk in the park, or just simply enjoy the afternoon and evening with Max. She needed some time alone. It was something she rarely had.

Chris was ready and waiting for me at the mall parking lot. She was like a kid in a candy store, excited for Cathi, and eager to "shop 'til we drop" or at least until the charge card was tapped. When I told her $1,200 was the max for clothing and that I never went into Cathi's clothing drawers or knew what size she was, I truly stunned her. Fortunately for me Chris knew Cathi's sizes but teased me profusely. She could not believe that after all the years we were together, I never once disrespected Cathi's privacy.

By 8 P.M. that evening, Chris and I completed the shopping extravaganza. Chris, still excited and in disbelief of what she was taking part in, insisted on taking all the clothing home to wash and iron them in preparation for the trip. "Leave the luggage too, I want to pack for her." Chris insisted.

All that was left was to get the packed luggage to the limo driver. "We can take it to him," Chris offered, "but I might need help from Scott, so he may need to know what is up."

I liked Cathi's brother Scott, and didn't think he would have a problem with keeping this secret for the next five days. "Yeah, it's okay to let him in on the plan," I told her. "Just tell him to keep quiet."

Scott knew our limo driver and he and Chris delivered our luggage to his home Sunday night before we left.

My covert operation was right on track. On Friday night, prior to leaving, I informed both families of the vacation plans. As expected, I was met with concerns about money and health, but when they all learned of the doctor's approval, the concerns were somewhat diminished. My demanded secrecy of Chris made both families realize, at least temporarily, the psychological toll we endured. No one insinuated anything to Cathi or further questioned the necessity of the trip.

Monday morning was cold and I was up before Cathi to be sure everything would happen as planned. When Cathi got up, she went through her usual routine of preparing for work. She entered the kitchen like clockwork, right at 6:45 A.M. Rick, our Limo driver pulled into the driveway unnoticed by Cathi.

I stood quietly in shorts and a T-shirt.

"It's a little cold for shorts, don't you think?" Cathi commented as she went for her coffee.

"Well, you're probably a little overdressed," was all I said in response.

"What do you mean, overdressed?" She had no idea what was about to happen and instinctively was concerned about the effects my medicines might be having on me.

It was a struggle, but I did not allow my expression to change. "You're not going to work today, you know, kiddo." All I had to do was act a little strange and Cathi would worry. But this allowed me to prolong her confusion and the suspense of the surprise.

Cathi's constant fear of another day at the hospital, or losing her job, were the first thoughts that entered her mind. "Why?" she asked, controlling the panic she felt. "Did they call and say not to come in?" she asked, to see if I was thinking clearly.

"No," I said nonchalantly. "We're leaving town."

"Come on," she snapped, "I'm in no mood. What are you talking about?"

"Look outside."

"Fine," she said, annoyed with me.

As she leaned toward the kitchen window, there, sitting in the driveway, was long, sleek limousine. Our friend, Rick, dressed in his chauffeur uniform, stood beside the limo with a big smile. He called to Cathi, "Your chariot awaits you with a new wardrobe inside!" As he pointed to the trunk.

"What?" she stuttered. "What's going on?"

"We're going to the Bahamas! I arranged for you to take the week off, and we're out-a-here! Happy anniversary!" I announced proudly.

Cathi stood speechless, letting her startled brain absorb the information. "The Bahamas. But, I'm not even packed."

"Yes, you are. Chris and I bought you all new clothes and luggage last weekend. She packed for you and everything is already in the limo. Just look outside, Scott and Chris are here."

Cathi was bewildered with excitement. She ran outside to greet Chris and Scott and see if all new "stuff" was really in the limo.

We were all laughing and Cathi was still running about in disbelief. Finally, I stopped her. "We'd better get going. You don't want to miss the plane, do you?"

Chris grabbed Cathi and opened her luggage to show her everything was going to be okay. "You're all set. You don't need anything. So get in the house and get changed. Because if you guys don't get in that limo soon, Scott and I are!" Cathi was still in a panic but ran into the house and was changed in minutes.

Cathi shouted, "Chris, I'm really going to the Bahamas! "

"You sure are," Chris answered. " And I got to go shopping with Richie for all this stuff. By the way, Scott, when are you going to do something like this for me?"

Scott needed to change the conversation, and quick. "Hey Cath! I got all this stuff to Rick's last night. Wow, it's after 7; you guys better get going."

Cathi was ecstatic the entire drive to the airport, and as we drank champagne, our limo driver got to hear the details of the plan one more time.

The vacation was exactly what we needed. Getting away from treatments, attorneys and financial worries was the best therapy for the both of us. For the first time in five years of *Fighting Cancer and America's Failing Justice System,* we relaxed.

When we arrived at the Bahamas well-advertised Paradise Island,

Atlantis Hotel and Casino we could not believe its beauty. Our room overlooked the ocean and the meticulously tended water gardens. Directly below our 7th floor room we spent our evenings at fine restaurants and watched swordfish, stingrays and sharks swim in the huge environmentally correct holding tanks.

The days were spent swimming, scuba diving, snorkeling, jet skiing, fishing and just relaxing on the beach with one of many "Bahama Mama" drinks. Although this smooth drink was definitely not an approved part of my medical schedule, we toasted each of my primary clinicians many times with *"thanks for keeping me functionally alive."*

Mid-week I rented a boat for half a day to go fishing. George our captain and local owner of the 24-foot skiff was familiar with Cathi from fishing trips with her Dad years ago. He was also the local that knew where to go for the fish. No wasting time. Cathi hooked the first fish and spent better than an hour reeling in a 100-pound plus Bull Dolphin.

After she had some time to relax, she rubbed some salt in my wounds and reeled in a 38-inch Barracuda. Cathi was tired after fighting the two fish and wanted George to take us to the reefs to snorkel and explore the area. Reluctantly, with my empty hook in hand, I agreed.

Later that day Cathi and I were walking on the beach, still in our bathing suits. A little boy was playing in the sand and caught sight of the gaping scar on my hip. He ran to his mother's side and hugged her leg with terror on his face. His mother, not knowing what he had seen, instinctively said to the boy, "don't do that that's not polite."

As I was putting my t-shirt back on, the mother looked up, apparently getting full view of my "battle" wounds, her entire body and facial expression changed to fear. She squatted down to look to her son and said, *"Michael, he's been hurt really bad and it's very impolite to stare at people like that."* Michael's Mom probably could not have made a more accurate comment to her son. But often people forget what it's like to be the one that caused such fear.

We continued to walk down the beach and as I got my shirt on Cathi walked with her body against mine. She knew I usually kept my shirt on so as not to draw attention and the last thing I wanted to do was to frighten kids.

A man approached us from behind and asked how I received such an injury. Politely and jokingly I said, "It was a shark attack."

I stunned him and showed him my many other scars, then, I told him my real story. Well, not all of it.

It turned out that the Regis and Kathie Lee Show was filming there that week and he asked if I would like to be interviewed to tell my story. I was now the ecstatic one in the group. There was nothing more I wanted to do than to go public with all that was happening to me, but he was not the first to make such an offer.

My civil action attorney, Art, always told me he did not want me to do such a thing. Usually his excuse was that most TV stations cause more harm then good, but often I wondered if the investigative reporting would threaten his self-confidence. I trusted Art, and in one effect with my life; therefore, I *very reluctantly* turned down the opportunity.

The representative left in a hurry and as he met with others where the stage was being set up, Cathi and I could see him pointing us out. Apparently he was quite interested and told them all that I said. Later that evening we went to the show. Cathi was thrilled to see Kathie Lee but I told her I wanted to stay in the back. If I was approached again, I may not be so respectful to Art. Although I was not approached, we did not stay long; both Cathi and I felt that Regis and Kathie Lee looked directly at us more then once. They knew.

The evening before we were scheduled to leave, Cathi and I enjoyed a private poolside dinner. We reflected on the week and the fun we had. It was easy to conclude it was as good as good could be expected for us. I suggested that we have drinks at the aquatic fish park and enjoy the swordfish teasing the stingrays one more time.

As we approached the tank-side bar I stepped on a small piece of glass that went through the side of my sandal and into my foot. Cathi switched into her medical protective mode and ordered the bartender to direct us to the hotel doctor.

The bartender asked what I was going to order and called the doctor. He made Cathi and I our drinks (on the house) and said the doctor would be waiting as he directed us.

Cathi was worried and needed the drink. She knew all too well that even a simple infection could kill me. The hotel doctor gave me an antibiotic injection as Cathi told him my medical past.

I displayed scars and tumors candidly and the doctor sat in awe. After all he was just the hotel doctor. He assured me that the antibiotic would hold me over for the weekend but Cathi and I knew that once we were home, my hematologist, Dr. Martinez, would be the first to hear from me.

Our vacation to Paradise Island was perfect to us. The island lived up to its name. While we were packing the evening before leaving, Cathi told me that it was the best time of her life and she couldn't have asked for a bigger surprise or better anniversary. I knew she needed this surprise and trip, and I was pleased that she accepted it for what it was meant to be. She certainly earned it, but the way she took care of me for years without question, just for the sake of love for me. I just did this for her, out of love.

50
Back to Front Lines

March 1997—Reality hit hard when we returned home to New Jersey. From the time we boarded the airplane to leave the Bahamas, to the quiet drive home in the limo, we were aware of the realities and responsibilities that my disease demanded. Our brief vacation only represented a moment in time away from it all.

Rick, the limo driver, was genuinely interested in our trip and wanted to hear all about it. Our short, but polite answers to his questions alerted him that we needed privacy. As curious as he was, he respected the complexity of our lives, something he knew he could not possibly understand.

The family was happy to see us and also wanted to hear all about our vacation. Cathi and I chose not to share the incident with the glass in my foot, and told only the doctors.

My parents visited mid-morning that next day. It was a Saturday, and they spent a few hours talking about the well-needed trip. Cathi was happy sharing her adventures with my parents.

Mom and Dad realized that their son and daughter, as they often referred to Cathi, still had to make the hour and a half drive down to the southern Jersey shore to visit Cathi's parents. Dad's parental concern got the best of him as they prepared to leave. "You two ready for the doctors and lawyers this week?" he asked.

"Sure Dad, we're ready."

"Well, let us know if we can do anything," Dad continued, "or, if you need some money. Just don't let the bastards get to you."

"Come on, Bob," Mom interrupted before he could continue. "Don't bring that up. They had a good week. Let it last the weekend. Monday will come soon enough for them."

"It's okay, Mom," Cathi interjected. "We had a great time last week, and we're ready for Monday. Dad, we'll let you know if we need help. Thanks."

The drive to the Jersey shore was pleasant, and we could not help but talk about the plan of attack for the week. I scheduled two treatments, plus my appointments with two different attorneys, one with Eric, for the Social Security fiasco, the other with Art, for the civil trial. I also had extensive research to prevent my various adversaries from getting away with screw-ups or the manipulation of information.

Monday came too soon, and I experienced a particularly difficult treatment. Upon returning home I became sick. I attempted to sleep for a couple of hours but the nausea and chills prevented any relaxation whatsoever. Drained of all energy, working on trains or medical and legal work was simply not part of the day's plan. I ended up in bed, losing another day to the television and bathroom. It was now my turn to pay for a week-long splurging of rich foods and alcohol. Chemotherapeutic medicines simply do not mix with that lifestyle.

51
Spying, Theft, Harassing
Leave No Way Out

October 1995–1998—Beginning the first week in October 1995, I began a long series of depositions for the civil trial that would last over the next three years.

It was necessary to work my treatment schedule around the dates of the depositions. The Oxsoralen Ultra and PUVA treatments continued to cause reactions. I was back in the routine of getting sick and sleeping after each treatment. I was still very sensitive to light and had to wear sunglasses during most of the depositions.

At the beginning of each of them, the attorneys would ask if I had taken any medication that day. They would also reiterate that "if at any time you need to take a break for any reason, just let us know and we'll accommodate that."

By the middle of November, I had sat through five sessions of manipulative, repetitious questioning, and knew there would be more to come. Thankfully, Art informed me that we were going to take a hiatus during the holidays, and we would not resume until after the first of the year.

I had long suspected that Cathi and I were being watched. Mail, mostly our telephone bills, had disappeared from our mailbox.

Initially, we thought it was a simple mistake by the phone company, but our naïveté only lasted a short while. Realizing that there was more to it, I placed a call to Art and let him know about the missing bills.

It was essential that Art remain objective, but even he had to agree that the defense team might have had something to do with the missing mail.

During the depositions for the civil trial, it was obvious that Michael Eaten, the attorney for Cincinnati Milacron, would do anything to protect his client and win the case.

Michael Eaten was a personal injury attorney with the firm of Foster Richards of Hackensack, New Jersey. Mr. Eaten was physically disgusting to look at, with no redeeming value supplied by his odious personality. He was easily over four hundred pounds, and his slovenly manner of dress and disgusting personal habits did nothing to enhance his image.

It was obvious that Eaten was threatened by my friendships with so many of the employees who were to testify. I couldn't help but think that Eaten believed that if the case was ever heard, the attorney would lose.

If I was caught speaking to any witnesses about the case, Eaten could accuse me of manipulating their testimony. If Eaten could prove this, the testimony would be thrown out and my case would be weakened.

The questions Eaten often asked during my depositions led me to determine that the attorney might be behind the missing phone bills. Eaten would constantly ask me if I was having any conversations with others about the case.

The attorney would even ask if I had spoken with a certain person, and I knew that only the phone bill would give the attorney that kind of information. "Can you explain, Mr. Sabb," Eaten asked on one occasion, "why you have had so many conversations with Tony Haye?"

This ploy continually failed and the other defense attorneys were disgusted by Eaten's feeble attempts to discredit me.

Once, we found Max trapped beneath the deck. "Why would they put Max under the deck?" Cathi asked me, bewildered by this behavior. "They must have lured him with some meat. I found a bone under the deck, and I know we didn't give it to him."

"My guess," I said, "is they just wanted me to know that they could get to the house without me knowing. They might have been trying to get in the house, but I doubt it. They're just trying to make a point."

Another tactic the defense team attempted was to blame my cancer on my personal lifestyle. Our hot tub might have been a good ploy, because most people use chlorine to keep the water clean and germ free, but it didn't work with Cathi and I. Cathi never used chlorine in the hot tub, only baking soda.

After Max had been trapped, I suspected that someone was hired to sneak onto the property and take a water sample from the hot tub, and trapped the dog to keep him out of the way.

It would not have been a difficult task to lure the dog with food or to gain entry into the deck area. Our home was on a dead end street and was heavily wooded. The hot tub, located on the secluded deck, faced the park. Any intruder was well protected from sight.

Cars often cruised slowly past our house.

I had heard a car drive past the house, but paid little attention. It was only when I got up to go into the kitchen for a drink, that I noticed the activity across the street. I stopped to watch. The man was unloading elaborate photography equipment from the trunk of the car and carefully setting it up. It was obvious to me that the man's subject was our house.

What the hell does he think he is doing? I wondered to myself.

It took the man a full twenty minutes to get all the equipment set up. I was not sure, but it looked like the guy even had some kind of high-powered listening device. The distant intruder began to scan the house with his camera.

It was time for me to make my move. I went to the closet where I kept some rifles, and picked out a shotgun. I watched as the man panned the house again. When I was sure the camera was not focused on the front entrance, I quietly stepped out onto the porch, standing with my shotgun in full sight. I watched as the camera slowly made it's way back across the front. I knew the split second that the photographer spied me through the lens. The man's head popped up from behind the camera. My timing was perfect. I cocked the shotgun and yelled, "You ready to die today?"

Across the street, the trunk of the car flew open. All the intricate equipment was thrown helter-skelter into it. Within minutes, the engine roared and the peeping tom raced off. I simply stood and watched. I still didn't feel well, but my spirits were improved.

When I went back in the house, I called Art. "Art, a very interesting thing just happened," I began.

Art could not help but chuckle as I related the incident to him, but sobered when he asked, "Have there been any other suspicious things happening?"

"Yeah," I said, "I didn't think too much about them at the time, but several things have happened that seemed strange." I shared my suspicions about Cathi being followed during her lunch break, Max being blocked under the deck and the disappearance of mail.

"Well," Art responded, after digesting the information, "for every time you believed there was something amiss, there was, more than likely, two or three other times you were not aware of it. We obviously have them scared if they are spying on you. My guess is they are trying to find something to blame your cancer on. Just be very careful."

"We've got nothing to hide," I answered. "My cancer was caused by the failure of that machine and the chemicals we used on the project. They can watch and spy all they want, but they'll not find anything to help their case."

When I told Cathi, later that evening, about the photographer, she freaked. "You mean they've been watching us? They may have even been in the house?"

"It's possible," I replied, trying to stay calm, "but there is nothing to find. Art said we have them scared, because they are reverting to such tactics. We'll look into a security system for the house."

It took awhile but I was able to calm her down. I knew that without any proof, there was little we could do. We would just be more aware of what we did.

As if the stresses caused by the Social Security Administration were not enough, I was still in preparation with Art Rush for the civil trial. I sat through hours and hours of redundant questioning. The chemotherapy treatments continued to cause adverse effects.

It was when the attorney for Cincinnati Milacron, the manufacturers of the injection-molding machine, began to harass me and falsely accuse me of things, that I lost my temper.

Eaten, the Cincinnati Milacron attorney, had arrogantly commented to me, during a break at one of the depositions, "I love this case, and I'm just drawing it out as long as possible for billable hours. You and my client are paying my kids' way through college." His sordid grin displayed his un-brushed teeth.

During Dad's deposition, Eaten had fallen asleep, snoring loudly. Dad, angered by this inappropriate behavior, asked loudly, "Am I keeping you awake!?"

Their colleague noticeably embarrassed the others in the room. The attorney next to Eaten nudged him back into consciousness. Not phased by his rebuke, Eaten motioned for the questioning to proceed.

During this one particular deposition, there were no less than 14 attorneys sitting at the huge conference table. I sat with Art on the end. Eaten was asking the questions, and he was suggesting that Cathi might have been responsible for causing the cancer.

He was a master of the language, never stating outright what he was suggesting, but the inference was clear.

He speculated that Cathi was not caring for me properly and I had gotten an infection, causing the cancer. Or, because of her overzealous cleaning habits, the products that she used caused the cancer.

It was when the attorney's lewd and extremely personal questions about our sexual habits began that I could feel myself begin to seethe. Eaten as much as accused Cathi of sleeping around and engaging in group sex, and the cancer was a result of this behavior.

I could stand no more of this despicable line of questioning. Infuriated by the attorney, I jumped up, pushing the heavy, plush leather chair against the wall. I slammed my fists on the huge table with such force that the entire table jumped. I leaned out, glaring directly at Eaten. I had to clench my teeth to keep from saying what I was thinking.

You fucking son of a bitch, my mind screamed, I'll rip your goddamned lungs out if you ever speak to her or me like that again!

The young, black female attorney accompanying Eaten seemed unaffected by my outburst. With the arrogance learned from him, she looked at me confidently and was about to speak.

With my fist clenched, I glared at her. I was ready to permanently change the course of her life, but I said nothing.

Terrorized by my intense anger and my still wounded body's expressions, with no words spoken, everyone in the room froze. I turned and grabbed the heavy, ten-foot wooden door, slinging it open as though it was made of rice paper. I stormed down the hall and out of the building, cursing.

Once outside, I released my rage on a tree, striking it over and over with my fist, until I was able to regain composure. The ulceration on my right hip was again bleeding.

I was pacing up and down by the tree, my knuckles bleeding, when Art finally appeared.

"I think we probably need to call it quits for the day. But," Art tentatively said to me, "no one is leaving that room. Do you think it's okay to tell them they can go?" He could tell that I had regained my composure. "You know, you really scared the shit out of them! I think what scared them most was that you never said a word." He was smiling slightly at me.

"Yeah, but if anyone attacks Cathi like that again, I'll change the rules to this bullshit game you all play," I told Art, smiling too as I imagined all the overpaid, useless attorneys sitting like chastised children. "Tell them they can go."

Dr. Turner had been brought in by Art to be deposed. The doctor remembered very little from the day that he "examined" me. He could not remember having met with Carolyn Fox prior to examining me, although by her own admission, she and the doctor had met. Turner could not remember Carolyn Fox being in the examination room. He did not remember reports he had sent to Carolyn Fox and the insurance company.

When Art asked the doctor general medical questions, Turner was succinct and articulate. When asked questions specific to my case, the doctor repeated questions, and orchestrated answers to conform to medical studies that pertained to his client's needs. He never considered the case as it applied to the individual. The defense attorneys continually objected to the wording of Art's questions, resulting in even more confusion.

Drs. Lambert, Yang and Gochfeld had, also, all been deposed. Their individual testimonies could have won the case, but with the strength of all three, the medical testimony was indefensible.

Eaten, in his zeal to discredit Lambert, was only able to make himself look the fool. In his questioning of Lambert concerning the 1980 Cohen study in which Turner was one of the authors, Eaten asked, "Now, he," speaking of Turner, "was part of that Cohen/Turner study?"

"Yes," Lambert answered.

"And do you recall," Eaten continued, "in his deposition where he says that the Cohen/Turner study is out of date?"

"Yes, I do," the doctor acknowledged.

"Do you agree with him?"

"No." Lambert's answer was simple.

Eaten was unperturbed. "So, the man who participated in the study says it's out of date, and you disagree with him?"

"That's correct."

"Why do you disagree with him?"

302

Here Lambert was able to make his point. "Because he refers to two more recent studies that he uses to conclude that his material is out of date, and those are the Tuyp, et al., that's the paper from Scotland, and the Whittemore, which is the paper from California. I believe both of those papers are flawed."

When Eaten asked him to explain why he believed these studies to be flawed, Lambert continued. "They're both flawed for the same reason, because they make a very critical assumption that I think is not correct. They both assume that Mycosis Fungoides is a single, uniform, non-heterogeneous disease. The method of statistical analysis relied on that heavily, that concept, and I think that Mycosis Fungoides is not a homogeneous disease. By contrast, it's a very heterogeneous disease." A powerful statement from the man who headed the NATO Advanced Studies Workshop.

Lambert was able to counter all of Eaten's attacks, bombarding the attorney with solid references and extensive and undeniable personal experiences.

Lambert landed his final and forceful blow, when Eaten asked, "Why is the basketball project the key to Mr. Sabb having MF? Why can't it be any of the other things that occurred to him over the years?"

"The reason I think the basketball project was important were several fold," the professor patiently explained. "One of the most important of those is the fact that the distribution of lesions that were MF when I saw him so precisely coincided to the areas that were exposed during that incident. And, I thought they weren't really the precise areas that you would expect MF—or para-psoriasis, because it can be early MF—to correspond to, even though the hip girdle is where the early lesions of MF typically arise in many cases. This was not exactly in those distributions. One usually sees lesions that are primarily over the buttocks, not on one side under the belt. That's different. And one does not see lesions arising on the foot at the same time, and that was present. And one does not usually see lesions in the groin, essentially sparing the buttocks where you usually see the lesions arise, but in the groin and along the flank, as well as along the foot. This is a very unusual distribution to me, even though the area, the general part of the body, is where you often see MF."

Eddie Roman, Sam Golding, Tony Haye and Mike Krall from Hayward Pools had each been deposed. Mike conveniently forgot or lied about the dates and participation of employees, trying to protect Hayward. Sam waffled on his testimony. I believed that he knew the truth, but felt he had to protect his job. Sam's testimony was of no value to either side. Tony, now retired, stood his ground and supported all of my claims.

It was Eddie's hands-on experience with the injection molding machine, and discovery of the fractured pin during the cleanup after the June, 1986 accident, that provided the strongest testimony. He testified about the lack of instruction Cincinnati Milacron provided the operators and maintenance personnel to enable them to evaluate the tolerance levels of the metal and the effects of the resulting stress on the parts.

Dwight, the other maintenance employee who worked on the machine after the accident, had died. After his motorcycle accident, he had been through numerous operations and became addicted to painkillers. When his doctors refused to prescribe any more pain medications, he started doing cocaine. He died of a heart attack not long after.

52
Never Happened, Never Existed

During the myriad of depositions, the defense attorneys presented Art with some potentially devastating evidence. Hayward had provided the attorneys with a list of machines that were at the plant. *The 200-ton Cincinnati Milacron machine that had been in use during the accident was not on this list. Hayward claimed that they had never owned a 200-ton Cincinnati Milacron.*

"Richard," Art said, his face creased with worry, "this looks bad. It makes it look like you made up the entire accident. It could end the case. If there is no proof that the machine exists, there is no case."

"This is stupid! Everyone who works there knows that machine was there!" I was angry. "Goddamn it! I didn't imagine that accident! I'll get some proof. I don't know how, but I'll get some proof!" There had to be some way to prove that the machine was real.

I made several calls to coworkers, but kept hitting dead ends. None of them were able to get the information I needed.

It was not until several days later that I remembered someone who might be able to help me, and the guy was an executive. I knew this man liked me; we had always had a good relationship. Plus, the executive had access to the computer codes that could produce the equipment list I needed for my case.

I placed the call to the man and told him about my predicament. I was very careful not to ask him for any help. I just wanted him to know what Hayward was saying. The man apologized that he was not able to help, but wished me well in my case.

Two days later, I was sitting in my living room and heard a loud thump at the front door. Suspecting that my neighbors were playing ball, I went to check it out.

Sitting by the door was a large, manila envelope. I picked it up, but there was nothing on the outside. I tore it open and pulled out the single sheet of paper that was inside. It took me a second to comprehend what I was reading. It was a list of machines at the Hayward plant. On that master list was the 200-ton Cincinnati Milacron machine. I looked up, hoping to see who might have left this answer to my prayers, but the street was empty.

As quickly as I could get to the fax machine, Art had a copy at his office. When I gave him a call, I could not help but gloat. "Show that to the damned defense attorneys. That should make them squirm!"

Art looked at the paper carefully. "Where did you get this?"

"It was left on my front porch," I said. "I don't know for sure who brought it, but I have a pretty good idea. But it's ours to use."

Art played it like a scene out of a movie at the next meeting with the defense attorneys. The report from Hayward was brought up almost immediately. With the finesse and timing of Sir Lawrence Olivier, Art pulled out the computer printout and announced, "I find it interesting that the machine is listed on this internal company readout that Richard had."

The defense side of the table got very quiet. One attorney held out his hand and Art placed the undeniable evidence in it. He quickly perused it, nodded his head to the others, and handed it back to Art.

One of the other attorneys finally spoke up. "Well," he said, clearing his throat, "let's move on to something else."

As an expert witness, Art brought in Joseph Shelley, Ph.D. from Princeton. He was a mechanical engineer whose experience included work on the space shuttle with NASA. Rush asked Dr. Shelley to evaluate the toggle clamping system and the pin that held the mechanism together on the Cincinnati Milacron machine. Art was almost embarrassed to ask such a respected scientist to offer his opinion on a simple, elementary engineering question. I remembered learning about toggle clamps in a high school course. However, Dr. Shelley produced a sixty-page report, complete with detailed drawings of the machine and offered a complex engineering discussion assessing the safety factors involved. In the report he stated:

" . . . it is my professional engineering opinion that the Cincinnati Milacron Toggle Injection Molding Machine is defective in design, and that these defects make use of this machine unreasonably dangerous. It is my further specific engineering opinion that these defects include:

Use of a toggle mold clamping mechanisms with links pins and bearings that experience foreseeable wear to a condition where the toggle mechanism becomes unsafe for use.

Failure to provide any type of instructions, information or measurable specifications, in the Operator's Manual.

Failure to provide instructions on how to measure the amount of wear of the toggle pins and/or bearings.

These defects were the direct cause of the failure of the toggle clamping mechanism, and the subsequent injury to Richard Sabb."

This report was more supportive to my case than any of us expected. Eddie Roman's testimony would provide the layman's point of view and Dr. Shelley's would provide the expert's.

A representative of Cincinnati Milacron was also deposed. The gentleman, whose position with the company would warrant extensive knowledge of the machine in question, displayed a complete lack of details as to the design of the machine and the pin and it's functionality over time. Instead he focused on the actual workings of the machine and the possibility of improper maintenance. He was unable to even explain the possible result of a shattered pin, as in this case.

Dr. Shelley's report included a reference to the testimony of this representative. "It might be expected that a person in his position would have a better than average understanding of the design and construction of injection-molding machines."

Art was ecstatic about the undermining of the defense's supposed authority.

Cathi, Mom and Dad had their time with the panel of attorneys, each sharing the physical anguish and mental duress the disease had caused to my life and to their own.

I endured eleven different sessions of deposition, each time the defense attorneys trying to twist my answers and distort the truth. Remarkably, I contradicted myself only five times over the four-year period, and only on minor points. Considering the effects of the medications and treatments I sustained throughout the process, my consistency of testimony was considered no less than miraculous.

When asked to tell about the accident, I was able to describe, in great detail, the events of June 18, 1986. "At the moment of the accident, a combination of things happened. The winding sound that the lead screw made had a change in pitch, and it was becoming more abrupt or a high squealing pitch, as if it was coming to a grinding stop. At the same time, I heard what I describe as the explosion, as a toggle bolt sheared."

"What do you mean when you say 'sheared?'" James Williams, the attorney for one of the chemical companies, asked.

"Well, at that point, the lead screw sounded like it was grinding to a stop," I responded. "I'm going to say like it was metal on metal."

"To the extent you can describe it, what did the shearing bolt sound like?"

I thought for a moment. "Well, it was like a bang. I would have been a lot like somebody using a hand-held sledgehammer, like a five-pound sledgehammer, and the person may be trying to peen steel on an anvil."

"And the sounds of material escaping, what did that sound like?" Williams asked.

"That was more like a swishing sound," I explained.

The attorney continued his questioning. "Did anybody at Hayward tell you on the day you were going to use this injection machine, 'hey, we've been having problems with it,' or, 'it's been running fine?'"

"No, sir," I replied.

"Did you discuss with anybody at Hayward on that day or preceding week, the suitability of the mixture with the machine, whether it would work?"

"Yes," I told him. "I know there were various discussions about the heating coils maintaining the temperature in the lead screw, and actually, injecting the material."

The attorney paused to look at his notes. "After you heard the bolt shear, as you describe it, what happened next?"

"This was all in an instant, in the way that when something severe happens, it almost seemed to happen in slow motion. But the fumes and the resins that came out, I have to say that the lead screw emptied, 'cause it just went all over the place. I do recall seeing the mold itself and hearing the swishing sound, I guess from the hydraulics, and the mold slowly opening. I was the one who took the impact of this when I got hit with the resins and the fumes. I took the impact. Henry and Harold were on the sidelines."

"How far away from the machine were you?"

"I was right next to it; I was actually leaning on it," I answered.

The attorney continued. "You used the term 'spew fumes' and 'spew resin' earlier when you described the accident. What do you mean by 'spew?'"

"When the product came out," I began, "it didn't come out with a very high velocity. It came out sloppily, as if a child tossed a thick chocolate shake at you. The product had density to it."

"When the accident took place, did coworkers come running to the site, or come to the site?"

"No," I explained, "the way I recall it, the coworkers in the general area had started to leave, 'cause maybe you should have asked me about the fumes first."

"Okay," Williams complied, "tell me about the fumes."

"When the fumes came out, that entire building had to be evacuated," I recalled.

"And what did the fumes smell like?"

"Bad," I said. "It was an extreme irritant in that I did immediately feel nauseated. It immediately went to your head, causing light-headedness, somewhat of a disorientation effect. And to maybe help you realize the power or magnitude of the fumes," I went on to explain, "that was a big area, 150 feet by 300 feet about, and people tend to go toward an accident out of curiosity, not away from it."

"And you say you reacted to the fumes almost immediately?"

"Yes," I responded.

"Where on your body did the material get on?"

"Well," I explained, "the first area that I felt was my right hip, as far as actually receiving the material. Then, probably the second area I felt would have been my groin area and my right thigh. It was a burning sensation, because the material was heated. There was that delayed reaction, because it had to absorb through the clothing. That's why I say it happened kind of like in slow motion; the fumes hit you first, and even though the material probably hit you at the same time, you didn't feel it right away."

I went on to describe my reactions. I told them about my moment of shock when the accident occurred, the confusion, the brown-yellow fumes, and trying to whisk away the burning material with my bare hands. There was little doubt that the accident had been traumatic, and the burned area definitely correlated with the cancerous sites.

Carolyn Fox reappeared briefly in my life during her deposition. I was no longer a victim of my own naiveté, and listened intently during her questioning. She contradicted herself several times, causing even the defense attorneys confusion on different points. I wrote notes for Art, pointing out the discrepancies in her testimony.

It was during her deposition that we discovered how underhanded Ms. Fox had been. She was acting as a private contractor, hired by the insurance companies, but was also a employee of Zurich American, allowing her to utilize the information she garnered as a private contractor to benefit her full-time employer. New Jersey laws permitted such an arrangement provided the individual worked less than 20 hours per week as a private contractor. In the eyes of the law, she was able to provide an unbiased opinion as long as she abided by the less than 20-hour rule.

In reality, Ms. Fox, acting as a private contractor, had complete access to my attorneys and doctors and all the information we provided, some of this information she would not have otherwise been privy to. She would then share this information with Zurich, affording them with a much stronger and unwarranted position.

Art and I were not the only ones surprised by the duplicity of the woman. Most of the defense attorneys were stunned by the revelation. During a break, I overheard the comment, "You can be deceptive and unethical, but you just have to do it in 20 hours or less per week."

I had personally done a substantial amount of research for my case. I scoured the University of New Jersey Medical Library for articles and studies, which supported workplace environment and chemical exposures as causative factors in the development of cancer, and specifically CTCL. And, I found that there was no shortage of supporting evidence. I additionally researched other court cases similar to my own and shared all this information with Art.

I contacted the widows of Kenny, Henry and Harold to try to convince them to have their late husbands' bodies exhumed and examined for evidence of CTCL. I was certain that all three had died of the cancer.

Each widow had received a pittance of a settlement when her husband had died. Harold's wife had received the largest amount of

$40,000. Compared to Harold's salary of $175,000 at the time of his death, the settlement was nothing. Henry and Kenny's wives each received only $10,000.

I told the widows that there was the potential for receiving much more if we could prove that their husbands' deaths had been a result of this same cancer. More importantly, I attempted to describe the potentially staggering effect it could have with the medical community.

But the widows were not interested in my proposal. Revisiting the painful deaths and the prospect of legal battles both outweighed the prospect of potential monies and/or medical advancement.

Ed Fryer, owner of WebbTool and my former employer, initiated a restraining order against me, and convinced Kenny's widow to enforce it.

"Why are you opening up old wounds?" Ed demanded when he called me to warn me to stay away from her. "It is a terrible strain on her and you are making life worse for her. Just stay away!"

"Ed," I countered, "we both know why you are doing this. You're just trying to protect your pocketbook, because you know what we can prove." The click on the other end of the line ended the phone call. I knew I had hit home with my accusation, but I could not prove it without her cooperation.

Although it was of no consequence to my case, I received support from an unexpected source, several of the defense attorneys. More than one of the lawyers approached me privately during the deposition process to confide that I deserved to win the case, but they had to do their jobs.

Even one of Eaten's team could not understand why their client was not willing to offer a settlement. "I just think that you are being victimized and treated unfairly," the team member confessed.

Another attorney revealed that he was looking for any loophole possible which might relieve him of this case. He believed my case was solid and he told me, "I don't want to be any part of the screwing of someone in your situation."

Two or three other defense attorneys attempted to be removed from the case also, filing motions citing a conflict of interest. They had each known someone who suffered from cancer caused by a workplace environment. In all cases, the requests were denied.

The secret support of members of the opposition made me feel good, but did nothing to help my case. Reality and the truth are often contradictory and are expected to be a pain in the ass. Reality was:

- Insurance fraud costs the public billions every year
- Corporate defense attorneys have to do anything to win, to prevent fraudulent misuse of precedent setting cases
- The truth was more frightening, they knew my doctors were correct in the etiology of my cancer
- New medical discoveries supplied the evidence
- I had to rely on the testimony of those who could speak out

Selection of the judge was on a rotation basis, and allowed the attorneys from both sides to briefly question each judge candidate. One judge had a family member who actually died of CTCL, and she was immediately released. The odds of this were amazing and shocked us all. One statistical analysis determined that a person working in the *mechanized field* would have approximately a 1 in 300,000 chance of developing this rare disease.

The judge who took the case was William Wertheimer of the Superior Court of New Jersey.

I heard that Wertheimer had a reputation for siding with business interests and he typically encouraged a settlement for significantly lesser amounts than was projected. I was concerned, having been burned by one judge already whose sentiments were swayed.

53
Battle Cry for Justice Unheard

For almost four years, I had been in preparation for the civil trial. After more then 30 depositions, they were finally complete, and the date was set.

After five different postponements, the trial began on March 16, 1998. The defense filled the first morning with motions, most of which centered on dismissing the case. Art objected on all points, stating the case should go to trial and a jury needed to be selected.

"Despite the fact," the judge stated, "that corporations usually win these types of cases, I can find no reason to dismiss the case at this point." I noticed that he stressed the words "at this point." The judge's comments hit hard, confirming the rumors I had heard about Wertheimer. We were told that the case had to be wrapped up the week of March 30, because the judge was going on vacation after that.

Art was livid; his face was dark red as he shook his head in disgust with the judge. During the lunch break, he demanded to speak to Cathi and I in private. We now had to re-evaluate our entire case strategy.

Originally, Art intended the case to be heard over a two-month period of time. Allowing time for all witnesses to be heard, but primarily, Art was making time for Mr. Eaten's courtroom antics.

Cathi and I were quite concerned as we listened to Art explain our only possibility of getting some form of a fair trial with the Judge's arbitrary limitations. Art summarized that of the 30 plus people to testify, he would narrow it down to:

1. Eddie; was to describe only what he had seen and repaired.

2. Dr. Shelley; was to give expert testimony as to why and how the pin actually failed (basic engineering concepts).

3. Dr. Gochfeld; was to explain the medical theories and facts for the etiology of my condition.

4. Dr. Lambert; was our medical "home run hitter" that would qualify and further explain the medical facts, discoveries, and controversies that were relevant to my condition or histopathogenesis.

5. Lastly, we decided, due to the time constraints that I would testify after Lambert, to describe the full spectrum of my experiences.

Cathi, although named as co-plaintiff in the case, would testify only if there was time or if the judge allowed.

After a lunch break, jury selection began. The slow and tedious process proved to be as redundant as my depositions. The defense dismissed anyone who made the slightest negative comment toward industry and business. They rejected all potential jurors who knew anyone with cancer or anyone who died because of cancer. Knowledge of the plastics industry would be cause for dismissal. Several doctors were dismissed. Anyone who represented a union was dismissed. I began to wonder if they were going to have enough people from which to even select a jury.

By 10:30 the morning of the third day, out of the pool of 150 candidates, 16 potential jury members were finally chosen.

The judge charged the jury pool members: "Now, if you are chosen as a juror in this case, what you really will be is a judge of the facts, whereas I am a judge of the law... It is my job to rule on motions during the course of the trial, and give you instructions on the law that govern this case at the end of the case, so that you can apply the law to the facts that you find for the purpose of arriving at a fair and correct verdict . . . If you are chosen as a judge of the facts, it is impera-tive that you be fair and impartial, as it is Imperative that I be fair and impartial . . . This case, it is anticipated will conclude the week of March 30. We will not sit on Friday and we will not sit on next Wednesday."

Today was March 18, and the trial was to conclude the week of March 30. If we went to the Friday of that week, April 3, we still had 10 days to complete all testimony; not just our witnesses, but the defen-dant's witnesses, and the jury deliberations, and the decision.

At the end of testimony in the trial, only six jurors would be ran-domly selected to determine the case. But none of the jury members wanted to be there. When Wertheimer asked if any juror wanted to speak with him in private about being released from duty, everyone raised his or her hands, with the exception of one black woman sitting over in the corner.

What irony, I thought. Of all the people on this jury, this woman is probably the one who needed to be with her family or at work and certainly didn't need to be in this courtroom. Yet, she is the only one who was willing to serve.

The judge began to weed through the people and denying them their dismissals. The excuse given by most was that they just didn't want to be there. Three ministers seated on the jury shared this sad excuse as well, a sad commentary on the religious community and these self-proclaimed upstanding men of God. "I guess filling their donation bucket is the real business, practicing what they preach certainly was not," I whispered furiously to Cathi.

I looked over the group of people who held my future in their hands. I had my doubts, but I could only hope that they were fair-minded people that Art could keep awake long enough to prove our case.

The actual trial began immediately. Art made his opening state-ment first. The burden of proof was on him in this very complicated case. He quickly explained why I was wearing sunglasses.

"My client means no disrespect to you or to the court. His eyes are very sensitive," Art told the jurors, "as a result of the treatments he must take for the cancer he suffers."

Art went on to relate the details of the basketball project, my involvement in it, and the machine that was being used. Art described Mycosis Fungoides, and that it was potentially fatal.

Art's statement was rambling and not well presented. Eaten objected throughout the statement, arguing that Art was getting into summation. When Art talked about the sadness Cathi and I felt, Eaten objected and Wertheimer stated, "Sadness is not a part of the damages."

Most often, Wertheimer ruled against Eaten. But Eaten succeeded in distracting Art's thoughts and caused the jurors to feel like their time was being wasted.

When it was Eaten's turn, he began by expressing the sympathy that he felt for me in my plight with cancer. "We will never dispute the fact that Mr. Sabb has Mycosis Fungoides, or that we should all be sympathetic to Mr. Sabb. That makes us all caring human beings. But the one thing I will ask you is not to let that fact ultimately affect you in this case."

He laid the groundwork for his side of the argument, explaining the innocence of his client and attempting to cast doubt on the validity of the upcoming testimony.

The first witness called was Eddie Roman. Eddie was obviously nervous. Art did not have his files in order and Cathi had to help Art's assistant in getting to the box of files for Eddie, which were on the bottom. This lack of organization concerned me.

For the next 40 minutes, he answered Art's questions about the injection-molding machines at Hayward and specifically about the Cincinnati Milacron machines he had so often worked on. Eaten continued his barrage of meaningless objections that again caused the jurors to lose interest. One juror had his eyes closed.

At one point, the judge chastised Eaten for his numerous objections. "You cannot object to him asking questions you don't want him to ask, only to the form. You don't seem to want any questions asked. Overruled."

After the lunch break, Eaten began his cross-examination. His ploy was transparent. He wanted Eddie to contradict himself. But Eddie, more comfortable now on the witness stand, stood his ground. Eaten insisted that the machines indicated on a sketch of the injection-mold department at Hayward were not Cincinnati Milacron machines. "Is it not, in fact, true that these machines are not Cincinnati machines?" the attorney asked.

Eddie would not allow the attorney to confuse him with the intentionally manipulatively worded question. Eddie stated emphatically, "Those machines were Cincinnati machines."

For an hour and a half, Eaten tried to find a hole in the testimony. He did bring up several discrepancies from the depositions to Eddie's testimony. Eddie was excused from the witness stand and the judge concluded testimony for that day.

I felt pretty good about the testimony. One of my concerns was that there was so much complicated detail to be covered, I was afraid that the jury members would not be able to follow it or stay awake for it. And we had to cover it in nine days.

Another concern was Art. He did not return the defense's harassment and I detected a shift in his attitude. Art's confidence seemed weakened. He was less articulate and his speech patterns were less coherent. Before we left the courthouse he suggested that I might consider settling out of court. The once "dynamic case" that we all wanted on record, was now being looked at as frustrating by my attorney.

But I still had faith in our case. I knew that if we could just present the testimonies to the jury, despite the complexity, we could win this trial.

The next day dawned dismal and rainy and the weather did nothing to help my sense of foreboding. I had not slept well. As strong as I believed my case to be, I was up against some heavy hitters. That, combined with Wertheimer's reputation and what I perceived as Art's lagging confidence, caused me to worry about the outcome. I just wanted to make sure that Cathi was taken care of, that she would not be burdened with huge medical bills when I died.

She was my primary caregiver, and had tended to my multitude of needs through the last six years. When I was confined to bed after a particularly rough treatment or after a surgery to remove the constantly growing and emerging tumors, she had always been there, nursing and caring for me. The medical costs and attorneys fees were huge, and growing daily. This trial was the only avenue to financial relief.

Both Cathi and I were nervous, talking very little as we dressed and prepared to leave for the courthouse. My parents and siblings were already waiting when we arrived. Other friends were in attendance, including Brian who had flown in from England to visit and watch the court proceedings.

Art's usual outgoing manner had diminished, and worry was etched on his face. He was fidgety and spoke little to us as we entered the courtroom. Family, friends, doctors and other witnesses were seating themselves, all anxious to start.

Cathi, Art and I went to the table and sat down. On the opposite end of the table sat Eaten and his assistant. Everyone stood as Judge Wertheimer entered and took his place at the front.

Before the jury was admitted, Wertheimer addressed the attorneys off the record. "It is obvious that this case cannot be finished in two weeks. I am going on vacation in two weeks, and you," he spoke directly to Art, "need to shoot for a settlement. Otherwise your client could be left without anything, and, in fact, may end up paying back some of his benefits."

I could see Art's resolve crumble as the attorney quickly jotted down what the judge said. I glanced at Cathi and could see the same shock and frustration that I was experiencing. Justice again was going to be crippled by the bias of an unfair judge.

Art stood to speak, nervously adjusting his suit jacket. "Your honor, we have witnesses here today ready to testify and would like to proceed with the trial." I knew Art well enough to recognize the lack of strength in his voice.

"Very well," the judge said, obviously annoyed. "Seat the jury."

Art called Dr. Shelley to the stand. The first thing to establish was the professor's expertise in the area of mechanical engineering. The doctor was undoubtedly an expert, having taught every course available on the topic over the past 25 years. He had also authored books that were used as textbooks in engineering courses. His credentials were impressive.

When it was Eaten's turn to question, the attorney focused only on Dr. Shelley's lack of experience with injection-molding machines. "Dr. Shelley, you are not an expert in the design of injection-molding machines, are you?"

"That is correct."

"Dr. Shelley, you have not ever seen an injection-molding machine, have you?"

"That is correct."

"You have not ever seen an injection molding machine run, have you?"

"That is correct."

"And, Dr. Shelley, the books you wrote, they are books used by students, correct?"

"Well," Dr. Shelley explained, "they are used by students who become engineers who design products."

Eaten continued. "None of those books we talked about dealt with injection-molding machines, correct."

"Correct."

"None of the items you talked about dealt with toggle linkages in injection-molding machines, correct?"

"Well, toggle linkages are basic mechanisms," Shelley patiently instructed. "You can't say 'toggle linkages in injection-molding machines.' They are fundamental mechanical linkages and are used for many, many purposes, mostly clamping."

"Maybe my question wasn't clear," Eaten recanted. "Did the books contain any chapter, page, upon which toggle linkages on injection-molding machine was discussed?"

"Not to my knowledge," the professor responded.

"Doctor, you have never designed a piece of machinery for anyone, correct?"

"Yes, that is correct."

"In fact, Doctor, the only time you do failure analysis on machinery is when you are asked to testify for a plaintiff in court proceedings, correct?"

"That is totally incorrect," Shelley stated firmly. "I think in my deposition and resume, I stated that for thirty years I was a consultant to the Department of the Army. I have performed many, many failure analysis of ordinance munitions prematurely exploding, killing friendly troops. This was a very sophisticated, high-level analysis of designs of products that the U. S. government had obtained from contractors."

Eaten stopped and shuffled through his notes. "Doctor, you do not even know the number of pins in the toggle mechanisms of an injection . . . "

"Objection," Art declared.

"Sustained. The question had nothing to do with his qualifications," Wertheimer stated.

"I will continue afterwards," Eaten said, sitting down. "Thank you, sir."

"Do you have any objection to his testimony," the judge asked Eaten.

"Yes, sir," Eaten confirmed. "I'd like to continue at sidebar."

"Sidebar," Wertheimer stated, standing and walking over to meet the attorneys.

It was obvious to me that Eaten had a problem with Dr. Shelley as an expert witness. I could hear portions of the conversation. The attorney wanted to reject Dr. Shelley's testimony because "he has never worked on the Cincinnati Milacron machine and therefore can not be considered an expert on the machine."

The attorneys and judge huddled for a few moments and then returned back to their places.

Wertheimer seated himself and stated somewhat reluctantly, "I'll allow Dr. Shelley to give evidence in the area of mechanical engineering."

We were astounded. A doctor of mechanical engineering was only needed to testify on the stress analysis of a pin, was now being questioned as to if he ever operated or designed a molding machine. The defense was successfully confusing the jurors as to why each person was testifying.

"Your honor," Art addressed the judge. "I would like to ask for a two-minute recess to confer with my client."

"Certainly," the judge agreed.

Art motioned to us to follow him.

The judge turned and addressed the jury. "A lawyer's two minutes is not a real person's two minutes," he said with a smirk. "If you would like to go to the jury room and relax, we will call you when we are ready to begin."

When we had gotten out of the courtroom, Art turned to me and said, "We have to talk. The judge is threatening to throw the case out of court."

"But why? What happened? We have a good case and I have a world-renowned scientist willing to testify on my behalf." I was still reeling from what he told me, because I understood what that meant to me. If the judge threw the case out of court, I could be liable for my medical bills, not to mention the astronomical attorney's fees. I could only wonder if someone had gotten to the judge with a threat or a payoff.

"Richard, you can see the direction this trial is going," Art began. "Eaten is going to object to every witness, and the judge is getting impatient with my questioning. He said that there is a perfectly good offer on the table and it's one you need to accept."

"No," I was adamant. "We need to regroup and continue to fight. You know we have a good case. I'm being discriminated against. That fucking piece of shit judge is not allowing me a fair trial."

Cathi, her eyes red from crying, agreed. "He's right. We can't just give up."

"Listen," Art reasoned, "do you think for one minute that you are going to get a fair trial here? We know where the sentiments of the judge lie—the company and his vacation."

"Goddamn it," I cried, furious and disgusted. "You sound like they've gotten to you, too." I felt as though Art had just ripped my heart out and thrown it on the floor.

But in a flash of insight, I realized what Art meant. It really didn't matter what we did. The judge did not want to hear the case. He was looking for a reason to throw it out so we wouldn't interfere with his vacation schedule and, also, my future was in the hands of the misfits sitting in the juror's box. Art was right. There was absolutely no possibility that I was going to get a fair trial. The odds were stacked against me.

"Richard, I know you don't mean that. And that is not the issue. You have got to decide right now if you are willing to take this offer or risk ending up with all the medical and legal debts in your lap." Art let his words soak in. "Let me go over the offer. I want you to talk to your family. I want you and Cathi to talk it over. But we don't stand a chance here. We have to settle."

I felt trapped. "Why are you so afraid of going public with this. This Judge should be disbarred for his conduct. We have witnesses." I was furious but continued, "what's the offer?"

"The offer is $250, 000." Art began. "They are offering to pay all your medicals, past and future. And, finally, they are offering to set up a fund to take care of any secondary medical problems that could be caused by the cancer or the treatment of the cancer. This will keep you from having to go to court on every single issue. With the $152,000 we collected from the other companies involved you have about $400,000. We have to subtract my legal cost and Workman's Comp. One way or another, even if it comes out of my firm's money, we are going to guarantee you $200,000 for you and Cathi to use at your discretion."

To the average person, $200,000 sounds like a dream come true. But I knew how quickly that could disappear with all the medical problems my therapy caused and insurers do not pay even when they agree to. Depending on how much longer I lived, and I was not planning to give up anytime soon, $200,000 could disappear overnight. It was a joke, but it was the only offer I had.

"Richard, I know it was not what we were hoping for, but you will have insurance for the rest of your life, and some money to fall back on when you should need it."

I looked at Cathi. She had been in the bathroom crying, beating the walls and sink. Fighting with me to go after the judge, file against Art if necessary, and get any of the state officials involved that we can. We both had all that we could take and were emotionally beaten. I could tell that she had been beaten down and was resigned to the settlement. I paced the corridor, struggling with the only decision I knew I had to make. I looked at Cathi, and was crushed by my failure to guarantee her future.

"Accept their goddamned offer," I spat out, and angrily strode back into the courtroom.

Our conversation lasted less than 15 minutes, yet the court did not reconvene for another 15 minutes. The judge made the statement, "Now let's get going, I want to get this jury out of here. Are we on record? All right, I understand that during the two-minute recess, this case has been amicably adjusted. Is that correct?"

Art said, "That is correct your honor."

"And, the terms of the settlement are?"

Art stated, "Your honor, the terms of the settlement are that my clients will receive a cash settlement of $250,000 from the defendant, Cincinnati Milacron. Some of that will be allocated to the Workman's Comp. claim. At this point I don't know how much the allocation would be. Mr. Eaten and I will be discussing that matter."

"Alright, you can submit a consent order on the total settlement."

"All I will need on the behalf of Cincinnati is a release to them from the plaintiffs and the compensation carrier," said Eaten.

Wertheimer had the jury brought in. "During the two-minute recess," Wertheimer stated to the jury, "this case was settled. So it is over. But I don't want you to think that your service has been wasted by the fact that the parties settled the case. Every time a case comes into the Superior Court, whether it is criminal where they just have to negotiate pleas or civil where they attempt to resolve the matter prior to trial, there is an attempt to settle the case prior to trial. In fact, a vast majority of the cases that come into this system are either pleaded or negotiated or settled, because we couldn't possibly try all the cases that are in the system. And during the course of a trial, this case is a 1994 docket number (we filed the case with the court in 1994, and did not come to trial until 1998); there are opportunities and conferences, and perhaps some arbitration to attempt to settle the matter. Before we call for you we attempt to settle the matter. And all of those proved fruitless. And what you did was put 16 sets of eyes up there and the parties looked into your eyes and decided it was time to get this matter resolved, and they resolved it. So it was your willingness to sit as judges of the facts that proved to be the catalyst of the resolution of this matter. So, I want to thank you for that. And, I want to thank you for your willingness to sit on a case that was going to go on for a period of time. I really appreciate that. We don't have a perfect system of justice in this country, but clearly we have the best that has been designed thus far. And, it is the willingness of people such as yourselves that take the time away from your families and your jobs and your obligations, to sit as judges of the facts that empowers our system of justice. We take people from various educational backgrounds, racial, ethnic, and nationality backgrounds, economic backgrounds and meld them together to serve as a conscience of the community. The system works pretty well. So on behalf of your fellow citizens and myself, I want to thank you for your jury service in this case. You are excused from further jury service at this time. And although it is only five after 10, I will see that you get your full $5.00 pay for the day. Try to stay dry and drive home safely, thank you very much."

The jurors were excused and left the courtroom.

Everyone else remained seated. Wertheimer spoke again. "I want to thank counsel for their professionalism during the course of this trial, and for their efforts in resolving this matter. There is an old adage in law that a case settled is a case won. There is another old adage is that a perfect settlement is when neither party goes away happy. I believe that both adages are accurate in today's matters. Take your time in clearing the courtroom. This case is adjourned."

I was shocked. In all previous justice proceedings, the judge had at least asked if I was satisfied with my counsel's performance. Judge Wertheimer never asked. This time my answer would have been a definitive NO.

Cathi and I spoke briefly with Art as we helped him with the 20 some boxes of my case files. We were in a state of shock, not sure what to do or say. After Art's Ford Explorer was loaded I returned to the front of the courthouse with my family and friends.

Brian, a friend from England who flew in with his son to provide Cathi and I with moral support, was as disgusted as we were and broke the tension first. "I can't believe what happened in there! That judge should be disbarred from all aspects of law. I don't think I've seen anything so dishonest in our English courts. I'm glad I don't live in America; your justice system is greatly overstated."

Brian was certainly correct in saying his piece. He stated what everyone there wanted to say but was too afraid to. He indeed "broke the ice" to a barrage of joint criticisms toward the judge, Art, and this country's judicial system. But as quickly as it started, it only took 10 or so minutes before it ended. Brian had a plane to catch and my family wanted to meet at our house to console Cathi and I and possibly devise a plan that would provide us some sort of stable future.

Cathi and I drove home alone, taking some private time to digest the day's tragedy and ponder our possible future. Cathi was devastated and could really only think about how we were going to survive and pay the bills. What she was certain of was that she wanted to find some way to have the judge disbarred. His vacation schedule was obviously more important than our lives or the medical discoveries my team so diligently derived.

54
Family Deception Begins

1998-1999—When we arrived home, my parents were already there and had dropped off Cheryl, her husband-to-be Mark, and my brother Ron.

Cathi's brother Scott had driven for two hours up from the shore to see the trial, but the mockery of justice had already been concluded. Scott drove back to our house and met with my father. My father, trying to protect Cathi and me from rehashing the events, asked Scott to leave.

This caused Cathi to blow the proverbial gasket and again an emotionally traumatic argument exploded. With apologies, my parents opted to leave rather than causing further hurt feelings or continue a losing battle.

Cathi and I made our way up into my home office and sat on the floor while Cheryl and Ron sat at my L-shaped desk arrangement. The objective was to devise a plan that would allow Cathi and I some sort of viable future and some income to, most importantly, grant us with some sense of personal gratification. Cheryl was the family financial advisor and directed her thoughts toward a logical format:

First, concentrate on my health. Therefore, with the last trial over, get me moved to a cleaner environment.

Second, what could they do to help me and Cathi become self-sufficient, while maintaining my health?

"Money is a key issue in life. Whether one is wise enough to admit to it is another factor. You can't live on love." Cheryl's comment was quite accurate in situations like this and, therefore, she was focusing on a plan to move forward. Her basic plan was for Cathi and me to move to the wondrous mountains of Breck, Colorado, then purchase a home that Cathi and I could live in, and that would allow us another section to rent out for income. This would allow us to gain financial stability to move out on our own over time.

Cathi deplored the idea of Colorado. It was too far from home and trusting my sister with her future was not what she wanted to do. Basically, Cathi still could not trust her after all the destructively manipulative situations she had caused during the harder times of my cancer survival. Cathi definitely made her feelings known during this "negotiation" and questioned, "Why can't we do the same thing in a place Rich and I love, like Stowe, Vermont?"

Planning the possible future of a couple "living with cancer" is one hell of an emotionally destructive process, especially when you are secretly using the situation to benefit yourself. Cheryl responded that she could not work out of Stowe, since there were no Tek Investors Office locations close by, and there was just not enough money up there to earn a living.

Cathi immediately realized she was being bullshitted. She angrily cornered me with, "We have spent enough time there to know that Tek Investors indeed has an office right on Mountain Road in Stowe and that if she is able to use her computer to conduct business in Breckenridge, why would it not work in Stowe?"

I knew Cathi was making very good points. I, also, realized my sister was using me to get her dream, of "owning a piece of the Rockies." Cheryl tried for years but couldn't afford a home in Breckenridge. She knew if I agreed to move there, our parents would supply her with the money.

My dilemma with this orchestrated argument was that I knew my parents wanted me to do a partnership with my sister. Their point of view was that, even though I still possessed a highly questionable life expectancy, my determination to live would allow me to outlive them. Therefore, my parents looked to Cheryl to guarantee that Cathi and I would be properly and financially cared for after their death.

During all this traumatic discussion, Mark skillfully prepared us a seafood spaghetti dinner and often ran up the steps to masterfully contain numerous arguments with logic. Mark typically did not conform to our arguing format. Often he thought before he spoke.

Ron was busy with phone calls from a close friend in California. On one of the worst days of my life, my brother received some great news. His class action case against California Bell, his employer, was settled in favor of the plaintiffs. He received about $200,000 on top of a recent family estate settlement of about $750,000. His life was justifiably turning for the better.

While he shared the good news to Cathi and I, he sat down on the floor to join us. I was very happy for my brother and Cathi too was pleased that one family member was seeing changes for the better. Ron interjected an offer to us. *"Well if you really want to go on your own, I could lend you money at whatever rate Cheryl would normally earn me— you know like 15 percent—and you can pay me back. But I expect you to collateralize whatever assets or collectables you have and stipulate it in your Will or estate plan."*

This is actually a generous offer to someone that may be starting a business or even anyone with a "dream" and no money to execute it. But for me, it was emotionally traumatizing. I have learned to control my emotions and rarely showed any signs of anger. This time my brain went into a fury of past thoughts and reminiscing of past conversations.

"You asshole. When the lawyers are talking about me receiving a truckload of cash, you ask for a boat, a truck to pull it with, and a vacation home to park it at. Now in my time of need, without any means of payback that couldn't jeopardize my wife's future, you offer me a loan. Screw you."

Emotions often cause actions and thoughts that are not meant. This situation was no exception. I maintained composure—showing no anger, and thankfully, making no negative response.

"Cancer often destroys the life of its patient, and more often destroys the lives closest to the patient."

Cheryl spent many hours convincing Cathi that she would indeed be taken care of after my death and that no one would take advantage of her again. Cheryl concluded that her plan for Cathi and I would be presented to our parents.

My parents called late that night to see how things went with my sister and brother and even suggested that Cathi and I take the drive to Vermont. Again Dad's credit card received "skid marks." They knew we were completely drained of all hope of a normal future and did not want to spend any more time around the families.

The next day Cathi and I left for Vermont. We knew my sister would be conceptualizing her ideas to my parents and that by the time we were back Mom and Dad would be totally brainwashed through the fear caused by love and concern for their son.

The trip was indeed another one of our four-day escapes from reality, but it also provided us time to think about our options and evaluate the possibilities of Stowe.

By the time we arrived back home from our emotional escape, Cheryl was ready for another meeting, this time, with the key players: Mom and Dad, and Cathi and I.

I started the conversation by bringing up the desires that Cathi and I had for some 10 years. We wanted to purchase a small hotel that included a small restaurant in Stowe. This way I could have my own radiation machine set up in one area, Cathi and I would have a source of income, a place to live, and if my parents chose, they could work with us. This setup gave Cathi and I control of our lives, control of my medical condition and an opportunity for my parents to spend some time with us establishing "a new life."

The concern that my parents still contended with was, "What if you take a turn for the worse, die or need long-term care from Cathi? This is a huge responsibility to trust to employees."

My sister was not interested in this idea at all. After all there was no "upside for her." The conversation was directed toward a home in Colorado. Her focus changed to my parents' weakness, devise a situation where Cathi and I would have minimal responsibility and maximize our "quality of life."

"Dad," Cheryl commanded toward our parents. "Since Richard is not able to swing his portion of a house in Breck right now, if you guys help with the down payment, I will make the mortgage payments and Richard and Cathi will only be responsible for the upkeep of the house. This arrangement would give them a place to live, expense-free, for the rest of their lives and it's in a non-polluted place that Richard likes to ski anyway. It's no secret," she continued, "I like that area, especially Breck, and I want to live there. If we work this together and you input some money, we can all get what we want. Plus, it's close enough to Denver so that you would easily have access to any medical care you might need. What I am proposing is that we look into buying a house together. Richard and Cathi would live there full time; I would only use it for vacations."

Mom and Dad had just been listening up to this point, but at the mention of something that might help my physical well-being with less responsibility for me, they became much more intent on what Cheryl was saying.

I was not opposed to the idea, it was just that I knew Cathi must be a part of this decision and I did not want to finalize it right then. "Look, could we discuss this later? I'm tired and Cathi and I need some time to talk about this."

"That's fine," Cheryl responded. "I just wanted you to start thinking about the idea. The most important thing is that you get away from the pollution, and a place like Breckenridge would be ideal."

My parents stood to go. "Richard," Dad said, "we will help however we can. We'll talk about this later."

It took a few more minutes for them to gather their things and leave. I watched as their car backed out of the drive. The house was quiet. Max padded up to me, in search of a scratch behind the ear. "Well, boy," I said to my dog, reaching down to pet him, "we got screwed out of millions of dollars, and now they want me to think about leaving." I felt a wave of exhaustion wash over me. It was still early, but I just wanted to go to bed and sleep.

As I trudged up the stairs, I thought about Cheryl's proposal. Colorado was a possibility, but it was so far away from all that Cathi and I knew. It was obvious that my sister was going to push this idea, and she could be tenacious.

Cheryl had been very helpful and supportive since my diagnosis, especially when we were in search of attorneys. She seemed genuinely concerned about Cathi's welfare. On several occasions she brought small gifts to Cathi, and to me, for no apparent reason: a tee shirt, a certificate for dinner at a seaside restaurant.

I heard Cheryl telling Cathi, more than once, how much she appreciated Cathi caring for her little brother. Cheryl was a cheerleader, encouraging me, but especially Cathi when things were rough, taking the time to sit and talk when Cathi needed someone to listen. She would work to raise Cathi's spirits after a bad day of taking care of me when I had been up all night, puking, or when the pressures of caring for me had become too much to bear. For this, Cathi was confused, but often placed her trust in my sister.

I also had seen Cathi devastated at something Cheryl said. I was never privy to the comments that upset Cathi. I couldn't understand how she could be so supportive one minute and so destructive the next. I really wondered if the problem was with Cathi, at least until I overheard an exchange between the two.

I only heard a portion of the conversation, and couldn't tell what it was about. But what I did hear was Cheryl belittling and demeaning Cathi about something. Cathi was standing there, taking the abuse, tears streaming down her face.

When I later confronted my sister, she defended her actions. "What I said might have hurt her feelings, but what I did, I did out of love."

"But, Cheryl," I insisted, "Cathi trusts you. What you said hurt her."

"Richard," she told me, "What I said was for her own good. Cathi needs to learn that she has to be responsible for herself."

Cheryl had said this with such authority that I let it go. I knew her "holier than thou" attitude would become destructive. After all, she was the one with a degree in psychology, yet needed the most help. Maybe this was some technique she had learned in one of her classes, maybe it was her way of feeling superior, or maybe cancer was taking the emotions of another loved one.

I didn't understand it, though. I always stood up for my sister and spent many hours convincing Cathi to trust her. Now she was caught. For Cheryl to demean her, it could only be interpreted as intentional destructiveness toward Cathi. If it was a learning situation, it was a harsh one that she did not have the right to conduct.

I knew that there was some jealousy on Cheryl's part, and that was what kept nagging at my consciousness. She had long been envious of the relationship Cathi enjoyed with me; the gifts I would give to Cathi, the trips the two of us enjoyed together. I always did things especially for her. When I gave Cathi a pearl necklace, it was of high quality.

What Cheryl did not seem to understand was that it had taken me months to save the money for the necklace. We, as a couple, would give up things to be able to afford the best. We would stay at home, when we had the opportunity to go out and spend money on lavish dinners and entertainment, just so we could afford the trips. All my sister saw was the end result. She never realized the sacrifices that had been made.

Since overhearing the exchange between the two women, I had

secretly wondered about Cheryl's motives on other things. She had introduced me to Tom Stange, which had led to my involvement with the Cancer Society's fund-raisers. But, I had also noticed that she had gained several new clients as a result of the event. I didn't see a problem with that, but maybe her motives were not quite as selfless as I had once believed.

And, I knew now that Cheryl's reasons for wanting a house in Breck were self-serving, too. Sure, it would give Cathi and I a place to live, but it would also provide her a way to finally afford a house in the resort area.

I wanted to believe that she had our best interests at heart. She was my sister. But…I just don't know, I thought. I just don't know.

The lethargy of depression shrouded the following weeks. Cathi went back to work, and I to my life of treatments and trains. Although there was still paperwork to do and there were phone calls to be made, the frenzy and anticipation of a trial were missing, leaving a hole in my time and spirit.

I had the opportunity to talk with Dennis Murray. I had spoken with the attorney several times over the past few years since the hiring fiasco. The attorney was always ready to talk to me and interested in the outcome of my legal battles. I shared with Dennis the events of the trial in Werthheimer's court.

"The judge actually said he didn't have time to hear the case?" Murray asked.

"That's right," I responded. "He said his vacation was starting in two weeks and we'd better settle this or I might end up with nothing."

"Did your attorney call his partners and discuss this with them?" Murray continued his interrogation.

"Not to my knowledge," I told him, "unless he knew about the settlement before hand, which I doubt. He would have said something to me. Art and the defense attorneys all gathered around the Judge in sidebar. Then we went into recess, and that's when Art told me that I had no choice except to take the settlement they proposed. I told him that

I was accepting it only under duress. I know he was really fighting to get my medicals covered, and he at least accomplished that. What I was most upset about was that we had a hell of a case, and the judge didn't even want to be bothered."

Murray thought for a moment. "Well, every attorney works differently, but I sure would have wanted to discuss it with my partners. And, I would have demanded that the judge dismiss himself from the case, and then I would have contacted the media and gone public. Your future livelihood is a damned sight more important than his vacation."

Murray's comments didn't help me feel any better. I knew that my attorney really focused on getting me lifelong medical coverage, and, of course, Art was worried about his fee. In the end, I had to believe that Art wimped out on me. He had caved in to the threats from an unscrupulous judge.

When I received the transcript and video recording of the civil trial proceedings, all of Judge Werthheimer's remarks about his vacation and threats to me about coming out of this with nothing were not there. As a matter of fact, two days worth of recordings were not supplied, March 16 and 17. The only proof I had of the judge's unethical behavior was the people sitting in the courtroom. I knew that altering court documents was highly illegal, but it had been done anyway. I felt battered and beat down by the system.

55
Enhancing My Health, Destroying My Soul

With nothing more to focus on concerning benefits and legal hassles, Cathi and I concentrated on our options for the move. Cheryl was pushing hard for Colorado. She made a trip out to Breck in May to check out the real estate market. She called Cathi at work, asking her questions about what she wanted in a house. And, Cathi kept telling her that she did not want to move to Colorado.

"It's not that I am opposed to Colorado," Cathi told me one night after another phone call from my sister. "It's just that Breck would not be my choice of location. It's too cold and they have winter seven months out of the year. Besides, it's so far away from our families, and I don't want to have to give up this house. If we lived closer, we could keep the house and you can spend time with your train buddies."

I had to agree. We both had a lot invested, financially and emotionally, in the house, and I didn't want to lose it either.

The doctors had actually given us several options: Maine, Vermont, Alaska, the Rocky Mountains of Colorado and Montana. They only wanted me to be away from the city and the high benzene content that went with the metropolitan pollution.

"What you need," Dr. 'Ricky' told me, "is someplace where there are not thousands of cars and you can get a few acres out in the trees. It's all the effects of civilization that's feeding your cancer."

I knew Dr .'Ricky' was right. On weekend trips to Vermont and New Hampshire, I experienced very little growth of the cancer. During my trip with my brother to Northern California and Yosemite National Park, I had not used any medications during the entire vacation.

My ever-present concern was having adequate medical facilities close by. Some of my doctors were concerned about my moving. If something happened to me, I could not afford to be stranded in the wilds of a place like Alaska.

Cathi understood and agreed with me, but any move was going to be traumatic for her. She was going to have to give up the home she loved, the job she enjoyed, and the closeness of her family. She also thought that her parents .would never travel to Colorado to visit. She didn't know if she wanted to be that far away from them.

I made the mistake of mentioning a symposium on lymphomas that was being held in Denver the latter part of July. Professor Lambert told me about it and invited me to attend. "Because one of the areas you are looking at is Colorado, if you were to be at the symposium, I could discuss your case during one of the sessions and introduce you. It is important that any doctors you might work with know your body type. They need to know what you can do on your own; that you are willing and want to take care of yourself properly."

Cheryl pounced on this opportunity. "Why don't you take Cathi out to Breck at the same time and show her around. It would be a perfect time to let her see how nice it is up there."

It was a plausible suggestion. We would have the opportunity to explore the area and maybe even look at some houses. It would give Cathi more information to work with.

Cathi agreed to join me during the second week. And, we had a great time. The summer in the mountains of Colorado was filled with wild flowers and mild days. We hiked and biked through the beauty of the high country. It was a welcome vacation from work and the stresses at home. Cathi enjoyed herself, and I felt good. The cancer grew very little.

Back home in New Jersey, Cheryl used my well-being to strengthen her case with our parents. "He was out there for two weeks," she told Mom and Dad, "and did wonderfully. This would be a good move for him, and Cathi will learn to love it."

Her arguments were hard to resist. Swept up in a swirl of manipulation and concern for my health, Dad told Cathi and me that he was willing to put up the money for the down payment on a house.

My sister immediately placed a call to her realtor in Breck and told her to start looking. When the call came from the realtor that she had several properties for them to look at, Cathi found herself on a flight to Colorado, accompanied by my sister and Dad.

"It is important," Dad insisted, "that Cathi make the final decision on which house to buy. This is going to be their home for the remainder of their lives."

The house Cathi chose was tucked away in the trees on Peak Seven. The deck had a view of the majestic Rocky Mountains, and the floor plan would allow for two living areas; one for her and I, and one that we could rent out for additional income.

We all agreed that I would control the rental, and the money would be split with Cheryl. Cathi still had reservations but, knowing that we might finally be able to have some control over our lives, she went along with the plan.

It took less than a week to close on the house. It was two months before we found a tenant for the Meeker house, and we busied ourselves packing for Colorado. What we didn't plan to take, we put in storage. Cathi and I, both felt better because we decided not to sell the Meeker house. We loved the house too much to part with it and need the security of knowing we still owned something.

On October 18, 1998, Cathi and I, along with my parents, took off in a 24-foot U-Haul truck, loaded with our possessions. It took three days to make the trip from New Jersey to Colorado, but it gave us all an opportunity to discuss the future.

"The only reason I agreed to this plan," Dad confided to me as we drove through the plains of eastern Colorado, "was to make sure that you have a place to live for the rest of your life. This house is your house," he continued, enumerating the specifics of the agreement. "Cheryl is only going to be there a few days out of the year. You control the rentals and get your percentage. If for any reason you and Cathi decide to move, you get half of the equity in the house. Cheryl has agreed to pay for everything except the phone and your food. It is important to us that you take care of yourself and have nothing to worry about that might affect your health."

Mom and Dad stayed two weeks to help Cathi and I get settled. Once the phone was hooked up, my sister called often. Little comments Cheryl made during these conversations began to concern Cathi and I.

"It may sound petty, but why does she refer to it as her house," Cathi questioned me, "if it is supposed to be '*our*' house to live in from now on?"

Two days before Mom and Dad were to leave, Dad was on the phone with my sister. I heard only a portion of Dad's side of the conversation, but quickly lost interest. I was more intrigued with the plans for the downstairs. I was going to build another room in the basement. It was going to be a major undertaking, having to dig out the area for the new room, but it was going to be worth it. It would make the house more valuable, justifying my percentage in the equity.

Later, after my dad had finished talking to Cheryl, I showed him what I planned to do. "My plan is to dig this area out and build an 18 x 24 foot room. It's a huge project, but I don't mind. Since I'm going to have 50 percent equity in the house, plus my percentage of the rentals, this expansion is going to help all of us."

Dad looked uneasy, hesitating before he spoke. "Well, let's see how things go, and just take it one day at a time."

What the hell does that mean, I wondered, as my father walked back upstairs. It was not until later, when Cathi and I were talking in bed that the pieces began to fall into place. "Dad had been talking to Cheryl for a long time on the phone," I told her. "What do you suppose she said to make him so uncomfortable when I mentioned the equity."

"I don't know, Rich, but Cheryl is beginning to make me really nervous," Cathi shared. "It would be just like her to renege on everything she promised, now that she has gotten what she wanted."

I knew that by now there was little love between my wife and sister. But, I was also aware that my sister's attitude was changing. She had even said something to me about Cathi getting a job and going to work so that she could "start pulling some of the weight." I was under the impression that Cathi and I could spend some time together re-establishing our life and our relationship. After all, money should not be a problem, if we have no bills.

What finally convinced me that my sister had manipulated both my parents and I into securing the house for herself involved some casual information shared by the next-door neighbor.

I met the neighbors within a day of moving into the new house, and, as always, quickly developed a friendship with them. I asked them the best way to advertise for a renter in the area. They warned me that the town had some very strict policies, and they had just been fined for an illegal rental. "It could be as much as a $10,000 fine if they catch you," the neighbor told me.

I was aware that purchasing this house made finances very tight for my sister, and a huge fine would make things worse. Cathi and I called to tell her what we learned. "My recommendation is not to rent the house. If we get caught, that's a pretty hefty fine."

Cheryl was not as upset as I thought she would be. "You're right, Richard," she told me. "The best thing is not to rent the house out. But, you do understand that this changes things."

"What do you mean?" I asked. "Changes what things?"

"Without the rental income, you won't have any equity in the house."

I realized that I had just handed her the perfect opportunity to change the agreement. "How does that change anything?" I questioned, getting angrier by the second. "The rental money is only one part of our deal. I've already started building that extra room downstairs and I'm going to redo the kitchen, too. And if I remember correctly you received money from mom and dad that could have been used for Cathi and I in Vermont."

"Well, your wife better get a job to help out," Cheryl sniped, changing directions, "so she can quit being such a burden on everyone."

"What? Cathi is no burden to anyone, especially you. And she has done nothing but stand by my side and care for me. You may want to try treating her with respect."

Cathi had been quiet throughout the conversation, but Cheryl's last comment caused a sharp intake of breath.

"We'll talk about this later," I told my sister angrily, and hung up. My main concern now was to make sure Cathi was all right.

"I knew she was going to do this to us," Cathi cried when I came to her. "She's been saying all along that this is her house."

"I'll talk to my parents," I reassured her. "They agreed to put up the money only if we had a place to live."

But, I quickly found out that my parents did not want to get in the middle of the disagreement. "Richard," my mother told me, "this is between you and your sister. The two of you should try and resolve this. And, there's nothing wrong with Cathi getting a job, but the money is hers. She is not responsible for any bills at that house and don't let her worry, you both can live there as long as you like."

I realized that my parents obviously could not get involved. They only wanted to help and now could only find themselves as hostages to the situation with no way to win. I knew, full well, that Cheryl's motives were nothing but self-centered and my parents and I played right into her hands.

Cheryl could not afford a house in Breck on her own, so she used me as bait. My parents, only wanting the best for Cathi and I, had not hesitated to dole out the financial means for my sister's scheme. And, now, Cathi and I were caught in the middle.

"Damn," I muttered, as I hung up from talking to my parents, "Cheryl has no intention of honoring the agreement."

But I also knew that Cheryl would not chance forcing Cathi and me out of the house. My parents would not stand for that. I didn't like this turn of events, but I knew that Cathi and I had a place to live.

As concerned as I was about my sister's lack of ethics, I had to admit that the move had been a good one . . . for me, at least. I was still taking two treatments a week, but I was able to get by with lesser amounts of the medicines. I began feeling much better. The constant pain in my ankles and other joints was subsiding quickly. I felt like a new man. I regularly went to the local recreation center to exercise. When the snow came, I went skiing almost every day for half a day. I loved hiking and snowshoeing. I felt great and wanted to take full advantage of every waking moment.

Life was wonderful for me, but Cathi's life had become a living hell. She would ski or hike with me, occasionally, but she could not tolerate the cold weather. She would end up spending most days in the house alone. She had no friends to talk to, and no job to distract her. When she did talk to her parents, she would end up feeling miserable. They would tell her how much they missed her and that she needed to come home. She would be upset for the next two days.

Cheryl, too, would call, and because I was so often gone, Cathi would have to speak to her. My sister would tell her that she needed to get a job and support herself. "Quit being such a leech," she would sneer. "You are just mooching off of me and my family. It's about time you try to do something with your life."

Cathi started a house cleaning business that rapidly supplied income, but quickly found that the work was physically too difficult for her. She would come home in pain. I helped her on many jobs, and when I saw the toll it took on my wife, I told her to quit. It just wasn't worth it. Besides, this was the first time in years that I had been able to spend any quality time with her.

But closing her business gave Cheryl more fuel with which to degrade Cathi. "You had a perfectly good business going, and just quit. Are you afraid of a little hard work? Well, sweetie, it's time to grow up."

I tried to tell Cheryl that she was not helping the situation by harassing Cathi all the time, but my sister would not listen.

The perpetual guilt from her own family and the constant badgering from my sister did nothing to help the relationship between Cathi and I.

I was excited and eager about life. I couldn't understand why Cathi never wanted to do anything. All she wanted to do was stay in the house.

We began arguing about petty things, but the disagreements would always revert back to Cheryl and her broken promises. "She's going to do it. She's going to kick us out of here," Cathi would rail. "This is not our place. She used your parents, and she used you."

Unaware of my sister's continual rebukes toward Cathi, I could not understand Cathi's defeatist attitude. Cheryl was no angel, but Cathi and I had survived the most difficult time, a time when cancer causes 80 percent of couples split up.

Now, when things were easier and we could enjoy life, our relationship was disintegrating. Getting out of the house and away from Cathi was a relief. I didn't like feeling this way, but just being around her was depressing. I didn't want to fight. Why couldn't she lighten up? It wasn't so bad; in fact, I was having a great time, why couldn't she?

Things improved somewhat once the weather began to warm up. But, phone calls from her parents and my sister continued to have a devastating affect. She would be upset for days afterward, and we would inevitably end up in a fight over the dumbest of things. Every word I spoke meant another reason for an argument. Often, we both said things we didn't mean.

"Quit being such a bitch! If you hate it here so much," I would snap, "why not just go home, that should make your family happy."

Although these statements were not meant, it demonstrates how emotional turmoil can lead to verbally vicious attacks on our loved ones. I always felt bad after such arguments and certainly did not want to hurt the person who had unconditionally done so much for me. My sister and her parents were doing quite well at that. Occasionally, I would apologize afterward, but the damage was done and the apology only led to more bickering.

Cathi also realized that emotions were getting out of control and that our problems were not self-inflicted. She was able to rationalize that our outside influences were destroying all her best personality traits. But this rational thought process never lasted. Emotions and anger prevailed.

Secretly, I sought help from two of my doctors and from the Cancer Societies services on ways to handle the psychological and emotional turmoil that we both experienced. It was my intention to mend the emotional bleeding that was sucking the life from Cathi and I.

My doctors recommended that I try to listen more carefully, and then try to decipher or pinpoint each problem. Once this was identified, make suggestions as to how we can solve the problem that satisfies both our needs.

Another added suggestion was to actually write this book. They believed that in doing so it would help Cathi and I recognize how much we really accomplished. It would also give us a venue to help others and other Cancer patients and their families.

Finally they recommended that I put all of Cheryl's promises to my parents and us in writing. This should give Cathi the basic sense of security that was missing in her life.

I was also warned that Cathi might have reached an emotional point that will not allow forgiveness. Seven years of verbal abuse from others and caring for me could have changed her permanently.

The doctor continued, stating that, in his experience, less than 20 percent of cancer patient spouses endure the magnitude of turmoil she has experienced. I assured him, and promised myself, I would try to do the right thing.

It was the beginning of August and I was conscious that Cathi was going through another critical phase of depression. She seemed to constantly be on the verge of tears. The only topic that she could focus on was Cheryl's betrayal and manipulation of my parents and us.

I tried to reassure her. "If she tries to kick us out, we'll just take her to court. We do have some rights in this situation and, besides, it's my job to make sure she keeps her promises to you after I die. So I taped many of our important conversations. She wouldn't have a leg to stand on in court, if she tries to do anything against you."

But Cathi still was not satisfied. Every day she was confronted with the joy she felt about the improvements in my health and the negative thoughts of: "What is going to happen to your parents if we strike back at Cheryl and they find out the truth about her? They will be devastated by this." Cathi's innate concern for me and my parents was now also destroying her.

One particular morning began as most of our mornings did. We were both up early. I worked in my office on things that could help Cathi and me. Things like rewriting my will and estate plan, organizing a plan for starting a business or foundation that assists young married cancer families. This was something she and I had wanted to do, almost from the time of my diagnosis. Cathi and I didn't want others to experience what we had.

I assumed Cathi was off doing something around the house or just took a relaxing walk. About 10 A.M. Cathi came to the office door. One look at her and I could tell that she was obsessing about Cheryl again.

"What are we going to do, so that in a year, we can get out of here?" She asked me with tears in her eyes. "And, how are we going to protect your parents?"

I really did not know what to say; she knew I was working on a plan.

Before I could say anything, Cathi continued. "This isn't going to work. I don't trust your sister. We're going to get screwed and your parents are going to get screwed, too." Her tears were now spilling down her cheeks and her lips were quivering with emotion.

As I got up from my desk to hold and hug her, she began to wave her arms hysterically. "Don't come near me. Cheryl's going to screw us all and I'm going to end up homeless when this is all over with."

Her voice reached a pitch of hysteria and her bodily movements where becoming very erratic. I was not sure of what was happening to her, but she was indeed getting worse. Her violent strikes to my upper body hurt, and I realized she out of control and might hurt herself (This was something I had done to Cathi when I went into convulsions from medication reactions.).

I maintained an iron grip on her shoulders, as she continued to kick and scream. I picked her up and ran down the hall and into the bedroom where I pinned her to the bed. I thought this was the safest thing to do for her, and then I realized a fear she had with caring for me. "What if she swallows her tongue?"

For what seemed like 10 to 15 minutes Cathi uncontrollably and violently tried to break my grip. The entire time she raged about Cheryl's deception and how my parents and she (Cathi) would suffer.

Suddenly she relaxed. I loosened my grip and asked how she was feeling. She did not answer but her "little girl" smile formed on her face and she went to sleep, or passed out. I really don't know which. I stood beside her for sometime, checking her breathing and setting her favorite "Teddy Bear" in her arms. She remained sleeping peacefully with a smile.

I was not sure what exactly happened, but I hoped her convulsions represented an end to her anger. For about 3 to 4 hours Cathi slept. I attempted to continue to work on making our dreams of a normal life happen, but to no viable avail. About every five minutes I found myself checking on her. She lay there calm and serene, like the angel I perceived her to be.

When she awoke I was sitting at my office desk. I hoped she was feeling better but with one look at her glaring face, I knew something unpleasant was about to happen.

"What are we going to do? I don't trust your sister. We're going to get screwed, and I'm going to end up homeless." Again, she began to wave her arms and express bodily actions of hysteria.

I kept my voice calm and mundane. "Well, Cath, I think we'll be okay. You know I am working on some good ideas here. But it will take a little time for me to organize things."

"Now you're not paying attention to me and turning against me!" she mumbled. "I'm going to be alone and homeless, and you and that bitch don't care."

It was like a rerun from the morning, except this time her comment insinuated that I didn't care. She confused me with that, but in seconds she was out of control again. I forcefully grabbed her tight to control her, but calmly asked her, "are we going to do this again, like this morning? Do you have more to let out?"

"What the hell are you talking about?" she screamed, with tears pouring down her face. "I didn't do anything this morning. I didn't bother you, I didn't talk to you!"

Somewhat bewildered by her statements, I knew I couldn't take any chances of her getting hurt. Her strength was equal to her first fit, so I immediately picked her up, ran her down the hall and pinned her to the bed. Amazingly she fought to break free for another 10 to 15 minutes and raged about Cheryl and how my parents and she (Cathi) would be screwed. Every word she stated appeared to be exactly what she said in the first bout. And again she exhausted herself and peacefully went to sleep.

Although I am considerably stronger than Cathi, she physically wore me out. Emotionally I was drained. Not sure of what was happening to her, I decided I had to figure a way to get her away from Cheryl and this house. Cathi felt everyone was against her, abandoned, and that she would have no place to live. I had to make something happen.

While I worked in my office, Cathi slept for about another three hours. I was completely frustrated with the situation and uncertain what I could really do to help her. I was doing great health wise. Cathi was rapidly deteriorating. I only spent time with her when I thought she wanted me to, in the attempt to give her time to herself. I made it a point to do things together, but the extenuating family matters eventually marred her thoughts.

It was 5:30 when Cathi awakened and came back down the hall to the office. I looked closely at her face. She seemed fine.

"God, you shouldn't have let me nap so long," she said sleepily. "I can't believe how late it is."

All the anguish that had ravaged her face earlier was gone. I was cautious not to mention our episodes and suggested: "Feel like going to the Wellington for dinner?"

"Sounds good," Cathi calmly responded. "Let me just freshen up and we can go. I'm starving."

Dinner was wonderful and Cathi was relaxed and talkative. We discussed our various possibilities of starting a business and ways to continue our life. She very coherently rationalized all the problems that "*Living with Cancer*" allow us no choice but to contend with. Finally I relaxed, Cathi had released all her anger and my wife was back. The dinner outing went perfectly.

On our drive home Cathi looked over to me with a blank face. "You know, we should go out to dinner one of these nights, maybe to the Wellington, or someplace nice like that."

Stunned, I couldn't believe I had heard her right. Maybe I had misunderstood her. I glanced at her, and the vibrant expression that she had during dinner was gone, still blank. Casually, I brought up topics that we discussed at dinner, but she was clueless. She was still cheerful and I was not sure what was happening so, I further tested her by saying, "You know, you didn't have to push me around today."

"What are you talking about?" she responded, completely puzzled by the remark. "I didn't do anything with you today. All I did was sleep."

It was then I realized something might seriously be wrong. She did not remember the dinner and discussion we just had enjoyed, and she didn't recall anything about her emotional explosions either.

As we entered the house, Cathi sighed, "My chest hurts."

"Do we need to go to the emergency room? You took me plenty of times when my chest hurt." I wanted to keep the situation light-hearted as she always did with me. I knew she put herself through a lot of strain earlier in the day and wanted to take her to the hospital. But like me, she stood strong saying, "No, I just want to go to bed. I can't believe how tired I am today."

I went into the kitchen for a drink of water and then went to the bedroom to check on her. She was sound asleep in only a few minutes. I looked at the clock and couldn't believe it was only 8 P.M.

For the rest of the evening, I wrestled with what to do about Cathi. I knew she needed rest after such a hard, emotional day, but I was unsure if I should wake her and force her to go to the doctor the way she had done for me. As I looked upon her serene face, I thought, hopefully tomorrow would be better.

That night I barely slept and continued to check my placid wife. The next morning I was up early and tried to busy myself with projects around the house. Every so often, I would go in to check on her as she slept. Finally, at 10 o'clock, she got up.

She shuffled into the room where I was working. I wanted to tell her "good morning" but I noticed that her face was showing the ravaged signs of torment.

"Cheryl doesn't want me in this house. She is going to make me leave and she is destroying us. I'm going to be homeless, and you don't care." Again she went into a hysterical fit.

Swiftly, I grabbed her and propelled her back to the bedroom. This time I controlled the situation. Every time she made a statement of panic, I forcefully responded, "You're going to be okay. We'll do whatever we have to do, even if it includes suing Cheryl. You will not be homeless. My parents will protect you if I die first. You're going to be okay."

When she looked like she would fall to sleep from the exhaustion, I gently slapped her and kept her talking. I did not want her to forget that I was on "her" side and I did not want her to worry about her future. I wanted her to remember so we could talk about it and not let her feel threatened by my sister. This second day, it took all my strength to hold her down for an hour, and I kept her talking. I continued with my barrage of factual reassurances. It seemed to be sinking in and she calmed down.

Wearied by the emotional and physical workout, I let her go to sleep. I sat on the side of the bed and had to admit this was too much. She saw me through many life and death situations, nursed me back to health after the big surgery and unconditionally cared for me. I couldn't help but think that letting her go would be the best thing for her. She deserved a decent life.

Frustrated, I decided to call some of my doctors and ask for their opinion of all that happened over the past two days. This was something I knew most of them could help me with, because they had seen me through the emotional psychology of my therapeutic pitfalls.

After explaining the events of the past few months, and the last two days, the consensus was quite shocking for me to accept. Most thought it might be best to send her home for a month or two. Get her into therapy and let professionals help her to get over the traumas.

One doctor told me, "She needs psychological attention and might do better with the security she perceives with her family. As difficult as it may be for you to understand right now, she has lost confidence in you, and whether it is real or not, it is what she currently believes."

"Look at it from her perspective. She was the caretaker for over six years, and a damned good one. Now that you're doing so much better, she no longer can assume that role. You suddenly don't need her to the extent that you did before, and she is floundering with that lost identity. Think about how rewarding it all was to her. She was present for some of your operations; normal wives do not do that, Richard. She needs to focus on herself, and my guess is, with her family background, she does not know how to do that. It is a serious change going from a caretaker to a self-provider. She's going to need a professional to help her find her way."

It was times like this that I hated, but my doctors talked sensibly to me and I knew I had to try what was suggested. It was the least she deserved. I sat and stared out the window.

The world outside was green and lush. The majesty of the mountains met the brilliant blue of the sky. It was a perfect picture of God's handiwork. But God had dealt me an unusual hand of cards, and so far I thought I met the challenge. I could not go back to New Jersey and jeopardize my health, and I would not jeopardize Cathi's well-being or sanity.

Now it was time for me to do what was right for her. If I had to send her home I would. And, to protect her from any future liabilities connected to the family, or me, I would dissolve the marriage.

I could not believe the pain I felt inside, now my mitral valve caused me anguish, but if it would make things right for her, then so be it.

Cathi slept the entire day and into the evening. About 11 P.M. she woke, complaining her chest really hurt. It was my turn to be the caretaker. I ordered her out of bed, made her get dressed, and told her I was taking her to the hospital—whether she liked it or not. Obediently she got dressed and, in minutes, we were quietly on our way.

I brought her into the emergency room and informed the nurse Cathi was having chest pains on and off for two days. Immediately Cathi was brought in to the doctor. After the examination, which included an EKG, the doctor asked to speak to me in private. He wanted to know what she had been doing the past two days and I gave him a full recap. He was not happy with the events in our life and asked many questions. Then he described his findings.

"Her blood pressure is very high, and she may have strained her heart; it could last a few days. The heart is a muscle, and like any other muscle, if it is overexerted, it will hurt. You need to keep things calm around her and let her rest as much as possible. I suspect at this high of a stress level, you may want to take your other doctor's advice and send her home for a while. This could have developed into something much worse, even a heart attack."

That night when I took her home, she wanted to know what the doctor talked to me about. I didn't want to upset her so I responded honestly. "Well, he wanted to know what has been going on in your life. I think we are going to have to make some changes that will benefit you and allow for some time away."

Cathi looked at me with understanding and sadness. I continued, "Hey, you know how often the doctors told you most wives couldn't do what you have. Some time might be what we need. Let's talk about this tomorrow." To my surprise, Cathi knew.

She asked, "Do you think I should go home for a while?"

"Well it doesn't seem like a bad idea. Let's relax tonight and talk tomorrow."

That morning when Cathi was ready to talk, she knew what I was going to say. "We both know you're not happy here. You miss your family, and Cheryl has made your life hell. I might not have been much help either. I've been focused on all the things I can now do and your desires were forgotten or ignored. I guess I didn't realize how important the job of caring for me was. Out here we needed to start over and you were pushed aside. So now we spend our time fighting about nothing or something pertaining to Cheryl. It doesn't leave much of a relationship for us. And I think you deserve more."

Cathi said nothing, but I could tell she was agreeing.

"I want you to be happy; I think you should go back to your family. Spend time with your parents and make sure you see my doctors or see one on your own. But remember my doctors are yours and they will help you in any way they can. Whatever you decide is fine with me. As you know, because of all the legal and medical problems I have, I think it would be best if we dissolved the marriage as the lawyers suggested."

I could see the tears building in her eyes, but again she agreed. Cathi wanted to be happy and knew, from experience, this was something she had to try. That evening she called her parents to let them know she was coming home for a while, maybe a vacation.

We spent the next week talking about how we would always be there for one another. Cathi also assured me, even if she were to remarry, should I feel I needed her care during the cancer dying process, she would be there. She promised to see the doctors and we went to the courthouse to sign the dissolution of marriage papers.

Continually, tears were in her eyes, but the aura of relief was in her face. This was the hardest thing I have ever had to do, but I thought it was right for her.

"Thank you," was all she could say.

About one week after her nervous breakdown she sat at my side for the two-hour drive to Denver airport. The entire time we both felt a sense of relief, yet renewed promises made to protect one another and help one another in a time of need. We were still close but worn out from life's trials and tribulations.

We arrived at the airport terminal just before the flight was boarding. It didn't allow for a long good bye, and rightfully so, reality was sinking in. A 19-year relationship was coming to an end.

When the announcement finally came over the speaker, I walked her to the gate and with only a touch of the hand, asked, "Call me and let me know you got home alright."

"I will."

We stood for a brief moment looking into each other's eyes. All the joys and laughter, pain and tears of our life were reflected.

Cathi turned and handed her ticket to the agent. I watched as she disappeared down the skyway and onto the waiting airplane.

I sat at the terminal to "see her off" and waited until the plane started to taxi away. I relived all the times we shared and felt tranquil in that I was doing this for her, as she had done so much for me.

As the plane taxied, I stood at the window to watch. I was in the best health I had been in seven years. I looked at my reflection and realized this was the most unselfish thing I have ever done.

I turned to walk down the concourse toward my life alone. Ready to continue my battle with cancer but not ready for my broken heart.

They say that if you really love someone to let them free, if they return to you then it was meant to be.

God, let the caring, giving, loving beauty that Cathi brought to my life, be brought back to me.

Epilogue

Losing Cathi in August of 1999 forced me to do some re-evaluation of my life's goals and relationships. As I moved through the remaining months of 1999, I continued to concern myself with doing what was right for her.

I also knew that I wanted to do something to help others who faced the ordeals of cancer. I took the ideas that Cathi and I shared at the Wellington and decided to bring those worthwhile goals to reality.

This book is the finalization of one effort to let others know that they are not alone in their battles with Cancer and the American legal system. It is scheduled to be sent to the printer's on October 2, 2000, the eighth anniversary of my diagnosis.

The second goal, a website where the victim, family and friends can reach out to the world and share their stories is just a short time away. See the section following on TrueStoryNetwork.com.

Both of these endeavors had false starts, restarts, and have evolved over these many months.

The year 2000 brought many changes to my life, the most important being that Cathi has returned to me. She and I are working on our relationship. We know that we can never go back and pick up with the innocent love, sharing, and trust of the first two years of our marriage, but we hope that we can rebuild on a more mature and stable foundation.

My health continues to be my major concern. Through Professor Lambert, I was able to purchase my own PUVA machine. This allows me to do the two treatments per week on a more convenient schedule. I no longer travel to Denver with a two-hour drive each way, with the threat to others of the possibility of my blacking out. At the time of this writing, I have done over 600 treatments and broken down four additional tumors.

Cathi is working on a book telling her story of how the loved ones pay a price during the battle with cancer.

TrueStoryNetwork.com

"The Information & Publishing Network that
Educates & Exposes All"

TSN offers on-line publishing for aspiring, creative people from children to adults, to share their knowledge and life experiences. Our desire is diverse; through our web site, we intend to educate and expose the general public to the information and truth that is usually obscured by the system.

TSN's founder is a cancer survivor since 1992, still undergoing treatments, who also spent 6 1/2 years in various courts attempting to prove the industrial causation of his condition. It is for these reasons he has started this web site, designed to provide a learning resource that empowers individuals of all ages to take charge of their lives.

A Foundation Under Construction

Help Wanted

Having fought the battles with cancer and the legal system, the founder is building a foundation to assist others who face these horrendous financial and emotional damages. The goals include providing the proper psychological, medical, and legal support for the victim and loved ones as they face these battles, and eventually, adding the sponsorship of research work at universities.

Unfortunately, he faces the reality that he cannot help everyone the way he wants, and that he cannot start immediately, but must plan and prepare appropriately. Watch the TrueStoryNetwork.com web site to see the Foundation's birth, growth, and achievements as they transpire. Contact information will be available on the TrueStoryNetwork.com web site.

The Foundation needs volunteer professionals to assist in preparing programs and fundraising.

TrueStoryNetwork.com Start Up Team